BRITISH UNIVERSITIES PAST AND PRESENT

British Universities
Past and Present

Robert Anderson

**hambledon
continuum**

Hambledon Continuum
A Continuum imprint

The Tower Building
11 York Road
London, SE1 7NX

80 Maiden Lane
Suite 704
New York, NY 10038

First Published 2006

ISBN 1 85285 347 6

A description of this book is available from the
British Library and from the Library of Congress.

Typeset by Carnegie Publishing, Lancaster,
and printed in Great Britain by Biddles Ltd, King's Lynn, Norfolk

Contents

Introduction

In the last fifty years, the position of universities within British society has been transformed. For centuries they served only a small social elite, and as late as the 1950s were attended by only about one in twenty-five of each generation. Today this figure approaches one in two, and where once there were two dozen universities now there are over ninety. University expansion is associated with the Robbins Report of 1963 just as the welfare state is with the Beveridge Report of 1942, though in fact growth was under way well before Robbins reported. Equally important, though less well assimilated into common views of the recent past, is a second wave of growth which began in the 1980s and has continued since. This rather than the 1960s marked the real transition from elite to mass higher education, and was reflected in the transformation of over forty polytechnics and colleges into new universities in 1992. The same expansion has taken place in all advanced countries, many of which spend more on their universities and attract more young people to them than does Britain. But national university traditions remain different and distinctive, and have had a strong influence on the ways in which modern university systems have evolved and responded to contemporary problems. In a globalized world, an Oxford or Cambridge graduate is still distinguishable from a product of Harvard or Stanford, or a French technocrat. Layers of past history underlie the present, and successive waves of creation – colleges in London in the early nineteenth century, Victorian civic universities, 'greenfield' universities founded in the 1960s, former technical colleges with their roots in the work of elected local authorities – can be easily discerned in the current hierarchy of university prestige, which is further complicated by the nationally distinctive traditions of Scotland, Ireland and Wales.

For over 600 years, Oxford and Cambridge were the only universities in England, and it was difficult for new foundations to escape their

influence, to establish a different ethos, or to challenge their role in educating the social elite. The Victorian civic universities have been accused
of abandoning their distinctive provincial character to conform to this
metropolitan ideal. The Oxbridge model then seemed to find new
endorsement in the campus universities of the 1960s and in the Robbins
Report, which sought to extend the traditional university experience to
a new clientele. The post-Robbins expansion soon ran into financial
trouble because of these ambitions, and in the 1970s higher education
entered on a period of prolonged crisis, later exacerbated by the hostility to the public sector of the Thatcher and Major governments. The
changes of 1992 introduced strains of a different kind as all universities,
old and new, were treated with the same stringency. Attempts to square
the financial circle, and to compensate for the state's reluctance to support universities in the style to which they had become accustomed,
have included targeted financial incentives, student contributions to
fees, and semi-marketization to stimulate competition between institutions. These measures remain contentious, reflecting as they do the
conflict between the American social model and the European one to
which British universities have historically been closer.

An understanding of the present university situation means looking
at the evolution of policy since 1945, on which original historical
research is only now beginning. But it is also relevant to pursue the story
back into the nineteenth century, and – however briefly – to earlier ages.
Issues from the past have a habit of reviving: at one time the movement
from autonomous corporate status to dependence on the state seemed
natural and irreversible, but today there may be new lessons to learn
from the balance between state and market and the sources of university finance in the past. Another controversial balance, that between
teaching and research, looks very different when seen in historical perspective, for the research ideal is a comparatively recent development.
Over the centuries universities have had many functions, but as institutions which served the state and trained the national elite they have
never been far from the centre of power. Once, their function was to
instil political and religious conformity. In the nineteenth century, as
Britain became an industrialized and democratic society, they were
reformed and developed as agencies of social cohesion, forming an
intellectual aristocracy through a common elite culture. In the process,

a distinctively British university ideal was shaped, combining an emphasis on the broad education of the individual student with the new rigours of academic specialization. Universities were also crucial to the formation of national identity, at British and imperial levels, as well as in Scotland, Wales, and (much less harmoniously) Ireland. For much of the twentieth century, especially its second half, university policy was dominated by social and economic issues – equality of opportunity, social mobility, access for the poor, and the contribution of science and technology to national prosperity. In the new century the social issues remain far from fully resolved, and international economic competition has given urgency to the university's role as a powerhouse of knowledge and original research. But older questions of secularism, shared culture and national identity have also risen up the national agenda, and universities are not immune to these debates. Their ideals of objective inquiry and academic freedom have to share the field with the ancient forces of state, religion and nationalism, and the newer one of corporate power. There is no single, predestined line of university development, and there is still a place for the lessons and the surprises of history.

1

Serving Church and State

Apart from the church and the monarchy, universities are the oldest and most international of British institutions. The European university traces its origins to the twelfth century, or even before – 1088 is the traditional foundation date for Bologna, and Paris followed soon afterwards. These two universities provided alternative models of authority, Bologna as a 'university of students' (the election of the rector of the older Scottish universities by their students is a relic of this), Paris as a 'university of masters'. More significant in the long run was that universities in Italy, and in southern Europe generally, came to focus on professional training in law and medicine, while Paris, the model for Oxford and then Cambridge, was devoted primarily to philosophy and theology. But this was only a matter of emphasis, for there was a common European pattern of teaching and degrees based on four faculties: the preparatory faculty of arts led on to the professional faculties of theology, medicine, and law – including both the canon law of the church and the civil or Roman law which trained servants for the state. The international character of medieval universities was reinforced by the need for papal sanction, by the migration of students and scholars, and by a common heritage of learning.

The full course of arts and theology required a long progression through a series of tests and exercises. The central discipline of medieval universities was logic, based on the works of Aristotle as interpreted by Christian commentators, which covered most existing knowledge of the natural and human worlds. Pupils studied texts and commentaries under the guidance of masters, and proved their ability through formal, oral disputations in which propositions were expounded and defended. The system was designed to develop analytical and expository skills within a framework of orthodoxy rather than to encourage critical or original thought, but at its best it provided a subtle and rigorous intellectual training.[1]

Oxford University took shape toward the end of the twelfth century, and Cambridge was founded by a secession from Oxford traditionally dated to 1209. Both began as informal groups of scholars, but soon acquired privileged status, from king as well as pope. European universities were never purely religious bodies – they also depended on the protection of the state and served secular interests, and the English ones were especially favoured by the monarchy. Since state and church were often in conflict, the universities could carve out space between them. They were not subject to the direct control of the local bishops, while in the secular world they enjoyed autonomy and privilege as property-owning corporate bodies with their own legal rights, not least exemption for members of the university, both masters and scholars, from the jurisdiction of the towns in which they were situated; these exemptions lasted well into the nineteenth and even twentieth centuries.

The medieval university was a community (the original meaning of *universitas*) of study and learning. At Oxford and Cambridge the communal ideal seems strikingly represented by the colleges, whose chapels, dining halls and quadrangles or courts survive as built evidence. But colleges were a comparatively late development, borrowed from Paris. Early students lived in lodgings in the town, or in halls (Oxford) and hostels (Cambridge) which provided basic accommodation but not teaching. Colleges differed from halls in being corporate bodies enjoying legal privileges, with a permanent financial endowment, usually in the form of land, provided by the founder and added to by later pious benefactors, who included aristocratic and royal women such as Lady Margaret Beaufort, mother of Henry VII. The endowment paid for the buildings, for the maintenance of communal religious worship, and for scholarships to support promising young men, especially those who aimed at careers in the church. In the earliest colleges, which appeared in the thirteenth century, scholars and fellows were advanced students, 'postgraduates' in modern terms. The first colleges to admit undergraduates were King's Hall at Cambridge (*c.* 1317, an ancestor of Trinity College), and New College at Oxford (1379).[2] New College, founded by William Wykeham, bishop of Winchester, was a joint foundation with his school at Winchester: 'Wykehamists' proceeded from one to the other, and often back again as teachers. Henry VI established a similar connection when he founded Eton College along with King's College, Cambridge in 1440; non-Etonians were not admitted to King's until 1865.

The links between schools and universities have always been important in defining the social function of higher education, and the foundation of grammar schools in towns of all sizes was a favourite field of action for wealthy philanthropists from the late middle ages to the seventeenth century, encouraging new links between the universities and urban merchants or lawyers. Grammar schools taught the Latin which was essential for any university education, and often had scholarships tied to particular colleges. The boundary between schools and universities shifted over time: in the sixteenth century boys were still going to the university at fifteen or sixteen, but the typical age rose to seventeen in the seventeenth century, and eighteen subsequently. The youth of university students, and their reputation for indiscipline and violence, led the universities to insist by around 1400 that all students must reside in a hall, hostel or college. But it was only in the Tudor period that the colleges came to predominate, and that teaching and housing undergraduates became their main concern.

In the middle ages the universities were comparatively little used by the aristocracy, who had their own system of apprenticeship to military and chivalric values within noble households, or by the lesser landed gentry. Information about the social origins of medieval students is scanty and difficult to interpret, but it seems to show that most of them came from the middle ranks of society – from the families of prosperous farmers or yeomen, of small traders and merchants, perhaps of urban artisans. The church had an interest in recruiting its priesthood as widely as it could, and was an important channel of social mobility. Scholarships and family resources supported students through their long university years, and colleges developed connections with specific counties and regions, recruiting their students through local endowments and personal contacts with schools and patrons.[3] But students from really poor backgrounds were rare. An overwhelmingly rural and illiterate society possessed only rudimentary mechanisms for discovering and promoting talent. The stereotype of the poor medieval student thus needs to be qualified. Nor was the romantic image of the student as an international wanderer much more accurate: many English scholars went on to European careers, but they received their first degrees in England, and the English universities (unlike Paris, Padua, and other continental counterparts) attracted few students from abroad.

If there is one point on which historians of medieval universities agree, it is their essentially vocational and utilitarian character. The pioneering authority Hastings Rashdall poured cold water on the cult of 'liberal education' in his own age, the 1890s, and pointed out that 'the rapid multiplication of universities during the fourteenth and fifteenth centuries was largely due to a direct demand for highly educated lawyers and administrators' to serve the state.[4] The intellectual skills of logic and disputation were valuable in a wide range of occupations, especially as society became more urbanized and royal bureaucracies expanded.[5] The intellectual elite cultivated scholarship and learning, to maintain and honour which was one of the purposes of the university, but teaching future servants of church and state was equally important: to suppose that medieval universities were ivory towers devoted to pure scholarship is a misunderstanding. Theology was itself a practical study in a society which saw the salvation of souls as a central concern of life. Most arts graduates became parish priests or schoolteachers, while a higher degree in theology or canon law was almost indispensable for influential posts in cathedrals and church administration. University students included many monks and friars, sent by their orders for a training in scholarship and administrative skills, and living in separate monastic colleges or local convents; but the spirit of the universities was not a reclusive or monastic one, and they always served the lay professions as well as the church. The medical faculties were not as important in England as in many continental countries (though they never completely lost their foothold), but the law faculties provided secular servants for the state, and this was one reason why monarchs favoured the universities with endowments and legal privileges. The crown also drew heavily on the higher ranks of the church for its servants, and worldly clerics were among the most generous of the universities' benefactors – most spectacularly in the case of Thomas Wolsey, whose Cardinal College at Oxford was planned on a lavish scale. It was confiscated by Henry VIII and refounded as Christ Church;

Trinity College was the corresponding Henrician foundation at Cambridge, enriched by monastic plunder.

Henry VIII's break with Rome was a decisive episode, putting both the English church and the universities under closer royal control. In 1535 the king sent commissioners to 'visit' the two universities and impose changes, a mode of intervention followed by other rulers over the next century and more.[6] Henry expected the universities, as arbiters of religious orthodoxy and nurseries of the clergy, to fall into line with royal policy, and this was enforced by Henry's powerful minister Thomas Cromwell as chancellor of Cambridge. In subsequent years, as policy shifted towards a more explicit Protestantism under Edward VI, then back to Catholicism under Mary I, the universities underwent a further series of reforms and purges.

The first concern of Henry VIII's visitors was religious conformity. The universities were required to acknowledge royal supremacy in the church and to renounce the authority of the pope, which they did without much resistance. But the visitors were also concerned with the curriculum: the teaching of canon law was entirely abolished (though civil law remained), various books were prescribed or proscribed, and the teaching of theology was to rest in future on scripture rather than on medieval authorities. The visitors' edicts reflected Renaissance as well as Reformation. The influence of classical humanism had been apparent well before 1535, marked not least by Erasmus's visits to both English universities. Both before and after the Reformation, humanists aimed at purifying religion by putting it on a rigorous scholarly and scriptural basis, requiring the study and teaching of Greek and Hebrew. The rediscovery of classical authors also led to a new stress, in schools as well as universities, on studying literary texts, on elegant composition in Latin and Greek, and on the arts of rhetoric and persuasion.[7] Appeal to classical authorities was combined in the new humanist curriculum with the traditional Aristotelian logic, and although the latter was increasingly criticized the basic blend of classical and Christian influences and ideals dominated educated culture until the advent of the Enlightenment.

Academically, the sixteenth century was the decisive period when teaching moved from university to college. In the medieval universities, teaching was carried out largely by 'regent masters', recent graduates for whom teaching duties were a part of the course leading to higher degrees. In the fifteenth century this system began to break down, and new posts were created for salaried professors, readers, or lecturers (the terms were more or less interchangeable). The Tudors tried to build on this innovation to revive university-level teaching, and Henry VIII founded five 'regius' chairs at each university, in divinity, Greek, Hebrew, civil law and medicine; other donors followed suit. But this came too late to counter the more intimate and flexible forms of teaching developed in the colleges, where there was also a chance to study fashionable subjects not on the official curriculum such as modern languages, literature and science. Although the university system of disputations and exercises retained its vitality well into the seventeenth century, and those who wished to graduate still had to jump these hurdles, the authority of the university itself dwindled. The colleges effectively controlled admissions, and decided who was allowed to present himself for a degree. The universities' buildings, consisting essentially of examination schools and libraries, and their revenues from matriculation or graduation fees, were overshadowed by the wealth of the colleges, which became the focus of loyalty and everyday life. New colleges were founded, often with distinct religious agendas, since all parties in the church saw the training of godly parish clergymen as the key to religious regeneration. The tradition of regional links also thrived, with foundations like Jesus College at Oxford (1571) for Welshmen. The number of halls and hostels declined sharply: at Oxford, there were fifty-two halls in 1505, only eight by 1537, a few of which survived into the nineteenth century.[8] Most halls and hostels vanished, or their sites and buildings were absorbed by the colleges. The latter also benefited from the abolition of monastic colleges and the diversion of church revenues which followed the Reformation. The rise of collegiate life reflected the desire of both university authorities and parents to impose more discipline on undergraduates; the college fellows now acted as tutors supervising the morals and finances of their charges, and answered to families for them. Discipline at this period included corporal punishment as well as attempts to curb student activities outside the college walls.

The attractions of the college system, combined with the focus of humanist education on the moral and cultural formation of the gentleman, underlay the so-called 'educational revolution' of the late sixteenth and early seventeenth centuries, marked by a huge influx of lay students from the upper classes.[9] First the aristocracy, then the broader mass of landed gentry, became enthusiasts for university education as a way of training their sons for leadership of their local communities, for service in the expanding state bureaucracy, and for careers in the more prestigious professions such as law and the clergy. The educational balance within the universities shifted from the higher, vocational faculties to the general liberal education given in arts, and it became common simply to attend the university for a few years to acquire social and cultural polish, without necessarily taking a degree. For intending lawyers, for example, or for landed gentlemen seeking a smattering of legal knowledge for the management of their estates, the legal education given at the universities was of limited value. Civil law was relevant for some specialized branches of the legal system, and encouraged by the state because of the support it gave to monarchical authority, but the far more useful common law was not taught, and a barrister needed to be trained at one of the Inns of Court in London, themselves a late medieval development. It thus became normal to seek a general education at Oxford or Cambridge, and to follow this with professional study at the bar. In the case of medicine, university qualifications were even less useful: surgery was still essentially a practical skill, taught through apprenticeship; an MD degree was needed for the more prestigious qualifications given by the Royal College of Physicians, but the university's own medical teachers could not offer practical training.

The sixteenth century thus consolidated what was to remain a feature of the English universities – the atrophy of the professional faculties, and the centrality of general or 'liberal' education. This contrasted with the importance of law in most continental universities, as a form of general education for laymen as well as for the expanding bureaucracies of the state. For a time, the growth of 'offices' under the Tudor and Stuart monarchs took the same direction, and helped to make university qualifications more attractive. But British political developments cut short the growth of bureaucracy, one reason why growth before 1640 did not resume after 1660. What remained was the role of the ancient universities as finishing schools for the upper classes, grafted onto corporations devoted to learning and religion.[10] Their national role in giving the governing elite a set of common experiences and values was of lasting significance.

Historians have disagreed about the timing of the 'educational revolution' and about how to interpret the ambiguous social descriptions given in college and matriculation registers. Like the influence of humanism, the aristocratic influx of laymen was probably already under way in the fifteenth century. Growing numbers may have included boys from the urban middle class as well as from the gentry.[11] And while contemporaries were already grumbling that the wealthy were squeezing out poorer boys and taking over the endowments intended for them, it is probable that the older machinery of scholarships leading to careers in the church survived alongside the growth of 'commoners' (those not holding scholarships but paying fees), and continued to allow some social mobility.[12]

What seems beyond doubt is the sheer growth in numbers. It has been estimated that in 1400 there were about 2000 university students (1500 of them at Oxford, 5–600 at Cambridge), and that by 1450 numbers had risen to 3000 (1700 and 1300 respectively).[13] For later years, when continuous records of matriculation became available, it is easier to establish the number of students entering each year than the number in residence at any one time. Matriculations, after fluctuating in the sixteenth century, began a steady rise in 1600, which reached a peak in the 1630s. There may have been 6000 residents in the 1630s (3000 in each university, about one-third fellows and two-thirds undergraduates), a remarkably high figure for a country with a population of about five million.[14] It appears that, counting both universities and Inns of Court, some 2.5 per cent of the male age cohort was then receiving higher education.[15] The Civil War led to a sharp fall, especially at Oxford, which was the royalist headquarters, but in the 1650s numbers recovered, and reached a new peak around 1670, not much lower than that of the 1630s. But then a long decline set in, and for most of the eighteenth century numbers continued to fall, reaching their lowest point around 1760.[16] Revival then began, but growth was not steady, and the actual number of students did not pass the 1630 (or indeed the 1450) level until the 1860s, and in terms of percentage participation English higher education did not get back to the level of the 1630s until the twentieth century.[17] These long-term fluctuations are a reminder that continual growth is not a natural feature of university history, though it came to seem so in the late twentieth century.

After the upheavals of the Reformation period, the reign of Elizabeth I marked a return to comparative peace. In 1559, as part of her attempt to achieve a stable and balanced religious settlement, the queen issued further commissions of visitation for both universities, and she later visited them in person, staying for a week and attending learned disputations. James I made a habit, during his visits to Newmarket for racing and hunting, of summoning the Cambridge officials to account for the enforcement of royal instructions, and both James and Charles I used their hunting expeditions to Woodstock to monitor Oxford in the same way.[18] This close royal interest was accompanied by the growth of oligarchic government within the universities, replacing the self-government of the medieval masters. The heads of the colleges, or 'heads of houses', became the effective power, ruling through the Hebdomadal Board (Oxford) and the Caput (Cambridge). The chancellor, formerly elected by the masters, became in practice a royal nominee, the post usually going to a great nobleman with influence at court. It was not yet a purely ceremonial office, and the chancellors exercised much patronage, but they did not live on the spot, and everyday administration was in the hands of the vice-chancellor, normally a head of house. In the reign of Charles I, Archbishop Laud at Oxford was exceptional in being a clerical chancellor, and a former don; his ecclesiastical policies led to his downfall and execution, but his statutes of 1636 governed Oxford until the Victorian age.

Closer ties with the Crown strengthened the political and social position of the universities. An Act of Parliament of 1571 confirmed their corporate status and privileges, and in 1604 they acquired the right to elect university MPs (not abolished until 1948). The universities, said Charles I, were 'the seminaries of virtue and learning from whence the better part of our subjects by good education may bee disposed to religion, virtue and obedience of our lawes, and enabled to do service both in church and commonwealth'.[19] They were intimately connected with the governing elites of the country, and academic posts became a favourite field for royal and aristocratic patronage. But in this Faustian bargain, the state expected in return the universities' unquestioning support for political and religious authority, and for the hierarchical social order.[20] The universities were there, after all, to uphold the current theo-logical orthodoxy, and had to follow its twists and turns. Very broadly, Oxford was more sympathetic to the old religion, while Cambridge was a stronghold of reformers, and later of the Puritan wing of the Church of England. The Catholic Queen Mary made the point in 1554 when she sent the Protestant heretics Cranmer, Ridley and Latimer, all Cambridge men, to be tried by the Oxford theology faculty; the memorial erected in the 1840s on the site of their martyrdom was to have its own place in the religious controversies of nineteenth-century Oxford.[21] Elizabeth reigned with a rather lighter touch, and the different parties within Anglicanism coexisted in their university and college strongholds.

In the mid-seventeenth century religion and politics again divided the nation, and the universities once more underwent successive purges. Unlike the sixteenth-century visitations, these showed relatively little interest in changing what was taught, or in reforming university consti-tutions; their main effect was to eject, replace or reinstate college fellows. The personnel changed, but the property and corporate privileges of the colleges survived. The Grand Remonstrance of 1641 proposed to 'reform and purge the fountains of learning',[22] and in 1644–45 a parliamentary visitation of Cambridge ejected about half the heads of houses and fellows, and replaced them by scholars with more sympathetic religious views. Similar measures followed at Oxford, and both universities underwent further extensive purges during the most radical phase of the revolution. Once Oliver Cromwell was in power, some stability returned, despite the appointment of reforming commissions for each university in 1654. This period also saw various radical projects and pamphlets advocating wider university reform, including the idea of a university in London, and a college to serve northern England, at Manchester or Durham. The Durham project had Cromwell's support, and a start was made in organizing it. But even the radicals were more concerned to impose their own religious preferences than to change the social basis of education, and they had little support within Oxford or Cambridge.[23] Besides, subversive ideas provoked a conservative backlash. Thinkers like Thomas Hobbes argued that the expansion of education before 1640 had itself been a cause of social upheaval ('the Universities have been as mis-chievous to this Nation, as the Wooden Horse was to the Trojans').[24] Not only did they teach dangerous ideas, but too many men had been encouraged in ambitions which could not be satisfied, and as professions like the church became overcrowded their frustration turned into political and religious radicalism.[25] This was not the last time that 'alienated intellectuals' were to be blamed for revolution; if university numbers never fully recovered after 1660 to their previous level, this owed something to a deliberate policy of discouraging recruitment from classes outside the wealthy and the landed.

After the restoration of the monarchy in 1660, there were fewer wholesale ejections of personnel, but those who had suffered for their loyalty to king and church were naturally restored to their posts. Religious orthodoxy was more narrowly enforced than before, and former dissidents within the Anglican fold were redefined as 'Dissenters' or Nonconformists and excluded from the universities. The religious tests introduced in the universities under Elizabeth, requiring students and dons to subscribe to the Thirty-Nine Articles and other criteria of Anglican orthodoxy, were now rigorously applied, eventually leading the Nonconformists to develop their own form of higher education, the 'Dissenting Academies'. In the 1680s, religious politics again reared their head. The Roman Catholic James II was determined to extend tolerance to his coreligionists, and attempted to appoint them to university posts. The resistance of Magdalen College, Oxford, to the intrusion of Catholic fellows was celebrated in the nineteenth century by Thomas Macaulay as a heroic episode in the making of the 1688 revolution, though the affair could be seen more justly as part of a long and continuing history of royal intervention and pressure. After 1688 the sanctity of property, including the privileges of corporate bodies, became entrenched in English political thinking, and this was one form of defence for university autonomy; but it carried the danger that universities would no longer respond to changes in the outside world.

When James's reign ended in disaster, there was a natural reassertion of Protestant loyalty, but this was a difficult period, as many Anglicans also opposed the deposition of a legitimate king, and Oxford was a stronghold of these 'non-jurors'. The Whigs who dominated politics after 1688 behaved with relative moderation, and the last real university purges took place after 1715, when Oxford was again suspect as a centre of Jacobite resistance to the Hanoverian succession. For a time politicians contemplated a new 'visitation' of the universities, 'to reform and correct all excesses and defects so that these places of public education may be made in the best manner to answer the end of their institution',[26] and there was a parliamentary Bill in 1719, but these plans were dropped. Some politicians may have shared the view of Speaker Arthur Onslow that the purpose of universities should not be the defence of orthodoxy, but 'the search of knowledge, which can only be had by the freedom of debate, and without which an university would contradict its nature and shall I say its name';[27] but a more common reason for leaving them alone was that both Whiggish Cambridge and Tory Oxford could now be relied on to sustain the social order.

These experiences were shared by the Scottish universities. The first Scottish universities were founded in the fifteenth century: St Andrews in 1410–11; Glasgow in 1451; King's College at Aberdeen in 1495. All were situated, unlike Oxford and Cambridge, in the shadow of cathedrals, and were under the thumb of their bishops. They had the usual four faculties, but by this time collegiate life was also in vogue; St Andrews had three colleges, founded between 1450 and 1537 (but reduced to two in the eighteenth century), while Aberdeen and Glasgow were universities composed of a single college. The same was true of the University of Dublin, better known as Trinity College, founded by Elizabeth I in 1592 to ensure Protestant supremacy in Ireland by training clergy for the Irish Anglican church; it also came to serve the landed class, and the Protestant professional and merchant classes of Dublin itself. Trinity College developed on 'Oxbridge' lines, with an endowment supporting celibate fellows, and students living in the college. In their early years the Scottish universities were also residential, and traces of this survived until the early nineteenth century, but they never had rich endowments and retained much of their original character as seminaries for the priesthood. The Scottish upper classes, and ambitious scholars, often preferred continental universities, weakening the over-numerous native institutions.

The Reformation reached Scotland later than England, in the 1560s, and took a more radical, Calvinist form, which placed even more emphasis on training a learned clergy to bring the Bible and its teachings to the people. To this end, many bursaries were created to recruit students from rural and relatively poor backgrounds, laying a foundation for Scottish 'democratic' traditions.[28] The Reformation stimulated a thorough overhaul of the existing universities, notably at Glasgow, and there were two new foundations. At Edinburgh, the university founded in 1583 was financed and controlled until 1858 by the town council, an arrangement unique in Britain. Marischal College at Aberdeen (1593) was the work of a powerful local nobleman, and was to remain separate from King's College until 1860. Marischal was in 'new Aberdeen', the mercantile port distinct from the old cathedral town, and like Edinburgh it represented a new urban conception of higher education, perhaps reflecting Scotland's own version of the 'educational revolution'. The religious function of the universities still predominated, but they also attracted laymen interested in public office and liberal education.[29] As in England, this movement seems to have reached its peak in the 1630s, when Glasgow University felt confident enough to embark on a complete rebuilding. The politico-religious conflicts after 1640, however, were especially disruptive in Scotland, and continued until the end of the century, with the struggle between episcopalians and Presbyterians for control of the Scottish church. After 1688, when Presbyterianism triumphed, the Scottish Parliament set up visiting commissions which dismissed many teachers and overhauled the curriculum, even trying to impose a common philosophical textbook. The Act of Union of 1707 preserved the Presbyterian religious settlement in Scotland, and the legal position of the Scottish universities was guaranteed. But the 1688 revolution had created Jacobitism as a new political threat, and this was harshly dealt with by further purges after 1715; at Aberdeen, where Jacobitism was strong, Marischal College was closed down for two years.[30] As a result, the universities became thoroughly Hanoverian and proved loyal during the rising of 1745. Thus in Scotland the state firmly established its right to regulate the universities as a national system, and the restoration of calm after 1715 allowed them to modernize themselves and to develop as centres of enlightened thought, in marked contrast to the English ones.[31]

It is natural to think that the political interventions and upheavals of the Tudor and Stuart periods damaged the intellectual vitality of the English universities – for scholarship seems to depend on academic freedom. Yet their historians are agreed that the seventeenth century was something of a golden age.[32] The very fact that religion was at the heart of contemporary concerns, for the lay elite in parliament as well as for prelates, religious radicals and the state, gave intellectual and scholarly debate within the universities a vital importance. If by the end of the seventeenth century the curriculum was beginning to fossilize, it was certainly still capable before that of producing sharp minds as well as learned scholars. The academic inhabitants of Oxford were already demonstrating the robust and quirky independence of mind which became characteristic of the place, just as the puritanism of Cambridge might be seen as a forerunner of the 'plain living and high thinking' traditionally attributed to the fenland university. This was also a period, like the reigns of Edward VI and Mary, when many academics endured exile, often teaching or studying in continental universities, and bringing back fresh ideas – a cosmopolitanism which was to be lost in the eighteenth century.

It is sometimes claimed that the universities failed to take account of new developments in science, which were centred in London, where the Royal Society was founded in 1660, or to promote what one of their contemporary critics, Francis Bacon, called 'the advancement of learning'. But 'learning' was not the same as modern science or research: preserving and passing on inherited knowledge was more valued than originality, and the universities were carrying out this function effectively, refining and transmitting the science and learning of their time.[33] They fed well-prepared men into London's speculative circles, and incorporated new ideas into their teaching once they had established their claim to truth. The courtly intellectuals in London had close university connections, and the universities helped to shape a broader learned culture in which country gentlemen cultivated classical taste and the study of local history and antiquities.

In the eighteenth century this responsiveness dwindled, for various reasons. The formal curriculum seemed increasingly irrelevant to the expectations of students, which were as much social as intellectual; social recruitment was narrower; aristocratic polite culture came to be centred on the literary world of the capital, the social life of the country house, and the grand tour; the rise of Whiggish anticlericalism and the decline of religious passions left universities with the useful but marginal professional role of turning out moderate-minded clergymen to preach reason and obedience to their flocks; and comfortable landed endowments removed any incentive to cultivate the market. Between 1715 and 1850, the state interfered less with the English universities than at any time before or after, satisfied with their loyalty and their social usefulness. Was it a coincidence that this was also the longest period of intellectual stagnation in their history? Or a paradox that it was the Scottish universities, impoverished and battered by events, that responded creatively to the new challenges of the age of Enlightenment?

2

Currents of Change

'The religious and academical establishments in some parts of Europe are not without their use to the historian of the Human Mind', remarked the Scottish philosopher Dugald Stewart in 1824. 'Immovably moored to the same station by the strength of their cables, and the weight of their anchors, they enable him to measure the rapidity of the current by which the rest of the world are borne along.'[1] Stewart was one of several Scots who contrasted the lethargy of the English universities with the liveliness of the Scottish ones. The *Edinburgh Review*, the organ of Whig reform, ran a series of attacks on Oxford and Cambridge in 1808–10, and in the 1830s Stewart's colleague at Edinburgh, William Hamilton, returned to the charge, especially targeting Oxford. Scottish critics attacked both the narrow curricula of the English universities, compared with the broader, philosophical Scottish approach, and their corporate privilege and inefficiency. For Hamilton, writing at the time of the 1832 Reform Act, when all aristocratic and clerical institutions were under scrutiny, the root of the evil lay in the college system. The colleges had usurped the 'privileges by law accorded to the public University of Oxford, as the authorized organ of national education', establishing a monopoly of teaching, and entrenching the private vested interests of the fellows.[2] The key to reform was to replace this 'tutorial' system by revival of the professorial university on Scottish lines.

The contrast between Scotland and England was a valid one. The Scottish universities had their own faults, which called forth a royal commission of inquiry in 1826, but they certainly seemed more efficient organs of education. While student numbers at Oxford and Cambridge had fallen (on extremely rough estimates) from perhaps 3000 in 1700 to 1500 in 1800, in Scotland, which had a tenth of the English population, they had risen in the same years from about 1200 to 2850. These numbers were handled in 1800 by seventy-two professors; Oxford and

Cambridge each had about twenty professors, whose lectures were largely unconnected with the curriculum, if they were given at all, while lavish endowments supported college fellows – some 400 at Cambridge – among whom only a minority taught or published scholarly books.[3] Defenders of the English system pointed out that fellowships had other functions, as part of the career structure of the national church, as rewards for academic achievement, and as a support for young men in the early years of professional life, but it was not only Scottish radicals who thought that this was a wasteful, even scandalous, diversion of resources originally meant for education and the advancement of learning.

One reason for the relative vigour of the Scottish universities was the very lack of wealthy endowments, for little of the plunder of the church at the Scottish Reformation had come to them. Liberal economic theorists like Adam Smith argued that this was why they were responsive to new needs, since professors depended for their income on lecture fees. The universities were located (leaving aside St Andrews) in Scotland's three largest cities, and in the eighteenth century there was a decisive shift away from college residence to living in lodgings or with families. Fees were moderate, and students could combine part-time study with work. Local elites – merchants, clergy, gentry from the surrounding counties – had a strong interest in promoting and modernizing their universities, and there was a feeling after 1707 that the exploitation of Scotland's intellectual resources would compensate for its loss of political independence; there was no equivalent of this lay influence at Oxford or Cambridge.

Revival from the troubles of the seventeenth century began in Scotland around 1720. Teaching had traditionally been given by 'regents', who took a cohort of pupils through all three or four years of the fixed curriculum. Edinburgh and Glasgow took the lead in replacing regenting with professorial lectures, which were soon given in English rather than Latin, and professors like Francis Hutcheson at Glasgow used the subject of 'moral philosophy' to discuss contemporary social, economic and political problems. The lecture system broke down the single compulsory curriculum, and allowed students to study what interested them; a fixed set of subjects was still required from candidates for the church, but formal exercises and graduation fell into decay. The universities provided the 'polite' and useful education favoured by the eighteenth-century elite, and student debating societies and the broader cultural life of the cities supplemented university lectures to promote (as a contemporary put it in 1774) 'boldness of disquisition, liberality of sentiment, accuracy of reasoning, correctness of taste and attention to composition'.[4] Combined with relatively tolerant and rational attitudes – there were no religious tests for students, and those for professors were loosely enforced – this liberal educational function put the universities at the heart of the Scottish Enlightenment. For a time in the late eighteenth century, they could claim to be the most advanced intellectual centres in Europe, as scholars like William Robertson, Adam Smith and Adam Ferguson illuminated the human sciences (though David Hume's scepticism barred him from a chair). Nor were the natural sciences neglected, as Joseph Black and William Cullen showed in chemistry at Glasgow and Edinburgh. In 1754 King's College Aberdeen launched a successful appeal to 'their Alumni, in Different Parts of the World, and others, who Wish well to this University, and the Improvement of Natural Knowledge', to pay for a museum, chemistry laboratory and dissecting-room.[5] It was not the last time that universities were to target their alumni.

As the mention of a dissecting-room indicates, medicine was now a key subject, for urban elites encouraged the development of the professional faculties, to train their own sons and to serve the community's general welfare. Scottish universities retained active theology faculties, and from around 1740 also expanded their schools of law and medicine, drawing on the Dutch models with which many Scots were familiar. James Boswell was only one of the many upper-class men who studied at Leiden or Utrecht before becoming lawyers, but once Scottish universities had modernized their own faculties this custom died out. The Scottish medical schools adopted the new continental practice of combining theory with clinical teaching in large modern hospitals, and became distinguished enough to attract students from England and overseas. Until the mid-nineteenth century, a British doctor with a medical degree was almost certain to have got it in Scotland. Medicine was also important because it supported the teaching of chemistry and botany. Chemistry professors soon became interested in industrial and agricultural applications (and Edinburgh had a separate chair of agriculture from 1790), serving another of Scotland's national aspirations, which was to modernize the economy and catch up with the prosperity of England. Thus the Scottish universities developed a successful blend of general and practical education.

A further notable feature was their wide social base. The universities were accessible to the broader urban population, and in Glasgow at least this meant local merchants and artisans as well as the social elite.[6] But rural Scotland also contributed students. Since 1696 there had been a statutory system of parish schools, whose masters were themselves expected to have some university education, so that they could teach Latin and send promising boys direct to the university, often very young. The typical age of entry in Scotland remained fifteen or sixteen, sometimes even younger, while in England it was rising to eighteen. The corollary of this, as English critics of Scotland pointed out, was that much university teaching was at an elementary level. It was among aspirants to the clergy that poorer students were most likely to be found, and in Scotland scholarships or bursaries still reached the class for which they were founded. Once they had graduated, these men could become ministers and schoolmasters, or take their chance in literature, journalism or science, Thomas Carlyle and James Mill being notable examples. The notion of the Scottish 'democratic intellect' can easily be exaggerated or sentimentalized: the system was a haphazard one which depended on luck and aristocratic patronage; it benefited the sons of farmers or craftsmen rather than the really poor, and had parallels in other Protestant countries like Germany; but it certainly contrasted with England.

The stereotyped view of the English universities at this time goes back to the criticisms of Edward Gibbon. The great historian was typical in being an aristocratic heir, but untypical in his thirst for scholarship. He went to Oxford at the age of fourteen in 1752, stayed for little over a year, and later regarded it as time wasted. Like Adam Smith and other Scottish critics, he indicted the decay of the professorate and the idleness of the college fellows, 'steeped in port and prejudice' by their 'dull and deep potations'.[7] Gibbon was right to focus on the status of the college fellows. They were the main beneficiaries of the university's wealth, but had little incentive either to teach or pursue original scholarship. Most fellowships required the holder to take holy orders within a certain time, and also to remain celibate. Thus fellowships were not seen as a lifetime academic career, but as a staging-post while waiting for a well-paid parish living, often one of those to which the college itself nominated. Many fellows had careers elsewhere and did not live in Oxford or Cambridge; colleges appointed one or two of the resident fellows as tutors to look after the undergraduates' education and their moral and religious welfare. The system would have been more defensible if fellows had used their ample leisure for research, but few did. Stress on religious orthodoxy, and the detachment of the universities from any kind of utilitarian concerns, meant that although there may have been an English Enlightenment as well as a Scottish one, the universities had little part in it; and if the central feature of the Enlightenment was its challenge to tradition and authority, these were not attitudes which eighteenth-century Oxbridge encouraged.

Yet Gibbon's judgements, and others like them, give only a partial picture, and historians have recently done something to rehabilitate the unreformed universities. For one thing, it was not only in England that student enrolments and intellectual life stagnated or declined in the eighteenth century. The French universities, with an equally distinguished past, were also dominated by the church. They had virtually no part in generating the ideas of the Enlightenment, their curricula were resistant to innovation, and formal graduation exercises had become rituals with little relation to students' ability or real knowledge. When the twenty-two French universities were swept away by the 1789 revolution, there were few mourners. The English ones at least retained their central position in the life of the governing class, and their function in providing ideological justification for the existing order. But in other respects, again with French parallels, they had become marginal to national life: both France and England were wealthy and intellectually dynamic countries, but the universities were simply bypassed by the new currents of thought, and seemed to stand apart from the changes taking place in society, especially the growth of commercial wealth and of a new middle class. As early as the 1690s, proto-utilitarians like John Locke (a former Oxford don dismissed for his political views) were writing off the universities as hopelessly traditional. London, with its literary circles, newspapers, coffee-houses, theatres and salons was now the centre of

English cultural life.[8] The exclusion of non-Anglicans became a serious weakness when so much new wealth, and so much of the progress of science and social thought, arose in Nonconformist circles, in London and in new centres of energy like Birmingham and Liverpool. Neither in France before 1789 nor in Britain were reform pressures strong enough to shake the state's reliance on the universities as bastions of religious and political orthodoxy. Attempts to dismantle the Anglican monopoly in the 1770s were easily defeated, and the political reaction which set in once Britain was at war with revolutionary France after 1793 only strengthened this conservatism, and discredited ideas of radical reform. In that year, the vice-chancellor of Oxford defined 'the sole purposes of our academical institutions' as 'maintenance of Order, the Advancement of Learning, and the furtherance of Religion and morality'.[9] He did at least include the advancement of learning, if not of critical thought.

If the universities were reinforcing the existing order rather than challenging it, however, this was precisely why their position in English society was so difficult to shake. The wider vocational role evident until the seventeenth century had decayed, and the church was now the profession into which about two-thirds of graduates passed.[10] The appeal of academic learning to the lesser landed gentry had declined. Yet Oxford and Cambridge did not lose their links with provincial communities, or the allegiance of the aristocratic landed magnates, whose elder sons were sent there to fraternize with their peers, make useful contacts, acquire the classical veneer needed to move in fashionable circles, and fit themselves for public life as leaders of local society and national legislators. After 1740, over half of all peers attended Oxford or Cambridge; half of all MPs continued to be graduates, and by the 1820s this had risen to 60 per cent.[11] This concentration of elite education in two institutions, creating an unusually cohesive set of shared values and social habits, had no parallel in other large European countries, and created a national consciousness that was increasingly 'British'.[12] The universities' appeal to the gentry and the younger sons of the aristocracy also increased as growing agricultural wealth made livings and offices in the Church of England more lucrative. The fact that landowners and clergy were educated together was seen as a strength: the rural masses were taught order and obedience through the preaching of the parish clergy; if the latter were in turn dependent on the landlords for their posts and shared their upbringing and values, social stability would be secured. One consequence, seemingly paradoxical when the universities were the chief seminaries of the clergy, was that specifically theological education declined: it was more important for the clergyman to be a 'scholar and a gentleman' than an expert in his profession.

Thus the universities had a single cultural role, as dispensers of a uniform liberal education, but a dual social one as nurseries of the clergy and the governing elite. In 1800 a few students of poorer backgrounds were still reaching the universities, sometimes as 'servitors' or 'sizars' waiting on richer students, but college scholarships were usually beyond their reach. One reason was that most local grammar schools were no longer serving their original function. Some of them, as charities left without state supervision, had fallen into deep decay; others, in a process which continued in the early nineteenth century – Thomas Arnold's Rugby being a notable example – had been converted from local schools to 'public' schools with national recruitment and high fees. A few grammar schools, like Hawkshead in the Lake District, which sent William Wordsworth to Cambridge in 1787, were still serving a wider middle-class or farming clientele.[13] But by the early nineteenth century a handful of public schools had established themselves as the main feeders of Oxford and Cambridge, and the intensive classical education which they gave allowed the universities to insist on a high level of preparation, which further repelled the poor. On the other hand, public schools and universities together allowed the richest members of the business and professional class to induct their sons into gentlemanly values and consolidate a family's position in society. The university could be a road to the highest positions in law and politics, as shown by Robert Peel (Harrow and Oxford) and William Gladstone (Eton and Oxford), sons of a Lancashire industrialist and a Liverpool merchant respectively. At a rather lower social level, the attraction of careers in the church or law made a gentlemanly education a good investment for modest landed or professional families who could scrape together the resources, linking the universities intimately with the world of country houses, parsonages and cathedral cities.

Though open only to Anglicans, the universities thus had a tenacious combination of social roles which kept them at the centre of English society despite their lack of intellectual vitality. Even on that point, historians have recently begun to correct the Gibbonian stereotype. There were always individual scholars, like the Cambridge classicists Richard Bentley (d. 1742) and Richard Porson (d. 1808), who used their positions to advance learning. In the early eighteenth century there was a thorough overhaul of the curriculum at Cambridge, which retained the classics, but eliminated the last traces of scholasticism. Locke and Newton were the new authorities, and Newton's influence now made mathematics the dominant subject at Cambridge. In the long run, conservatism set in here too, and Newton's prestige became an obstacle to adopting new mathematical approaches. But the subject became the basis of a new university examination system. The 'Senate House examination' began in the 1740s, was later renamed the 'Tripos', and by 1800 had become a testing examination. Although voluntary, it provided a competitive test for ambitious students, and success in it opened the way to college fellowships. Oral examinations were gradually supplanted by uniform written papers – a Cambridge invention with a big future.[14] Oxford was slower to discard the Aristotelian curriculum, but it set up a similar 'Schools' examination in 1800, based on classics rather than mathematics. These examinations became the main stimulus to intellectual revival; in an age of political and industrial revolution, they also represented a call to the traditional governing class to return to serious study and to justify their claims to leadership by proving their ability.[15] The reforming royal commission of 1850 noted with approval that even aristocratic youths had not 'disdained to adorn a noble lineage with the graceful addition of academic honours'.[16] The examinations were also a significant reassertion of the university's role as against the colleges, though the colleges had themselves, even before 1800, been using examinations to raise their standards, and encouraging undergraduates to follow coherent programmes of study and reading.

An important feature of the mathematical and scientific tradition at Cambridge was that it embodied an intellectual compromise with religion which has been called the 'holy alliance', a compromise which lasted until the mid-nineteenth century.[17] Within the Church of England, the prevailing eighteenth-century current was latitudinarianism, a form of churchmanship which avoided excessive religious zeal, tried to be tolerant rather than exclusive, and sought to base religion on reason as well as revelation. In Scotland, the dominance of the so-called Moderate party in the Church, and the elaboration of an intuitionist 'common sense' philosophy which sought to refute the scepticism of Hume, represented similar Enlightenment values. In this view, science was seen as providing evidence for 'natural religion', studying God's work as the creator and designer of the natural world. Thus it was possible for scientists also to be clergymen and college fellows, and mathematics seemed a suitable form of general education for future clergymen. William Paley's *View of the Evidences of Christianity* (1794) and his *Natural Theology* (1802) became standard textbooks at Cambridge, though high-church and Tory Oxford was always much more resistant to this Whiggish form of religion.[18] The breakdown of the holy alliance in the nineteenth century was to herald the end of the Anglican monopoly.

Among Dugald Stewart's tides of change, the most obvious might seem to be the transformation of Britain into an industrialized country and the growth of the middle classes. Yet the direct impact of these changes on universities was very limited. The progress of industry in its early years rested on empirical inventions and practical technology rather than scientific theory, and as long as industry was dominated by individual entrepreneurs and family firms there was little demand for trained scientists or technical experts. Universities simply seemed irrelevant to industry or commerce, and if there were demands for new forms of education they could be satisfied in other and cheaper ways. Nonconformists in England, Wales and Ireland often used the Scottish universities, or the dissenting academies, which spanned higher and secondary education and taught modern subjects, but could not award degrees; these might have developed into an alternative model of higher education, but in fact failed to do so, and later either disappeared or shrank into colleges for training Nonconformist ministers.

By the early nineteenth century, the English universities' educational machinery appeared disjointed and decayed. There were serious scholars and scientists at both, and serious students too, but neither had a real incentive to work, and whether teachers and students came together seemed to depend on chance and voluntary effort. The recreations of gentlemanly students were well documented in a university novel of the

1850s, *The Adventures of Mr Verdant Green*, by 'Cuthbert Bede' (a Durham graduate, as the pseudonym indicated). Verdant Green was a naive freshman, soon inducted into the idleness, drinking, indebtedness, and sporting habits – horses and dogs at that time rather than team games – of his aristocratic contemporaries. It was this image of dissipation, as much as the expense of university education and the dubious value of the archaic curriculum, which put off middle-class parents. Thus social pressure from outside was weak, and after a boom in numbers at the end of the Napoleonic wars enrolments at both universities stagnated until reform began to make an impression on public opinion in the 1850s.

In the political arena, the 1832 Reform Act seemed to shift power towards the middle classes, but political leadership remained in the hands of the traditional aristocracy. The Whig or liberal party had plans, often radical ones, for overhauling British institutions, but universities were not at the top of the list. Attempts at university legislation were made for Oxford and Cambridge in 1834 and 1837, and Scotland in 1836, but were defeated or abandoned. Various issues were involved in these debates, notably the archaism of university constitutions and curricula, but religion was the key political question. In 1828 the surviving restrictions on the civil liberties of Nonconformists were removed, and Catholic Emancipation followed in 1829. With the end of the 'confessional state', the exclusive Anglicanism of Oxford and Cambridge seemed increasingly anomalous. For religious tests were still in force: at Oxford all students had to subscribe on matriculation to the Thirty-Nine Articles; at Cambridge, similar declarations had to be made at graduation, which did allow non-Anglicans to study at the university, but not to gain much advantage from it; at both universities the colleges remained religious corporations, their fellowships and scholarships restricted to Anglicans. Middle-class spokesmen, including the strong Nonconformist element in their ranks, might not wish to transform the universities into utilitarian schools, or to destroy their privileged social position, but they did want to restore them as 'national' institutions, whose social advantages would be accessible to all. On the other side, churchmen were all the more determined to hold on to their control of elite education when they were forced to retreat from other strongholds, and they saw the universities as an integral part of the church's social and pastoral organization. Yet England now stood out in a European context, as the process of secularization started by the French Revolution and spread by Napoleon's conquests opened French and German universities to citizens of all faiths. Moreover, most British liberals ultimately shared the continental liberal belief that it was the function of the state to protect liberty of conscience and the rights of religious minorities, and to curb an overmighty church.

The most radical spokesmen for the middle class in the early nineteenth century were the utilitarian followers of Jeremy Bentham. Rational reform of British institutions was part of a project to replace an aristocratic system of government based on patronage and family influence with professional, bureaucratic, scientifically informed administration. To produce such experts, higher education of some kind would be needed – but Oxford and Cambridge perhaps seemed too irrelevant to the ideal to become the immediate target. A more promising venture, and one which filled an obvious gap, was the 'University of London', today's University College London, founded in 1828 by a group of reformers who included disciples of Bentham; the philosopher himself was only marginally involved, but after his death in 1832 the college acquired his remains and put them (clothed) on public display. The new college was to be secular, and was supported by Catholics, Nonconformists and Jews as well as intellectuals of a rationalist cast. It was not residential, and adopted a professorial lecture system inspired by German and even more by Scottish models. Its curriculum included new and practical subjects such as law, economics, engineering, English literature and modern languages; it was aimed, in the words of the poet Thomas Campbell, one of the founders, at 'the middling classes of the metropolis'.[19]

The new college had no religious tests for professors or students: this challenge to the established view that religion and education were inseparable made the 'godless university' highly controversial, provoking strong hostility from Oxford and Cambridge, and from the church party, who founded the rival and confessional King's College in 1831. Neither University nor King's College had the power to award degrees, a situation remedied in 1836, when the state founded a new University of London, a public, non-denominational body which did not teach but administered examinations and degrees for 'affiliated' colleges, of which

University College (as it was now renamed) and King's became the first. The 1836 Act was important in establishing both that state sanction was necessary to confer degrees, and that university education could be detached from religion.[20] Further reform of London University in 1858 allowed anyone to sit for the examinations regardless of their place of education. This external examination system was to be very important in promoting the development of higher education in provincial Britain and in the British Empire, while the idea of an impartial examining university, maintaining uniform academic standards, and standing above the tensions of religious sectarianism, became a model for later initiatives. It also embodied a split between teaching and examining, and an emphasis on external examinations, which deeply marked British academic culture in the nineteenth century. Outside London, a new university appeared at Durham in 1834, given degree powers from the start because it was Anglican, having been conceived as a way of using the surplus revenues of the wealthy bishopric of Durham. But it was not until 1851 that Owens College at Manchester brought higher education to the capital of industrialism.

The foundation of the University of London was influenced by continental as well as Scottish models, and the former were a growing presence in British university debate. Scottish universities had themselves been influenced by Holland, but later in the eighteenth century it was the Protestant universities of Germany, notably Göttingen (founded in 1737) which showed the way. As in Scotland, educational renewal was based on professorial lectures in the vernacular, but Göttingen also introduced the principle that professors were expected to carry out original research. They were recruited on the basis of scholarly ability from all over Germany, breaking down parochial barriers. Germany soon began to make notable contributions to humanistic study, and the Göttingen model spread elsewhere. University development, in Germany and many other countries, was then disrupted by the revolutionary and Napoleonic wars between 1792 and 1815. French conquest and occupation were usually accompanied by secularization and the confiscation of church property, destroying the financial independence of such universities as survived political reorganization, abolishing their corporate privileges, and making them dependent on the state. The insulation of the English universities from these changes made them stand out as archaic in a way which was new.

The political reaction to French rule was especially significant in Prussia. The new University of Berlin, founded in 1810, soon became Germany's largest university, an intellectual powerhouse and a focus for national sentiment. The official largely responsible for its foundation, along with the philosopher J. G. Fichte and the liberal theologian Friedrich Schleiermacher, was Wilhelm von Humboldt, and the university model developed at Berlin, building on the work of Göttingen, has come to be known (though only since about 1900) as the 'Humboldtian' university. The key principle, enunciated by Humboldt himself, was the 'union of teaching and research'. Professors should be both teachers and original scholars, and teaching itself should not be simply the transmission of facts, but a creative process in which the student learnt through discovery and was trained in the techniques of original research. Teacher and student were thus part of a 'community of scholars', allies in that search for truth which was the university's mission. 'So the university teacher is no longer a teacher, the student no longer a learner, but the latter carries out research himself, and the professor directs and supports his researches.'[21] It was an ideal which worked both ways: Humboldt saw teaching as sterile and elementary if it was not based on research, but research itself lacked life and a broader intellectual context if it was not subject to the test of teaching and transmitted personally to students. The German word *Wissenschaft*, meaning 'science', but with wider implications difficult to translate into English, described the objective and critical pursuit of science and learning and the establishment of truth through rigorous academic methods. This conception of the university remains the orthodox one today, though there is no simple line from Berlin in 1810 to the twenty-first century.

Not all aspects of the Humboldtian model proved adaptable to other countries, and in Germany itself it took time for various features to coalesce. It was customary at the time, and has been since, to contrast the German model with the French one established by Napoleon on the ruins of the old universities. In France, higher education was divided among specialized institutions, including schools of law and medicine and engineering schools like the celebrated Ecole Polytechnique, while scientific research was generally not united with teaching but pursued in separate institutes, mostly in Paris. The French system was highly centralized and bureaucratic. In Germany, universities were also run by the various states, but they retained corporate identity and autonomy; Berlin was significant because it reproduced the traditional grouping of arts, law, medical and theology faculties within a single body. Some British reformers, especially scientists, were attracted by the French model of specialized research institutes, but in the absence of a Napoleonic state it was the German autonomous university which was more relevant to both English and Scottish traditions.

The British universities retained far more legal and financial independence than the German ones. Academic freedom, though subject to the constraints of religious orthodoxy, did not generally have to be defended from political intervention by the state. In Germany, however, the idea of objective *Wissenschaft* was seen as an important way of securing 'freedom of teaching' (*Lehrfreiheit*) against both the state and religious dogma. Professors were appointed by the state, but it was the academic community which decided who was qualified for appointment, through the apparatus of disciplinary standards and protocols: the research doctorate, publication in learned journals and books aimed at fellow-scholars, membership of academies and professional associations; 'peer review' is a modern descendant of this idea. The professional university world became a guild which controlled entry to its own ranks; its senior members controlled the internal life of the universities, trained their successors, and enjoyed much power as patrons. Research was the criterion for appointment, not teaching ability, because it alone provided objective evidence by which rival candidates could be measured. The professor was at the centre of the system. Once appointed, *Lehrfreiheit* meant that he decided what research to do, following the internal development of the discipline and his own judgement of where the frontiers of knowledge lay. In Germany and other countries, this form of academic freedom was eventually protected by state constitutions. At Oxford and Cambridge, which controlled their own appointments, such guarantees hardly seemed necessary, and this was one reason for the comparatively slow growth of academic professionalization.

Disciplinary specialization and the stress on original work were developments of the Humboldtian ideal. What Humboldt himself meant by 'research' was a quest for understanding, leading to the spiritual growth and self-development of the individual, in the context of a half-mystical belief in the unity of knowledge. This ideal of *Bildung* was a German version of the theory of liberal education, and as such could be reconciled with both English and Scottish traditions. For Humboldt's generation, *Bildung* was closely allied with 'neo-humanism', the study of classical and especially Greek civilization as a source of timeless and harmonious values, and this hellenism had a strong influence on the rejuvenation of classical studies in Britain. But other aspects of *Bildung* were more alien. The German tradition stressed the 'freedom of learning' (*Lernfreiheit*) of the individual student, who should not be constrained by fixed curricula or examination syllabuses, but should map out his own path through the university's intellectual offerings. In an influential restatement of the German ideal in 1923 (republished in 1946 as part of the rescue of valid traditions in the aftermath of Nazism), the philosopher Karl Jaspers took it as an axiom that the student comes to the university 'to arrive at a well-founded *Weltanschauung*. He wants to arrive at truth, wants to gain a clear view of the world and of people. He wants to encounter wholeness, an infinite cosmic order.' Students are adults, not children, responsible for their own career in the world of ideas. 'Professors do not give them assignments or personal guidance ... No authority, no rules and regulations, no supervision of studies such as are found in high schools must be allowed to hamper the university student.' For 'the university would cease being a university if a properly qualified student body were shepherded through a fixed curriculum subject to periodical control by examinations.'[22]

This was not the British tradition, even in the nineteenth century. There the ideal of liberal education was based on prescriptive curricula and set exercises designed to train and test the mental powers, and although a modified *Lernfreiheit* later developed when students were given more choice of subjects, the dominance of examinations was to increase not diminish. There was also a practical difficulty: the supposed ability of the German student to work independently and carry out original work rested on a long and rigorous secondary education, which gave a thorough classical grounding and allowed other elements of general education to be completed by the age of eighteen. Training secondary teachers was a prime function of the arts or 'philosophy' faculty, and ensured that they shared the scientific spirit and values of the university itself. The English public schools, within their narrow social and intellectual limits, enjoyed a similar relationship with Oxford and Cambridge. But schools like the German *Gymnasium*, or the very similar French *lycée*, hardly existed in England for the bulk of the middle class, or in Scotland at all. This was one reason why students entered university so young in Scotland, and why on both sides of the border university reform was tied up with the improvement of secondary education, for which most reformers, notably Matthew Arnold, looked to continental models and to the state. Only when a longer and more academic secondary education became widely available towards the end of the century, teaching science and other modern subjects alongside the classics, were universities free to specialize.

Bildung was always a utopian ideal – the main aim of most German students was not to explore the cosmic order but to pass their professional examinations to become lawyers, doctors, pastors or officials. The real effect of the Göttingen and Berlin system, as German universities expanded after the restoration of peace in 1815, was to provide fertile ground for impressive intellectual achievements in 'philology' (the more technical aspect of classical and linguistic studies), theology and biblical criticism, history, philosophy, and science. The humanities saw the development of the 'seminar', a class in which advanced students learnt research techniques under the professor and could make their own contribution to knowledge. By the 1830s, Hamilton and other critics were already contrasting German achievements with the somnolence of Oxford and Cambridge, though the resistance of conservatives was only strengthened by the supposed role of German philosophy and biblical criticism in undermining Christianity.[23] In science, the equivalent of the seminar was the laboratory in which research and training were combined, and the chemist Justus Liebig at Giessen ran the most celebrated of these in the 1830s and 1840s. The value of a science like chemistry was increased by its industrial applications, and Germany seemed to lead other countries in harnessing science to economic development, though the tradition of *Bildung* remained hostile to purely technical education, which had to develop in Germany outside the universities. Many British scientists went to Giessen to be trained, and it was on this model that the British government created the Royal College of Chemistry in London in 1845 – a rare example of direct state provision.

It is was not only German intellectual achievements or the German form of university organization that attracted admirers. Benthamites and other practical reformers derived from both German and French models the principle of recruiting public servants by merit, using education to produce trained experts and a modern, rational bureaucracy, while cultural critics like Coleridge and Arnold sought to popularize the idea, particularly associated with Humboldt and Prussia, that the state had a positive cultural or 'ethical' role, and should use this creatively while respecting university autonomy. 'The state must understand that intellectual work will go on infinitely better if it does not intrude', wrote Humboldt. It 'must supply the organizational framework and the resources necessary for the practice of science and scholarship', but must also 'adhere to a deep conviction that if the universities attain their highest ends, they will also realize the state's ends too, and these on a far higher plane'.[24]

Continental states saw the support of education at all levels as part of their mission. In England the state began to finance elementary schools on a modest scale in the 1830s, but liberal dogma was against subsidizing middle-class education, and state intervention was seen as an example of the 'despotism' from which Britons were happily free. In Scotland, however, where there was a long tradition of public provision, from parish schools to universities, intellectuals tended to think that it was, in Hamilton's words in 1832, 'the duty of a government, not only to provide for the necessary instruction of the people, but also to promote the liberal education of the higher orders'.[25] John Stuart Blackie, professor of Greek at Edinburgh, who had studied in Germany and was an advocate of its methods, was a leading figure among those who campaigned in the 1850s to modernize the Scottish universities and raise their standards, resulting in legislation in 1858 which took up the abortive proposals of the royal commission of 1826. In Blackie's view,

despotism also has its virtues, and this is one of them, that the despotic King of Prussia ... has a much greater respect for high intellectual culture of all kinds than the money-makers and money-squanderers of this free commercial country ... It were a noble thing if a democracy of merchants in this free island would step into the arena and vie with the great Continental despots in the inducements which they hold out to men who wish to devote their life to the cause of literature and science.

But Blackie was not too hopeful: in 1846 he had railed against 'the undue devotion ... of the mass of the middle classes to Mammon, and of the landed proprietors to Pleasure'.[26] In the 1860s Matthew Arnold was to dub these two enemies of culture the Philistines and the Barbarians. But by then the liberal, middle-class state was well embarked on liberating the ancient English universities from the embrace of the church and adapting them to the currents of the nineteenth century. Reform in Britain had to come through compromise and cooperation with the institutions being reformed, not through revolution or central direction, but come it did.

3

Oxbridge Reformed

'Universities never reform themselves: everyone knows that', the prime minister Lord Melbourne told the House of Lords in 1837.[1] An attempt at reform in that year failed, but in 1850 royal commissions were appointed to inquire into Oxford and Cambridge, leading to legislation in 1854 and 1856 respectively, and inaugurating a complex process of change which continued into the 1880s. Why was the state now galvanized into action? Had the middle-class pressures released by the 1832 Reform Act finally worked their way through? Certainly, university reform reflected a broader Liberal agenda for modernizing British institutions and attacking aristocratic and clerical privilege. The universities needed to be brought under the sway of enlightened public opinion and opened to the whole nation instead of being the property of a caste. Oxford and Cambridge – the colleges even more than the universities – were sitting on large endowments which were essentially national property, and Parliament had a right to impose more efficient use of them, as it did with other archaic or misapplied charitable funds. Behind these political moves were a number of powerful social and intellectual forces: the growth of professionalization and the demand for trained expertise in public affairs; the reform of the public schools, spreading from Thomas Arnold's Rugby and creating a new middle-class clientele whose social ambitions and training in classical culture pointed them to the universities; the growing impatience of religious minorities of all kinds with an Anglican monopoly which seemed increasingly anomalous; the intellectual progress of secularization, which attacked the church on a different front; and new forms of scientific and scholarly knowledge, making a parallel attack on the dominance of classics. Some of these forces were penetrating the universities themselves, encouraging an alliance of external and internal reformers, and ensuring that radical change was diluted by compromise with tradition.

One important movement of the 1850s was the advance of professionalization. In England, unlike Scotland, the universities had virtually
withdrawn from professional education, and learning through apprenticeship to an existing practitioner prevailed. This was the case even in
a new and scientific profession like engineering: the London colleges,
Glasgow, Dublin and Durham all created chairs of engineering, yet practical experience as an apprenticed pupil was more valued by the
engineering institutions which controlled qualifications, imitating the
powerful medical and surgical colleges. There seemed to be a peculiarly
English prejudice against theory and against expertise tested only by
examinations, but this changed as the problems of an urban, industrial
society became more complex. One landmark was the 1858 Medical Act,
which set up a national register of doctors, the qualification for which
was a university degree or its equivalent. Another was the professionalization of the civil service, where the Northcote–Trevelyan report of 1853
recommended recruitment by competitive examination. Expertise and
ability should replace patronage and nepotism, and the defects of aristocratic amateurs were underlined by episodes like the Crimean War
(1854–56) and the Indian Mutiny (1857). The state began to dismantle
the patronage system and replace it by a merit-based one, a massive
piece of Victorian social engineering. Northcote–Trevelyan principles
were applied first to the Indian Civil Service, and later to most branches
of the service at home. The Civil Service examinations were at the same
level as university degrees, and came to enjoy great prestige as a target
for graduates, Scottish and Irish as well as English. As meritocracy
became established, and spread to a wider range of professions, secondary schools and universities assumed a central role as channels of social
mobility; both were expensive, creating a new set of social and cultural
barriers and new competitive anxieties for the middle classes. Oxford
and Cambridge were slow to revive strictly professional training, but
preparation for broader public service was seized on as a new rationale
for liberal education, and a way of reconnecting the universities with the
centres of power and the national elite. Moreover, professionalization
was central to university reform itself, as teaching became an expert
profession divorced from careers in the church.

Mark Pattison, a leading member of the reform party at Oxford,
told the 1850 Oxford commission that their aim should be 'opening the

University to the Nation and the world'; it should 'strike its roots freely into the subsoil of society, and draw from it new elements of life, and sustenance of mental and moral power'.[2] The idea that the universities needed to be reclaimed for the nation, and reconnected with its vital intellectual and social energies, was at the heart of reform. Politically, the way was cleared by the crisis of 1846 over repeal of the Corn Laws, which broke up the old Tory Party, the bastion of the Church of England. The revolutions in other parts of Europe in 1848 also underlined the dangers of resisting moderate change. 'Peelite' Tories who believed in reform and administrative efficiency now joined forces with Whigs and Radicals in a developing Liberal coalition. One of them was William Gladstone, a loyal graduate of Oxford and one of the university's two MPs from 1847 to 1865, a high Anglican who at first saw reform chiefly as a means of increasing the supply of efficient clergymen, and only accepted the need to open the universities to non-Anglicans after a long struggle with his conscience.[3] The removal of religious tests was excluded from the remit of the 1850 commissions, which were instructed to focus on educational efficiency. When a Bill was introduced in 1854 to carry out the recommendations for Oxford, by a government of which Gladstone was a member, there was no clause on religious tests. But Nonconformist MPs insisted on their abolition for undergraduates, and this was extended to Cambridge in 1856. The universities could hardly have claimed a national role while still excluding citizens who had full civic rights in every other area of life; but the admission of non-Anglican undergraduates did not itself transform them, as scholarships and fellowships remained closed until a more radical Act of Parliament in 1871, put through by a reforming Gladstone government after an election in which university tests had been an issue.

Radical reform was always limited by the entrenchment of Oxford and Cambridge men in Parliament, the press, and the establishment generally. National political divisions were reproduced in liberal and conservative factions within the universities, and reform became a matter of negotiation and collaboration between politicians and internal reformers, not something imposed from above. The method chosen, both in 1854/56 and in the Oxford and Cambridge Act of 1877 which introduced the final instalment of change, was through temporary 'executive' commissions which superintended the more or less willing overhaul of university and college statutes. The same method was used when reforming the Scottish universities, in 1858 and again in 1889. In the Scottish case, Parliament was willing to lubricate change with extra funding, but in England this was not on offer, and measures like the creation of new chairs by the state were ruled out. Reform thus concentrated on unlocking endowments and enforcing their more efficient use. Most of the wealth belonged to the colleges; conservatives claimed that these were private bodies, but reformers like Pattison insisted that they were as much answerable to the nation as the university itself.[4] Modernizing the universities' governance also depended on breaking the grip of the colleges, since in both universities it was the heads of houses who constituted the supreme authority. The reforms deferred to tradition wherever possible, but sometimes concealed profound change behind familiar forms.

The obstacles to reform were religious as much as political. There was no smooth, one-way movement of secularization, for the early nineteenth century was an age of religious revival and contending passions. The revival strengthened both Anglican resistance to change, and the case for religious pluralism: while liberals thought there must be 'free admission to the national universities for all members of the nation',[5] for conservatives the English universities were 'national' because they were the universities of the national church, and should remain so, resisting political intervention by the state. The religious revival was itself a force for university reform, bringing new vitality to their intellectual life and a new seriousness to their social mission. The broad movement known as evangelicalism saw the spiritual regeneration of individuals as the key to social problems, requiring a new race of earnest, devoted and well-trained parish clergy to minister to the poor and tackle the problems of poverty, crime and ignorance. Evangelicalism of a plain Anglican type was especially strong at Cambridge, but the Oxford or Tractarian Movement, at the other extreme in terms of churchmanship, was a product of the same impulses. This movement was at its height between the early 1830s and 1845, when J. H. Newman dismayed his supporters by going over to Rome. It was both a national movement, which sought to rediscover the Catholic roots of the Church of England, and a university party, resisting the end of the Anglican monopoly at Oxford, and insisting that religion and education, like church and state, could not be separated. While 'broad' churchmen, the heirs of the eighteenth-century latitudinarians, wanted to open up the universities yet to maintain Anglican dominance, through liberal theology and the fudging of disagreements, the Tractarians would have enforced conformity to what they insisted was the true apostolic tradition. For a brief period, these issues dominated religious controversy at Oxford. This did not last, but its legacy was the pastoral ideal, particularly associated with Newman, of university education centred on the personal influence, moral as well as intellectual, of teacher over pupil.

As we have seen, internal reform had been centred on the honours examination system, which became increasingly sophisticated and demanding at both universities. By 1850 it depended almost entirely on written papers, and was a test of endurance and concentrated preparation as much as intellectual ability. It was also intensely competitive. At Cambridge, candidates were initially ranked in numerical order, from the senior wrangler at the top to the 'wooden spoon' at the bottom. Later this was modified in favour of the grouping into classes which is still familiar, and which was the Oxford preference. By 1830 there were four degree classes at Oxford. The subjects tested also expanded to some extent: at Oxford philosophy was taught alongside classics, and from 1807 there was a separate examination in mathematics. Both classical and mathematical subjects had to be taken, and students could try for honours in one or both, making possible a 'double first' (later this term was more commonly applied to examinations, like the tripos, examined in two parts in successive years). The first double first, in 1808, was won by Robert Peel, and Gladstone got one in 1831. As college fellowships were increasingly opened to merit, a good degree became the key to academic ambitions; a dazzling university performance was noticed in the wider world and could launch a man on a political or literary career. In Thackeray's 1855 novel *Pendennis*, the hero's mother, the widow of a doctor who had prospered enough to buy a small estate, 'had not settled in her mind whether he was to be Senior Wrangler and Archbishop of Canterbury, or Double First Class at Oxford and Lord Chancellor'. His worldly uncle, Major Pendennis, sees the university more as a way to 'make his first *entrée* into the world as a gentleman, and take his place with men of good rank and station'. An investment in aristocratic acquaintances would stand him in good stead for the rest of his life. Pendennis goes to 'Oxbridge' (the novel is the source of this term) but disappoints both relatives, ruining himself by an extravagant lifestyle and scraping through his examinations only at the second attempt.[6]

The examination system provided an intellectual stimulus, an intensive 'trial of memory and nerves',[7] for the minority of so-called 'reading men', but it had several drawbacks. College teaching focused on it, and subjects which were not examined were neglected – this was one reason why professors' lectures had difficulty in attracting audiences. In geology, for example, the professors at Oxford and Cambridge, William Buckland and Adam Sedgwick, both of course clergymen, were central figures in the crucial religious and scientific controversies over the age of the earth and the evolution of species, yet those debates took place outside the universities, and were ignored in the curriculum. Students not intellectually stimulated by examination subjects had little incentive to work, perhaps especially at Cambridge, where many were repelled by the mathematical gymnastics of the tripos, unrelated even to the demands of the natural sciences. Macaulay loved Cambridge, but hated mathematics, and failed the tripos.[8] Moreover, for success in the mathematical tripos, and to a lesser extent in classics, it was necessary to employ an expensive private coach, which underlined the failure of the colleges to teach effectively. In classics as in mathematics, the emphasis was on performance in a set of established rituals, reflected in the cult of Latin and Greek verse composition at universities and public schools. Everyone agreed that the classics were central to liberal education because the ancient world provided unique models of truth, beauty and virtue, but 'scholarship' in Britain meant stylistic correctness and elegance rather than the sort of philological research which was the norm in Germany, based on the study of language and history. Thomas Gaisford, dean of Christ Church, Oxford, is supposed to have said in a sermon that 'the study of the ancient tongues ... not only refines the intellect and elevates above the common herd, but also leads not infrequently to positions of considerable emolument'.[9] And that was indeed its point: according to William Whewell, chief spokesman for the Cambridge tradition, the system was designed for 'the intellectual aristocracy of the land ... The characteristic education of the nation is *their* education.' If this did little for those who were 'dull of intellect, or idle or inert in study', of whom there were many, that was hardly the fault of the university, which did not choose its clientele; 'sometimes we are obliged to take almost idiots', complained one Oxford don in 1867.[10]

The Oxbridge examination system had two long-term consequences for British academic culture. One was that examinations came to be seen as a way of labelling and placing individuals on a scale, 'classifying' them in every sense of the word, rather than a simple certification of knowledge, as professional examinations were. Secondly, as the examination ethos was extended to new subjects, the 'single-subject' degree became the norm, and the 'pass' degree based on a combination of subjects had low prestige. It did little to stir the minds of the mass of gentlemanly undergraduates, and eventually died out. General degrees survived much longer outside Oxbridge, but in the twentieth century the honours degree was to triumph. In Scotland, where certification in the early nineteenth century was based on attendance at lectures rather than examinations, English influence now led to the revival of graduation and the introduction of written examinations, and reform in 1858 created a system of classified honours, though until 1889 only as an option after a general degree had been completed.

The specialized honours examination was one response to Oxbridge's critics. Another was the elaboration of a theory of liberal education to justify the unique position of classics, mathematics and philosophy, a theory expounded vigorously by spokesmen like Edward Copleston at Oxford and William Whewell at Cambridge. Theories of liberal education could take different forms, though they agreed in rejecting utilitarianism and in seeking to form the whole personality rather than preparing for a specific vocation. In the eighteenth century, liberal education stressed qualities of politeness and sociability; the Scottish version took an 'encyclopedic' view, moulding the mind by exposing it to a wide range of literary, philosophical and scientific modes of thinking; in Germany, men were to be ennobled and perfected by the search for truth through the scholarly techniques of *Wissenschaft*. The reshaped Oxbridge ideal stressed intellectual discipline and sharpening the 'powers of the mind' through the study of an established field of knowledge; 'to *exercise* the mind of the student is the business of education, rather than to pour in knowledge', said Copleston.[11] For the scientist Whewell (he invented the word 'scientist'), mathematics was 'the best instrument for educating men in reasoning'.[12] A rigorous mental training, tested by examination, and pursued within the social and religious framework of college life, produced the educated gentleman. These defences of liberal education were formidably argued, and accompanied by positive hostility to original thinking or research, and to German influences. The important thing, said Whewell, was to pass on the torch of culture, 'to transmit the civilization of past generations to future ones, not to share and show forth all the changing fashions of intellectual caprice and subtlety'.[13] For Edward Pusey, Newman's colleague in the Oxford Movement, 'the problem and special work of an University, is not how to advance science, not how to make discoveries, not to form new schools of mental philosophy, nor to invent new modes of analysis ... but to form minds religiously, morally, intellectually, which shall discharge aright whatever duties God, in his Providence, shall appoint to them'.[14]

Copleston was provost of Oriel College, and Newman and Pusey were fellows there. This college was a pioneer of reinvigoration, because it threw its fellowships open to intellectual merit, instead of confining them to the college's own members, as was usual at Oxford. Examination success was not all – Newman had performed disastrously in schools – but fellows were expected to devote themselves to college life and teaching. Newman's religious and educational ideal stressed the relationship between tutor and pupil, to which end the college must remain a religious community, centred on chapel worship. The intrusion of dons or students with different beliefs threatened this ideal of harmony, and the hostility of the Tractarians to the appointment even of men from rival brands of Anglicanism stirred up much resentment and controversy at Oxford. The intense religious atmosphere of these years, in which young men earnestly debated points of theology, was later depicted by Newman in an autobiographical novel, *Loss and Gain* (1848). Newman eventually gave up his teaching role at Oriel, where he was out of sympathy both with the liberalism of most university reformers and with the broad churchmanship of Copleston and others, but the pastoral ideal resurfaced in his celebrated work, *The Idea of a University*, and survived in more secular form as one of the characteristics of English education.

A more lasting moral and religious influence than Newman's came from the reformed public schools, notably the Rugby of Thomas Arnold. Arnold died in 1842, but his disciples continued to spread his influence, both to other schools, old and new, and to the universities. There was much movement in both directions between college fellowships and public-school headmasterships, not infrequently on the way to deaneries and bishoprics. Especially close links developed between Rugby and Balliol College, which took over Oriel's role as the pathfinder of intellectual meritocracy at Oxford. One purpose of reforming the public schools, like the universities, was to make them more religious and less raffish, in the hope of attracting the serious middle classes. Thomas Arnold's religious ideals were as earnest as Newman's, though his churchmanship was very different – he was a liberal who wanted the Church of England to remain 'national' through its comprehensiveness, and this became the Balliol creed as well. In the public schools themselves, Arnold's moral idealism did not last long, as in a movement 'from godliness to manliness' they took on the heartiness, philistinism and social and intellectual conformism for which they are better known. These attitudes, along with the cult of games, spread to the universities. In *Tom Brown's Schooldays* (1857) by the muscular Christian Thomas Hughes, set in Arnold's Rugby, the athletic idol Brooke declares that '"I'd sooner win two School-house matches running than get the Balliol scholarship any day" – (frantic cheers)'.[15] But Tom Brown did go to Oxford, and a sequel, *Tom Brown at Oxford* (1861), showed most of the features of Victorian and Edwardian undergraduate life (not least the cult of rowing) already in place. Contemporaries noticed and criticized the parallel between academic and sporting competition, both sustaining a 'shallow competitiveness' hostile to an ethos of true culture and learning.[16]

Tighter links with the public schools did little to broaden university access or to weaken the dominance of the classics – probably the reverse in both cases; the schools fed in a new middle-class clientele, but one which identified with traditional values and occupied the scholarship places once reserved for the poor.[17] Modernization of the curriculum would need outside pressure. The Oxford Hebdomadal Board refused to answer the 1850 commission's inquiries as they contested its legality

(Macaulay's account of Magdalen College's conflict with James II had appeared in 1848), and they resisted change on the grounds that the Laudian curriculum of 1636 was 'a system of study admirably arranged at a time when not only the nature and faculties of the human mind were exactly what they are still, and must of course remain, but the principles also of sound and enlarged intellectual culture were far from imperfectly understood'.[18] Such conservatism would have been more convincing if those features of the old curriculum found inconvenient had not already been discarded. Modernization could not in the end be resisted, but it immediately raised another problem: should the agency of change be a professorial system, which would shift the balance of power from college to university as Hamilton had advocated, or revived college autonomy, which would leave teaching in the hands of tutors? The outcome of a long struggle was to entrench the colleges, though professors and subject-centred departments were stronger at Cambridge than at Oxford, and at both universities stronger in science, with its need for expensive equipment and laboratories, than in arts.

The conflict between professorial and tutorial parties was further entangled with the rival claims of research and teaching. The German example could no longer be ignored, and by the 1860s champions of research in the universities, notably Mark Pattison, were part of a wider national movement for the 'endowment of research', which called on the state to subsidize fundamental research, both as an intellectual enterprise at the heart of the nation's cultural life and because of the new importance of science for industry and military power. For the ancient universities, the result was another compromise. They remained strongly attached to the ideal of liberal education, and extended it to new subjects, while resisting those which seemed too technical or vocational. Yet it became accepted that dons should be serious scientists or scholars as well as professional teachers, working at the 'frontiers of knowledge' (to use a twentieth-century cliché) and introducing their students to the results of research; for the students, this initiation into scientific or scholarly methods, and the critical and analytical skills which they required, would itself be a form of liberal education, useful in later life in any career. But students were not encouraged to do original work, and this was essentially a more flexible and searching version of the old ideal of exercising the powers of the mind. This alliance of liberal education with scholarship, it has been suggested, was closer to the original Humboldtian *Bildung* than to the specialized German scholarship of the later nineteenth century, and allowed Oxford and Cambridge to develop into great research universities while retaining intimate relations with their students and a concern for their personal intellectual and moral development.[19]

The 1850 commission observed that 'the fact that so few books of profound research emanate from the University of Oxford materially impairs its character as a seat of learning', while in 1877 an observer thought that 'over-anxiety to rush into print is certainly not a besetting sin of Cambridge residents'.[20] The 1877 Act included 'learning and research' among the aims of the universities, and this was soon reflected in revised college statutes, and in the spending of money on research grants, libraries and laboratories.[21] Some 'prize fellowships' for recent graduates making their way in the world survived, but only one college, All Souls at Oxford, retained a flavour of the ancien régime: it had no undergraduates, and its fellows, mainly in history and law, were free of utilitarian pressures. In more typical colleges, many dons cultivated the scholarship needed for effective teaching, but saw no need to do original research, and the universities remained deeply committed to undergraduate education as their most important function.

The secularization of the universities was linked both with the advance of disciplinary specialization, as religion lost its claim to be the point of reference for all forms of truth, and with the professionalization of teaching, which required an end to compulsory ordination and celibacy. Colleges abandoned celibacy more reluctantly than ordination, because the idea of the college as a community was weakened when dons married and moved into the villa suburbs which sprouted in both university cities. The secularization of fellowships was inevitable, however, if the universities were to retain a serious role in the country's intellectual life. In the early nineteenth century, clerical orders were compatible with active scholarship, but the challenges to orthodox natural theology posed by critical scholarship on the Bible, Darwinism, and the discoveries of geology ended this harmony. As religious doubts grew among the Victorian intelligentsia, men who would previously have taken orders as a matter of course were placed in a difficult position, while others, unable to reconcile their consciences with a clerical status in which they no longer believed, resigned their college posts; two celebrated cases at Cambridge were Leslie Stephen, who resigned his tutorship in 1862 to take up a career as man of letters and Bloomsbury patriarch, and the philosopher Henry Sidgwick, who resigned his college fellowship in 1869 (but retained his university chair). After 1871 such men were relieved of their dilemma, and religion was no longer a barrier to pursuing what had become an attractive career.[22]

The religious character of the universities did not disappear. Many colleges continued to insist on chapel attendance for Anglican students until the 1930s (it was a convenient way of checking that they were present and that they got up in the morning), and the overall secularization of the university actually paved the way for new colleges with a religious orientation, whether Anglican (Keble at Oxford, Selwyn at Cambridge, both intended as cheap colleges for prospective ordinands), Nonconformist, or Roman Catholic after 1896 when the hierarchy ended its ban on Catholics using Oxbridge. As in English life generally, the Church of England retained an undogmatic cultural hegemony.[23] A fifth of college fellows at Oxford were still clergymen in 1912, for it took time for Catholics, Jews or agnostics to work their way in.[24] But the change in academic ethos was fundamental and rapid: fellows now separated their scholarship and science from their personal beliefs, and subscribed to common ideals of intellectual objectivity and rationalism. The abolition of religious tests was thus an important step in the progress of academic freedom. Religious allegiance and religious passions moved to the margins of university life, and episodes like the prosecution for heresy of contributors to *Essays and Reviews*, a volume put out in 1860 by the leading liberal religious thinkers at Oxford, became impossible. The academic could now follow John Stuart Mill's injunction to 'follow his intellect to whatever conclusions it may lead', and compete with London-based literary intellectuals for national influence.[25]

For subjects like history and English literature were now professionalized and brought within the university fold, and colleges began to appoint fellows to teach them. At first new subjects could only be studied along with classics and mathematics, but independent schools or triposes appeared in the 1870s. In history, for example, a school of law and history was set up at Oxford in 1850, but a degree in history alone could not be taken until 1872; at Cambridge, history was first allied with law or philosophy, then gained its own tripos in 1873. The scientific prestige enjoyed by history at this time came from Germany, but the subject flourished because of its relevance to the training of men who were destined to be politicians, diplomats, civil servants or imperial proconsuls. Objective scholarship was combined effortlessly (as indeed it was in Germany) with the inculcation of national consciousness. For J. R. Seeley, professor of history at Cambridge from 1869 to 1895, history was 'the school of public feeling and patriotism ... the school of statesmanship'.[26] By 1914 it had overtaken classics in both universities, but classics retained its own unique prestige as a subject for the future governing elite: there were political lessons to be drawn from Rome, as an imperial power, and from Greece, as the home both of democracy and of Plato's enlightened governing class. At Oxford the 'Greats' school, which combined classical literature, ancient history and philosophy, became an instrument of education far broader than the old classical scholarship, though still dependent on the classical training given (often without much else) in the public schools.

As part of the college system, a unique form of teaching developed based on close contact between teacher and pupil, in the tutorial (Oxford) or supervision (Cambridge). Analytical and expressive skills were developed through questioning, discussion and the writing of frequent essays. Today this is seen as the essence of the Oxbridge tradition, but it was a late nineteenth-century development, for college teaching had previously taken the form of lectures or 'catechetical' work on standard texts. The 'striking and historic change' at Cambridge from college lectures to supervisions, replacing private coaches and drawing on their methods, took place between the 1880s and 1910.[27] The distinction between 'reading men' and passmen continued in modified form. Colleges now encouraged most of their undergraduates to take honours degrees, and became less tolerant of the idle. But there was always the element, identified by Leslie Stephen, for whom rowing came before books: 'Their sphere of thought is somewhat limited; but they are very good fellows, and are excellent raw material for country parsons, or for any other profession where much thinking power is not required.'[28] Stephen was one of the athletic dons who appeared on towpaths and touchlines to encourage undergraduate sport. Others, like the Balliol historian F. F. ('Sligger') Urquhart, a model for the character Sillery in Anthony Powell's *Dance to the Music of Time* novels, cultivated personal friendships with their students, took them on summer reading parties to the Alps or the more mountainous parts of the British Isles, and closely followed their adult careers. If the intellectual ideal of a community of scholars devoted to research was weak, the social ideal of a collegiate community, with 'senior' and 'junior' members, became stronger, sport being deliberately encouraged to promote loyalty and solidarity.[29]

At Oxford the average numbers graduating annually in 1910–14 were 159 in history, 144 in Greats, 75 in natural science, 73 in law, 50 in theology, 16 in mathematics, 16 in English, 12 in modern languages, and two in oriental studies. Comparable figures for Cambridge, this time for those taking the first part of the tripos in 1900, were 136 in natural sciences, 126 in classics, 82 in mathematics, 49 in history, 46 in law, 25 in modern languages, 18 in mechanical sciences (i.e. engineering), 13 in theology, and 9 in 'moral sciences' (philosophy).[30] The figures underline the division, already emerging in the eighteenth century, between Oxford as an arts university and Cambridge as a scientific one. The natural sciences developed, like other subjects, from the 1850s, and at Cambridge a world-famous school of research in physics grew around the Cavendish Laboratory, founded in the 1870s by a scientifically minded aristocrat, the seventh duke of Devonshire. There were similar developments at Oxford, where the university 'museum' was built as a centre for scientific research in the 1850s, Gothic in appearance but modern in intention. Science did not flourish in Oxford, however, for various reasons, including a professor of physics who held his chair from 1865 to 1915, retiring at the age of eighty, who believed that 'the wish to do research betrays a certain restlessness of mind' and did not encourage its pursuit.[31] Natural science nevertheless became the third largest school at Oxford; but it attracted few of the elite students destined for politics or the civil service, nor were there many links with industry. As the statistics show, the universities also revived professional training in law and theology, and in medicine, not included in the figures above but more successful at Cambridge. Cambridge also introduced engineering, a development resisted at Oxford until 1907.

Vocational subjects were acceptable in the gentlemanly guise of professions, but not if they were too closely tied to industry and money-making. This lack of strong vocational pressure was unsurprising given the nature of the universities' clientele, whose needs gave them an ample enough task. They still had their critics, but it was difficult to deny that they had successfully modernized themselves, were once more central to national life, and had striking achievements in research, even if this was not always united with teaching in the approved German way. And they had done this without sacrificing any of their social prestige or their appeal to the rich and powerful.

4

Effortless Superiority

It was H. H. Asquith, at a dinner of Balliol MPs to celebrate his appointment as prime minister in 1908, who spoke of the 'tranquil consciousness of effortless superiority' which was the Balliol hallmark.[1] Colleges varied in character and social profile, and Balliol best exemplified the late Victorian blend of intense intellectual competition, an ethos of public service and social responsibility, and connections with the London world of power and fashion. The cult of the 'first class mind' is associated above all with Benjamin Jowett, who was a tutor and later master of the college and a dominating Oxford figure. Jowett was at the centre of the *Essays and Reviews* controversy, and theological liberalism evolved into a new Balliol tradition represented by the social reformer Arnold Toynbee and the philosopher T. H. Green, whose idealist doctrines had a remarkable influence on a generation of the British elite. Green sought to move liberalism away from pure individualism to a sense of social solidarity and active citizenship, and taught a gospel of duty, self-sacrifice and service which made a special appeal to those who retained the moral impulses of evangelicalism while no longer able to accept Christian dogma.[2] Jowett himself had the rather more worldly aim of permeating the British elite through his personal influence on undergraduates, and though he held the university chair of Greek he was a prime champion of liberal education against research specialization; for him, as for so many college tutors of the time, the ideal 'was to train and sharpen young minds, using the body of knowledge already existing'.[3] Examination success was all, and it was no coincidence that Balliol specialized in training for the Indian Civil Service, the blue riband of the Victorian competitive system.

The reform of Oxford and Cambridge, and associated changes like the new civil service examinations and the reshaping of the public schools, were consciously intended to produce a public service bourgeoisie, or urban gentry, a new stratum of men blending elements of the aristocracy and the upper middle class, infused through their education with gentlemanly values: the concept of the gentleman, the all-rounder shaped by a liberal education and inspired by an ethos of professionalism rather than profit-making, transmitted the older aristocratic sense of public service to the new middle class and assimilated new wealth and social ambition into the existing establishment. For the historian G. M. Young, 'the Universities broke the fall of the aristocracy by civilizing the plutocracy'.[4] As early as 1846, speaking of the aristocracy, Jowett welcomed the way in which 'the Plutocracy and the aristocracy of talent, the latter partly through the professions, are ever blending with it, and as it seems to me becoming greatly improved by it'.[5] Charles Trevelyan, joint architect of the Northcote–Trevelyan report, wrote in 1853 that reform would secure for the public service 'the sons of gentlemen, or those who by force of cultivation, good training and good society have acquired the feeling and habits of gentlemen. The tendency of the measure will ... be decidedly *aristocratic*, but it will be so in a good sense.' Gladstone agreed that, combined with the internal university reforms which had stimulated intellectual competition, it would 'strengthen and multiply the ties between the higher classes and the possession of administrative power'.[6] The primary aim of recruitment by merit was to make the public service more efficient, rather than to provide new opportunities for the middle classes: those among the latter who gained admission would be filtered through institutions which socialized them into the appropriate values, manners and lifestyles.

The apparently anomalous survival of traditional or aristocratic values in an industrialized society, and the role of education in the process, has been much commented on by historians, and has been linked with cognate phenomena such as the idealization of rural life, the propensity of successful businessmen to install themselves in country houses, and the definition of English national identity in anti-modern and anti-urban terms; and linked beyond that to the thesis, pertinent to various phases of British university history, that education encouraged anti-entrepreneurial attitudes among the British elite and was a cause of economic decline. One school of thought argues that the industrial revolution failed to lead to a political and social revolution, that the

British bourgeoisie remained junior partners in a compromise with aristocratic power, and that the public schools and universities ensured the transmission of traditional values via the ethos of the gentleman. The other (and predominant) school considers that by the late nineteenth century the middle classes held the real power in a society which was industrial, modern, and set on the road to democracy. They remodelled aristocratic values and institutions for their own purposes, devised the gentleman ideal as a legitimizing concept, and allowed the aristocracy to share the spoils of the new society as long as they observed the rules of merit and competition, delegating to them those political, military and imperial functions best suited to their traditions and training.[7]

From this point of view, the universities had a central role in stabilizing a rapidly industrializing country and providing it with appropriate leadership. Oxford and Cambridge were not there to produce industrialists or technologists, and no one expected that they would. But administrators, teachers, the clergy and other professional men were just as essential to the workings of a modern society, and the universities gave Britain an unusually homogeneous elite.[8] The higher ranks in the professions, politics, law, the civil service, the press, finance, and to some extent also industry and commerce, shared educational experiences and values, and patterns of thinking and behaviour.[9] The value of this for social stability and political continuity should not be underestimated, and contemporaries pointed out the contrast with France, where the 1789 revolution left deep political and religious divisions reflected and exacerbated by the rivalry between state and Catholic education; or Germany, where rapid industrialization caused serious tensions between the business and professional wings of the bourgeoisie, and between the bourgeoisie as a whole and the authoritarian structures of political power. Foreign observers, who were fascinated by the picturesque antiquity of the universities, and tended to see the public-spirited 'gentleman' as the characteristic English type, appreciated the way the system tempered the aggressive materialism which was an equally striking feature of Victorian Britain.

Thus reformed Oxbridge blended old and new families into a united upper class which served an industrializing, democratizing and imperial country. Charles Trevelyan's grandson, the historian G. M. Trevelyan, exemplified the process, as a member of a landed family with a distinguished tradition of public service who became a professional academic. In 1955 he reflected on the 'new intellectual aristocracy, that dominates the scene in the last thirty years' of the nineteenth century.[10] He was accepting a volume of essays in his honour, which included a celebrated essay on this theme by Noel Annan. Annan studied the network of families which emerged to occupy the heights of intellectual and scientific life, closely tied by kinship both to each other and to the broader service class. Unleashed by the end of celibacy, the dons were now able to marry into these dynasties and found their own.[11] This integration into the wider elite helps to explain the absence, or at least muted presence, of a dissident or alienated intelligentsia, in a country where even the rebels and critics have often come from within the establishment. The status of dons as gentlemen and professionals also reinforced the alienation of the universities from utilitarian or business values.[12]

According to one critic in 1864, a former don and Catholic convert, 'it is at Oxford that a man learns to perfection "the gentleman heresy" and with it the adoration of national greatness and prosperity, of success, of rank and wealth, and social position, and of all that the World prizes'.[13] Matthew Arnold might speak of Oxford whispering the last enchantments of the middle age, but Oxford and Cambridge spoke more loudly of power and privilege, of ancient connections with state and monarchy, of more recent ones with the London world of bar, press and Parliament, of architectural beauty and the dignity of corporate life. The reformed universities, no longer tied to the church, were able to cast off the 'state of psychopathic withdrawal from society' apparent before 1850 to become the source of new national movements and cultural networks of which the idealism of Green was only one example.[14] Arnold himself, as visiting professor of poetry in 1857–67, and John Ruskin as professor of fine art a little later, were nationally-known prophets who could turn undergraduates into disciples, as did resident gurus like Walter Pater at Oxford, the apostle of late Victorian aestheticism. One admirer, Oscar Wilde, was able to 'launch his overwhelming personality upon the world from the uttermost pinnacle of Oxford celebrity' after getting the best first of his year.[15] The most famous university network, however, was the so-called Bloomsbury group, with its roots in Cambridge, in the select and secret society known as the Apostles, and in the influence of the philosopher G. E. Moore. While Green at Oxford taught a stern ethic of public service, Moore taught a private one which saw personal friendships and aesthetic experience as the supreme values. Bloomsbury men seem to have been peculiarly conscious of themselves as a university-educated segment of the upper middle class – both J. M. Keynes and Leonard Woolf commented on this – which may be why Woolf's wife Virginia, daughter of the former Cambridge don Leslie Stephen, felt so acutely the outsider status of women which she expressed in 1929 in *A Room of One's Own*.[16]

For men like Asquith, superiority was in reality 'not effortless at all'.[17] Asquith won a scholarship to Balliol in 1870; his background was in the Yorkshire middle class, and he had not attended a public school. As a Nonconformist, he was part of the new pool of students on which the universities could now draw, and could not rely on family wealth. Like many men of the same kind, he used university success to launch himself into the wider world: hard work as a barrister led to wealth, a political career, and (less typically) a second marriage into a family of Scottish industrialists turned wealthy landowners. In the 1920s Asquith chaired a royal commission on Oxford and Cambridge, and became chancellor of Oxford. His career symbolized the way in which the universities consecrated the path from the provinces to London, from a modest business background to the heart of the establishment – a location perhaps too readily supposed also to be at the heart of civilization, as in a revealing comment on Asquith's burial-place near Oxford by a biographer who later followed a not dissimilar path: 'a South of England resting-place, within ten miles of Carfax Tower, was ... wholly appropriate. He had always been faithful to liberal, humane ideas, and to civilized, even fastidious, standards of political behaviour.'[18] The social virtue of reformed Oxford and Cambridge was that they allowed middle-class families who could make the sacrifices needed to reach the university via a 'good' school to get a foot on what Jowett called 'the ladder of competition reaching from the gutter to the skies'.[19] They were the spiritual home of the professional classes, cultured but not wealthy, with their eyes fixed on the professions, public service and empire, depicted at their Edwardian peak of influence and complacency by another Bloomsbury connection, E. M. Forster.

No one displayed more effortless superiority than the aristocratic Conservative politician George Curzon, who became viceroy of India, the supreme proconsular post. Both universities had strong connections with the empire, through missions as well as administrative service, but Oxford made a more conscious effort to develop its imperial links. It has been estimated that in the four decades before 1914 at least 20 per cent of Oxford's graduates worked in the empire.[20] In 1910 a quarter of Oxford students were born outside Britain, and the Rhodes scholarships founded in 1902 under the will of Cecil Rhodes brought Americans (and until 1914 Germans) as well as men from the white dominions.[21] But dominion and Indian students were already quite numerous in Scotland and London as well as Oxbridge, even after universities were founded elsewhere in the empire. The first Congress of Universities of the British Empire was held in 1912, and became a regular institution. Imperial links in both directions meant that the sense of British nationality which the experience of university education encouraged was felt in terms of a worldwide 'greater Britain', a concept popularized by Seeley.

The connection of Oxbridge with the public schools tightened in the late Victorian years: they set the social tone, and in the view of many critics their philistine and conformist values spread upwards to the universities. But they never had a monopoly: about 65 per cent of students at both universities came from them in 1904.[22] Grammar schools, private schools, education abroad or study at other British universities accounted for the rest. Some colleges were more fashionable than others, and at a smaller Cambridge college like Gonville and Caius most students continued to come from local grammar schools and to be first-generation graduates.[23] Socially, data about students' backgrounds show a strengthening of the universities' middle-class character as the proportion from landowning families fell, and as business as well as professional families made increasing use of both public schools and universities. By 1914, as state secondary education became established, more students appeared from the white-collar lower middle class and even the working class, but they accounted for 10 per cent at most, and were hardly visible on the social radar.[24] Edwardian Oxbridge seemed to reflect the gilded, plutocratic side of the age rather than the vitality of its intellectual life, and much of this survived the Great War. It was a scene characterized by 'the sound of the English county families baying for broken glass',[25] and depicted in Max Beerbohm's Oxford novel *Zuleika Dobson* of 1911.

'It is the supreme function of the Universities', thought William Temple, the future archbishop of Canterbury, in 1912, 'to guide the thought of those who mould the destiny of the nation and the empire.'[26] This fixation with the education of a governing class was one of the obstacles to the integration of women into the ancient universities. The collegiate system allowed women to establish a foothold by founding their own colleges and seeking admission to university examinations. The first college, Girton, was started by Emily Davies in 1869 at Hitchin in Bedfordshire, later moving to Cambridge, where Newnham College was opened in 1871. At Oxford, both Somerville and Lady Margaret Hall started in 1879. The colleges had the support of progressive dons, and the women involved in them were often the wives or daughters of leading academic families. There were differences of academic and religious emphasis between the colleges, but the intimate family atmosphere which they cultivated harmonized well with the Oxbridge tutorial ideal, and their all-female staffs gave women scholars a sense of community and allowed them to establish their own academic careers. The classical scholar Jane Harrison, a student at Newnham in the 1870s and a fellow there from 1898, could not have enjoyed the same position in France or Germany. But women at Oxford and Cambridge remained outsiders, the colleges being denied full university status for many years.[27] Women were admitted to examinations at Cambridge in 1881, Oxford in 1884, and soon began to shine in the contest for honours, as they took brilliant firsts or came at the top of the Cambridge tripos, like Agnata Ramsay in classics in 1887 or Philippa Fawcett, who was placed above the senior wrangler in 1890. Yet they were refused degrees until 1920 (Oxford) and 1948 (Cambridge), because this would have given women a share in university decision-making.

There was rather more concern for those other outsiders, the poor, though little more positive action. The mid-century reforms made the universities respectable and affordable for the growing professional and business classes, mainly by cutting down the extravagances of college life. But an Oxbridge education still cost around £200 per annum, more than the total income of any manual worker; the cost in Scotland, including lodging, was nearer £50–60. By abolishing local restrictions on college scholarships and throwing them open to free competition, the reformers had closed off some of the surviving channels available to the poor, and favoured public schoolboys trained to compete for these prizes, not least because so many scholarships were in classics – 300 out of 500 at Oxford in 1900.[28] Through the tragic tale of its protagonist, Thomas Hardy's *Jude the Obscure* (1895) underlined how Oxford was cut off from the new working class, unable to open itself to the products of the new elementary schools or to respond to the yearning after knowledge of self-educated artisans.

This was one of the many issues which exercised Jowett, who was not from a privileged background, but entered Balliol in 1835 as an open scholar from a London grammar school. He thought that 'not a ... twentieth part of the ability of the country comes to the University', and that means should be found 'of giving the best education to the best intelligences in every class of Society'.[29] The question was much debated in the 1850s and 1860s, and two initiatives were the result. One was to admit students who would not live in college but in cheap lodgings or hostels, such as the one which Jowett attached to Balliol for a time (with T. H. Green as warden). For him, such measures would 'retain Oxford in many respects as it is, and ... add to it a Scotch university ... Such a change as would bring a greater number of the middle or lower class of people to Oxford would be analogous to the change that we see going on around us in society.'[30] Both universities admitted such 'non-collegiate' students in the 1860s, and the institution survived, but they remained on the fringes of university life, as distinctly second-class citizens.

The other initiative was university 'extension' – the idea that the influence of the universities should be extended to other English towns, particularly in the industrial districts. The movement had the endorsement of Gladstone, who declared in 1867 that 'there never was a period in the history of the University of Oxford ... when it was able to do so little for the poorer class of students ... Go into the great centres of industry and you will hardly find a trace in them of university teaching.'[31] Some champions of extension hoped that Oxbridge funds and staff would be used to set up permanent branches in these cities, creating a network of provincial proto-universities; in the event, extension took the more modest form, developed first by Cambridge in the 1870s, of evening lectures on university subjects, by dons and others, sponsored by local committees. The moving spirit at Cambridge was the Scottish-born professor of engineering, James Stuart, later a Liberal MP. Some of these lectures reached the working class, through trade unions or cooperative societies, but fees were charged, and most of the audiences were middle class. Nevertheless, the extension movement became well established, and was one of the few aspects of British universities to attract attention and imitation in continental Europe.[32] Provincial extension centres were often a kernel for the growth of the redbrick universities, and stimulated the interest of women in higher education. It was an Oxford extension class at Buxton in 1913 which gave Vera Brittain, the daughter of a wealthy businessman, the qualifications and confidence to go on to Oxford itself.[33]

A feeling that extension lectures were not reaching the working class led to the foundation of the Workers' Educational Association (WEA), and the 'Oxford and the Working Class' movement of 1907–8. These initiatives had roots in the idealism of Green and the traditions of social service inspired by Arnold Toynbee. Toynbee Hall, founded in the East End of London in his memory in 1884, was the first of many university 'settlements', which encouraged students or earnest young graduates to become cultural missionaries living among the working class. Although philosophical idealism was for many a substitute for orthodox religion, in this case it helped to inspire a group of Anglican social reformers, including the warden of Toynbee Hall, Canon Samuel Barnett, and his wife Henrietta, Charles Gore, bishop of Birmingham, and William Temple. In 1903 Albert Mansbridge, a self-educated London clerk, founded an organization which was renamed the WEA in 1905, and taken up by sympathizers at Oxford. Its special feature became the 'tutorial class', modelled on university methods of teaching, organized as a three-year course and backed up by summer schools at Oxford itself, a tradition taken over from the extension movement. By 1914 there were 145 classes nationally.[34] Working men proved to be especially interested in political and economic questions, and the economic historian R. H. Tawney ran a famous Oxford tutorial class at Longton in North Staffordshire.

After the First World War, the WEA became closely associated with Labour, and Tawney was the chief influence on the party's educational policy for many years. But before 1914 supporters came from all parties. They included Curzon, who was elected as Oxford's chancellor in 1907, and took an unusually active role in this ceremonial office. In the same year, Oxford set up a joint committee of university and working-class representatives, whose report appeared in 1908. It argued that Oxford must reflect the shift in power to the working classes which they identified (somewhat optimistically) as a feature of the age. 'The Trade Union secretary and the "Labour member" need an Oxford education as much, and will use it to as good ends, as the civil servant or the barrister.' The committee's idea was that these labour leaders would remain within their class to raise its intellectual level, not escape it by using university education to climb the social ladder. How this would work in practice was not very clear, but the committee enunciated a principle which was to remain fundamental to British adult education and Labour ideals: the workers should be heirs to the highest traditions of liberal education, not fobbed off with technical training. Liberal education through art, literature and history 'gives access to the thoughts and ideals of the ages; its outward mark is a broad reasoned view of things and a sane measure of social values; in a word, it stands for culture in its highest and truest sense'.[35] This 'nothing but the best' approach was in the traditions of Ruskin and William Morris; its connection with their moral critique of industrialism gave a left-wing twist to the Oxbridge bias against educational utilitarianism. Ruskin's name had indeed been given in 1899 to an independent college at Oxford for working men, founded to serve the trade union movement but not directly connected with the WEA.

The 'Oxford and the Working Class' campaign took up another long-standing complaint, the insistence of Oxford and Cambridge on Greek as an entrance requirement, a high barrier against all those, including women, without a public-school education. London University dropped Greek for matriculation in 1873, and the Scottish universities in 1892, but Oxbridge refused to give way until the end of the First World War. For many critics, this was a symptom of a wider complacency, as the dynamism injected by the Victorian reforms dissipated, and there were demands for a new royal commission to adapt the universities to the twentieth century. Letters were written to the *Times*, then a potent organ of establishment opinion, and Gore sponsored a debate in the House of Lords in 1907. The ancient universities, he told the peers, had become 'a playground for the sons of the wealthier classes' and were 'to a very large extent not in any serious sense places of study at all'. The resources wasted on them should be liberated in order to teach 'trained and sifted students' from all classes 'who are hungering and thirsting for that sort of knowledge and training which a University is able to supply'.[36] Some speakers, however, stuck up for the aristocratic passmen, and for the university as a school of character rather than an intellectual hothouse. Besides, Gore's vision of 'sifted students' seemed closer to individualist meritocracy than to the collective advance proposed by the Oxford report, and this was a controversial issue. Many socialists detected a plot to 'incorporate' workers into the capitalist system by absorbing the best individual talent, and in 1909 there was a breakaway from Ruskin College over similar questions. As Ramsay MacDonald put it in a parallel Scottish debate, the so-called educational ladder 'had nothing to do with the improvement of national education. It was individualism run mad', and there was nothing democratic about 'increasing the facilities given to working-class children to pass into the First Division of the Civil Service or into the managerial ranks in commerce through the doors of universities ... It was drawing lines across our social unity, dividing it up into a governing and a subordinate class.'[37]

It is unlikely that the bourgeois idealists behind the Oxford report had political designs to 'incorporate' the aristocracy of labour; it was rather that their concept of liberal education was in harmony with the values of the serious, self-educated artisans and politically conscious working men who used the WEA.[38] The future, however, lay with meritocracy and scholarships for working-class children, and whatever MacDonald may have thought, in later years practical Labour policies were to concentrate on removing the barriers to individual talent rather than on the collective cultural emancipation of the working class. The 'Oxford and the Working Class' episode looked forward to some of the dilemmas of democracy, but also illustrated the closeness of the link, even within a newly imagined democratic context, between the formation of elites and the idea of liberal education.

Hastings Rashdall saw the reform of Oxford and Cambridge as an example of 'that power of spontaneous self-development which is the happy peculiarity of English institutions'.[39] But it had taken a hefty push from the state to create this 'spontaneity'. It seemed generally agreed that the ancient universities were national institutions, elements in governing the country whose organization, social function and ideological direction were a legitimate subject of public concern. In the first half of the nineteenth century, this role was mediated through the Church of England and the attempt to maintain religious uniformity. When confessionalism became untenable, the liberal state assumed the role of guarantor of impartiality, and freed the universities from clerical control. But did this mean that the state took over the church's responsibility for sustaining common national values? And if it did not, from where was social coherence to come?

In 1854, opposing the Oxford University Bill, Benjamin Disraeli warned the House of Commons that, by intervening in the details of reform, 'you are degrading the University, and you are destroying one of those influences which, in the aggregate, forms one of the elements by which you govern this country ... I have said before, you will have much to answer for if you place the Universities of this country under the ... control and management of the State.' Gladstone's reply was that the Bill was an 'emancipating measure' which would liberate the university from the fetters of obsolete practices, restore the representative principle to its internal government, and allow it to meet the challenges of the age in the spirit of freedom.[40] In the short run, Gladstone's hopes were vindicated; in the longer run, Disraeli's warning has prophetic appeal. But the future lay with the development of a national university system, under the state's auspices. Given the wealth of the ancient universities, and the upper-class clientele which they had never lost even in their years of stagnation, it was inevitable that public policy would concentrate on reforming and modernizing them, redirecting the wealth locked up in their endowments, and restoring their truly national role, rather than on creating an alternative system directed by the state and based on entirely modern foundations. The alternatives which did appear, in London and the English provinces, posed only a feeble challenge in their early years, and by the time they gained strength Oxford and Cambridge had already been successfully reformed, allowing their conceptions of university education to assume an almost unassailable superiority within the national system.

5

Province and Metropolis

The reform of Oxford and Cambridge was largely complete before the civic universities in the English provinces got going in the 1870s and 1880s – initially as 'university colleges' which could not award their own degrees. The civic colleges were local where Oxford and Cambridge were national, had little appeal to the upper classes, and initially concentrated on science and practical, professional training. They were thus unable to challenge the social and intellectual prestige of Oxbridge, and a two-tier hierarchy was the inevitable result. In 1889 the state began to give grants to the English colleges, including those in London, and in 1899 London University was transformed from an examining body into a federal 'teaching' university. By the eve of the First World War, something like a national university system was emerging, and the state had a substantial financial stake in universities and scientific research. London became a powerful university centre for the first time, forming the third point of a south-eastern golden triangle which overshadowed the new creations in the north and the midlands. In the 1920s and 1930s, argued Edward Shils, the London–Oxbridge 'axis' won a decisive victory over the autonomous culture of the provincial bourgeoisie.[1] But Scotland, Ireland and Wales had their own university traditions, which complicated this hierarchy.

Statistics of student enrolments illustrate the dominance of Oxbridge and the slow development of the new foundations. The earliest national estimates are for 1861, and not very reliable, but in that year Oxford and Cambridge each had perhaps 1200 students, while London, Durham and Manchester together had only 985 – less than a third of the English total of 3385 – and Scotland still had more students (3399) than England.[2] It was not until the 1880s that numbers in the newer universities began to rise, but Oxford and Cambridge were expanding too. In 1910–11, there were 19,617 students in England, 1375 in Wales, and 6736 in Scotland (making a total of 27,728 for Great Britain). But of the English students, 4191 were at Cambridge, 3442 at Oxford, and 5344 at the various colleges and medical schools of London University. The 'axis' thus accounted for 71 per cent of the English total, Oxbridge alone for 40 per cent. Oxford and Cambridge were by far the largest unitary universities in Britain, bigger than Edinburgh (2911) or Glasgow (2637). One reason for expanding numbers was the admission of women, but while by 1910 18 per cent of English students were female (compared with 24 per cent in Scotland and 35 per cent in Wales), women students at Oxbridge were less than a tenth of the total.[3]

The early twentieth century saw a quickening of the pace of development, but it was around 1870 that a cluster of new pressures first made themselves felt. These included changes in school education, the advance of political democracy, and the movement for the higher education of women; but the most direct influence was the demand for more scientific and technical education, fuelled by the intensification of great power rivalries which culminated in 1914, and especially by the growing power of Germany, unified under Bismarck in 1871. Education and science were now seen as factors of national strength, and German models of technical and university education were constantly appealed to. A series of official inquiries and reports underlined the lessons from abroad and demanded state action, both to produce more scientists, technicians and experts, and because, in the words of the Cambridge physicist James Clerk Maxwell in 1873, 'original research' was now becoming 'the fountain-head of a nation's wealth'.[4] A royal commission headed by the duke of Devonshire, reporting in 1875, was particularly scathing about the neglect of science in schools and universities: 'The omission from a Liberal Education of a great branch of Intellectual Culture is of itself a matter for serious regret; and, considering the increasing importance of Science to the Material Interests of the country, we cannot but regard its almost total exclusion from the training of the upper and middle classes as little less than a national misfortune.'[5] The idea of science as a necessary part of liberal education was particularly identified with the biologist Thomas Huxley, a member of the Devonshire commission and the chief public champion of science. Another was the Scottish chemist and MP Lyon Playfair, who stressed the weakness of British technical education in an age of international industrial competition, and the need for universities to move into new fields and to provide the same intellectual grounding for modern occupations as they did for the old professions. Huxley and Playfair sat together on a royal commission on Scottish universities appointed in 1876, which recommended a radical overhaul of the curriculum.[6] But governments failed to act on either the Devonshire or the Scottish reports, and it was not until twenty years later, when there was a new scare about German commercial competition, and when Britain's weaknesses were underlined by her floundering performance in the Boer War, that state policy responded more effectively to these concerns.

Besides, the scientists had their own agenda, to increase their professional standing by the expansion of university posts. The real demand for specialized scientific training was limited, and industry was probably less important in driving the growth of science than medicine. Since the eighteenth century, medical education had emphasized clinical instruction in the hospital. In Scotland this was already combined with university training, but medical schools in London grew independently around the major hospitals, and private medical schools were also founded in many English provincial towns. By 1870 medicine was becoming more scientific, and here too continental examples were important, from France as well as Germany. Medical students now needed laboratory-based teaching for such 'pre-clinical' sciences as chemistry, physiology and microbiology. Access to expensive and sophisticated facilities and university degrees became essential, and academic medicine began to be separated from medical practice. The English provincial schools often became constituent parts of the new university colleges. In London they remained independent, but the University of London provided medical degrees, and was reformed in 1858 – which was also the year of the Medical Act, a landmark in medical professionalization, and of a major reform of the Scottish universities which included the overhaul of their medical schools.

Since 1836, London University had dispensed degrees to students in affiliated colleges. The 1858 reorganization, while maintaining London as a purely examining university under direct government control, opened its arts degrees to individual candidates wherever they were taught. The medical degree remained confined to affiliated schools, in London and elsewhere, whose university status was thus strengthened. The general degree, however, turned into a vital mechanism for promoting higher education in Britain and throughout the British empire (several parts of which created their own examining universities on the London model). The original purpose of London University as a neutral arbiter between religious denominations retained some value, but the London degree was now seen mainly as an external guarantee of academic standards. When the new civic colleges were small and weak, London graduation gave their better students a nationally accepted qualification. It was also important that in 1859 London introduced a separate BSc degree, soon imitated by the Scottish universities, a sign that the claims of science were not going unheard. When London University moved to new head-quarters in Burlington Gardens in 1870, the elaborate programme of statuary on its facade included Galen, Harvey and Hunter for medicine, and Galileo, Bacon, Newton, Cuvier, Linnaeus and Davy for science, as well as Plato, Aristotle, Cicero, Milton, Locke, Hume, Adam Smith and the university's own hero Bentham on the arts and philosophy team. (But apart from Hume, there were no historians.)

The demands of science and medicine were driven by intellectual and social change. A quite different factor was the extension of the franchise to most urban workers in 1867, seen as a decisive stage in the advance of democracy. It was no coincidence that it was followed by laws to make elementary education universal, in 1870 for England and Wales and 1872 for Scotland. In a modern democracy, the formation of citizens through mass education became essential to efficiency and social order, but so did the systematic organization of secondary and higher educa-tion, to provide a leadership class distinguished by competence and intellectual superiority, and recruited at least partly by merit. The rise of elementary education thus had indirect implications for universities, but little direct impact, since working-class education at this time had few organic links with the secondary schools used by the middle classes, and the 1870 and 1872 Acts forbade the ratepayers' money to be spent on the latter.

But middle-class education expanded independently. Between 1850 and 1870 the 'examination idea' won a 'very sudden and sweeping vic-tory',[7] due both to the growth of the professions and to the wish to make

secondary schooling more efficient and systematic. Unlike most continental countries, England had no system of state secondary schools.
What was available fell into three categories: the old public schools and
their many new imitators; local grammar or endowed schools, often
ancient and relatively wealthy, but ill-adapted to modern needs; and a
large number of small private schools, popular with the middle classes,
and teaching modern and commercial subjects, but of very varying standards. Of these only the public schools were effective in feeding students
into the universities, on the basis of a strongly classical curriculum, but
they were confined to those who could pay. Two lines of criticism were
heard: that the education of the elite was defective because it did not
include modern subjects; and that the broad middle classes lacked
schools of guaranteed quality. This should be remedied either by a radical policy of state provision, or by gradual levelling-up through
common standards. The universities contributed to the gradualist policy by setting up examinations for school leavers, especially at university
entry level. The London University 'matriculation' developed after 1858
as a generally available school-leaving examination, and Oxford and
Cambridge created similar 'local' or 'middle-class' examinations in
1857–58 as part of the extension impulse. These examinations, and similar ones developed by newer universities, were the ancestors of the
school certificate which was coordinated nationally in 1917, and of the A
Levels which replaced it in the 1960s.

The nine leading public schools (headed by Eton, Winchester and
Harrow, and including Thomas Arnold's Rugby) were investigated and
reformed, but with no attempt to change their class character, by the
Clarendon Commission in 1864: these elite schools were known thereafter as the Clarendon schools. Other public schools came under the
remit of the Taunton Commission, which reported in 1867–68. The
Taunton Report covered nearly all secondary schools in England and
Wales apart from purely private ones, and its elaborate investigations
included reports on foreign countries, notably Matthew Arnold's
Schools and Universities on the Continent. The Taunton Commission
tried to differentiate this mass of schools by classifying them into three
grades, the first grade being those which took pupils until the age of
eighteen and prepared them for university entry, which meant teaching
Greek as well as Latin. While Arnold and some others would have liked

a full-blown system of state secondary schools, like the French lycées and German gymnasiums, this was not politically practicable, and progress could only be made by reorganizing existing endowments. Under the Endowed Schools Act of 1869, a much watered-down version of the Taunton recommendations, schools were reformed on a piece-meal basis, and a number of improved grammar schools or high schools emerged from this process, usually with scholarships for poorer children based on the old endowments; but as they had no direct connection with the public elementary schools run by churches and elected school boards, there was still no real ladder of opportunity.

Many of the schools covered by the Taunton Commission already regarded themselves as public schools, developing their boarding side and repudiating a purely local role. From 1869 they could join the Head-masters' Conference, admission to which became the mark of public-school status. The Headmasters' Conference was, among other things, a pressure group which successfully fended off state control and has continued to do so until the present day. It can be argued that 1869 was one of the missed opportunities in English education, when an inte-grated state system might have bridged the class gap. Instead duality became entrenched: just as in the university sphere the modernization of Oxbridge precluded radical national reform and condemned newer foundations to inferior status, so the consolidation of the public schools and their successful adaptation to middle-class needs preceded the cre-ation of a state sector. When this sector was reorganized systematically after 1902, incorporating both new creations and existing local schools which received direct state grants, it was forced to compete and prove itself against rivals who had more prestige and resources, and to defer to their values. It was only the state grammar schools which had links with elementary schools and the scholarship ladder. England acquired a secondary school system unique in Europe, with its superior sector accessible only by payment. Some historians would see in these hierar-chical forms of 'systematization' the inexorable logic of social privilege reproducing itself.[8]

But the paths followed by secondary and higher education were not identical, and it is worth pausing at this point to consider some coun-terfactual history. In reforming higher education, the state had insisted on the national status of Oxford and Cambridge, and on opening them up to all, initially within the social limits dictated by nineteenth-century conditions, but eventually on a basis of impartial selection by merit. If the same approach had been applied to the public schools, these too might have become national institutions. London, for example, had five or six ancient schools (Westminster, St Paul's, Charterhouse, Christ's Hospital and others) which could have been remodelled as publicly accountable schools for the urban middle classes, like their counterparts in Paris or Berlin. But the power of privilege worked against this, and most of these schools moved to the suburbs, or out of London altogether. Conversely, if Oxford and Cambridge had been left to their own devices, they would probably have remained socially exclusive, and the civic universities would have developed as a rival state sector rather than as one level of a hierarchy in which Oxbridge set the standards. The relationship between a socially divided school system and a unitary national system of universities remains a distinctive feature of British (and especially English) education, with significant implications in the twenty-first century for policy and for social opportunity.

The Taunton Commission was notable for including girls' schools in its remit, and for taking evidence from some of the pioneers of women's education, whose efforts were gathering weight in the 1860s. University local examinations were opened to girls by Cambridge in 1865, London in 1867 and Oxford in 1870, and were a valuable stimulus at a time when most girls' schools were private and had no tradition of teaching academic subjects. Schools organized on more modern lines began to appear around 1850, and the expansion of academic secondary schools created a practical demand for university entry and for graduate women teachers. It was significant that most of the pioneers, including Frances Buss of the North London Collegiate School, the model for a chain of girls' day high schools, believed that women should compete with men on equal academic terms, an approach extended into higher education by Emily Davies. The demand for women's higher education was, of course, rooted in the wider women's movement. John Stuart Mill's *On the Subjection of Women*, which argued for complete equality of access to occupations and social functions, was published in 1869.

Champions of women's education were usually part of a broader provincial intelligentsia interested in the extension movement and the foundation of new colleges.[9] The late 1860s saw a transitional phase when women could attend university-level lectures given by sympathetic academics. In Liverpool, for example, a Ladies' Educational Association began in 1866, shortly becoming part of the North of England Council for Promoting the Higher Education of Women, which was also active in Manchester; at Liverpool it worked closely with the Cambridge extension scheme and other activists (notably a group of Unitarian shipping magnates) to create the university college in 1881.[10] In the capital, the London Ladies' Educational Association began its lectures in 1869, and its teaching was later absorbed into University College, the pioneer in coeducation. King's preferred a separate college for women, and there were also freestanding women's colleges: the first was Bedford (1878), developed from a secondary school founded in 1849, followed by Westfield (1882) and Royal Holloway (1886).[11] London University degrees, including those in medicine, were opened to women in 1877. In Scotland, informal lectures lasted for a good deal longer as the full admission of women to the universities had to await legislation and did not come until 1892. And even when medical qualifications were opened up, male medical authorities continued to deny women entry to their preserves. The Edinburgh medical school remained closed to women until the First World War, and the London hospital schools for longer, in some cases until the 1940s. Women pioneers were forced to create their own hospitals and schools.[12]

The demand for women's education, the claims of science and industry, the growth of provincial medical schools, the extension movement and the improvement of secondary schooling were all part of the prehistory of the civic universities. Until the 1870s, the striking thing about English higher education outside Oxbridge was its weakness. Lacking endowments or public subsidies, the London colleges struggled to survive. They were often seen only as a staging post for entry to Oxford or Cambridge, and few took the demanding London University degrees. By 1858 the University had only awarded 1469 degrees of all kinds since 1836, to students in affiliated colleges throughout Britain – an average of seventy a year.[13] Vocational courses attracted particular clienteles to the London colleges, but general education did not prosper, and the grip of the Inns of Court and the Law Society prevented them making a success of their law departments. Evening classes at a lower intellectual level were more successful. It was significant that both London colleges ran their own secondary schools, for the poor quality of English secondary education outside the public schools limited the demand for true higher education.

Durham was no more successful, despite its proximity to the industrialized north east. It appealed initially as an Oxbridge for the northern gentry, but once the railway system developed they deserted it for the real thing. By 1860 the university was at a low ebb: in that year there were only thirty arts students and twenty in theology. The appointment of a royal commission to shake the university up, and the opening to non-Anglicans which followed, did not make much difference.[14] In 1851 Owens College was founded in the greatest industrial city of the north, Manchester, but the rest of Lancashire and Yorkshire had to await the 1870s. At Owens the foundations of Manchester's later reputation were laid by appointments like that of Henry Roscoe in chemistry (1857), who introduced the German model of the research laboratory.[15] Yet numbers languished – at one point in the 1860s there were only nineteen full-time students – and Owens had to be virtually refounded in 1870–71. Those who made their money in industry or commerce, in the provinces as in London, might be interested in Oxford or Cambridge to give gentlemanly status to their sons, but otherwise universities hardly impinged on their world view.

In the 1870s opinion changed. The civic foundations were not the result of any central initiative or parliamentary interest, but the work of local elites with their roots in industry and commerce. Apart from Bristol (1874), the earliest ones were all in the industrial cities of the north and midlands – Newcastle (1871, as a dependency of Durham), Leeds (1874), Sheffield (1879), Birmingham (1880), Liverpool (1881), and Nottingham (1881). Most of these colleges started with a strong scientific emphasis, but it was never exclusive. There was frequently a background in Oxford or Cambridge extension classes, which created a taste for liberal and literary education. At Bristol, the influence of Oxford extension was especially strong, and Jowett's Balliol helped to sponsor and finance the college.

Progress was at first slow. Endowments were limited and capricious, and did not provide a secure financial base. In order to balance the books, much of the teaching, often of a technical or quasi-secondary type, was for part-time and evening students, and the number studying for degrees was small. At Birmingham, only 123 students took degrees between 1880 and 1898, seventy in science and fifty-three in arts. At Manchester, the strongest of the civic colleges, only 121 students took honours degrees in arts and 364 in science during the twenty years 1882–1903 – about forty-five graduates a year.[16] At first the only degrees available were from London, but in 1880 the Victoria University was founded as an examining university for the north. Manchester was initially its only constituent, but Leeds and Liverpool joined later. For a time this model (resembling the London of 1836 rather than 1858) allowed high academic standards to coexist with small student bodies and patchy teaching provision, but the future lay with independent chartered universities. When Birmingham gained its charter in 1900, the Victoria University lost its allure, and Liverpool broke away in 1903, Leeds in 1904.

In the 1880s poverty led the colleges to campaign for state grants, stressing the needs of science and industry: 'the experience of commercial nations throughout the world was that the competition of industries was a competition of intellect', Playfair told the Chancellor of the Exchequer in 1887.[17] In 1889 the Treasury obliged with an annual grant to be shared between the new colleges, initially £15,000 but periodically increased. In return the state acquired new powers: admission to the grant list, and later the grant of a royal charter, depended on minimum standards laid down by the Treasury and the Privy Council respectively – of size, of balance between subjects, of adequate endowment, and of autonomous academic governance.[18] By 1914, Birmingham, Bristol, Leeds, Liverpool, Manchester and Sheffield had acquired full university status, and university colleges at Nottingham, Reading and Southampton also received grants. But Nottingham was refused a university charter, and the university college at Exeter, though established in the 1860s, was refused a grant.

Treasury grants were not the only source of public finance. From the 1850s, when concern about Britain's comparative industrial performance began, there was a national system of grants for technical and artistic education, administered from South Kensington by the Department of Science and Art. South Kensington was also the site of various other institutions, mostly sponsored by the state, which could be seen as an embryo university. The School of Mines (1851) absorbed the Royal College of Chemistry, the Royal College of Science (so called from 1890) trained schoolteachers, and the central college of the City and Guilds Institute (1884) coordinated the efforts of a body which drew its funds from London charities and trained industrial managers and technicians. The Royal College of Science was where Huxley taught, and one of his last pupils was H. G. Wells, who became a popular propagandist for science, and recalled his time under Huxley as 'beyond all question, the most educational year of my life'.[19] Outside London there were no colleges of similar status, but technical education grants were stepped up in 1889–90 and administered by borough and county councils, whose art and technical colleges were often the historical ancestors of the new universities of the late twentieth century. These local authorities included the new London County Council, whose technical education board became an important force, and in London the name 'polytechnic' became established for adult and technical colleges. These multiplied in the 1890s, though the first, in Regent Street, could trace its history back to the 1830s.[20] The London polytechnics were hardly at the same level as their elite namesakes in Paris or Zurich, but by 1904 five hundred polytechnic students were working for London University degrees.[21]

Colleges like that attended by Wells, and the national network of technical classes, formed a distinctive alternative tradition of higher education, strongly practical, non-residential, open to part-time students, especially from the white-collar lower bourgeoisie, giving much of their teaching in evening classes, and allowing qualifications to be built up through a succession of examinations. But there was no clear line of separation from the civic universities, which did much work of this kind themselves and drew grants accordingly; in the 1890s state aid for agricultural education was a new source to be tapped, and several colleges entered this field. As they gained in maturity, and aspired after royal charters, the colleges sought to distinguish applied science, which was proper to a university if taught in a liberal spirit, from purely technical or vocational education, which was not – but the line was always blurred, and the term 'technology' spanned it somewhat ambiguously. In several towns universities and municipal technical colleges became partners, with affiliation arrangements to give access to degrees. At Manchester, the borough council's technical school became the university's Faculty of Technology in 1905; its reputation was so high that the future philosopher Ludwig Wittgenstein went there in 1908 to study electrical engineering.[22] This faculty was to become independent in the 1950s, then in 2004 to be reunited with the University of Manchester.

Another form of state support was income from training teachers. Traditionally elementary teachers were trained on the job, or in colleges without university status, mostly run by the churches. But from 1890 universities were encouraged to set up 'day training colleges', with scholarships which attracted students from working-class or lower-middle-class backgrounds. One such student at Nottingham was the miner's son D. H. Lawrence, who put this experience (through his female character Ursula Brangwen) into his novel *The Rainbow* (1915). Ursula Brangwen at first saw in the grimy college buildings 'a reminiscence of the wondrous, cloistral origin of education. Her soul flew straight back to medieval times, when the monks of God held the learning of men and imparted it within the shadow of religion.' But by her second year she felt it was spurious, 'a little side-show to the factories of the town' and 'a temple converted to the most vulgar, petty commerce'.[23] In fact the Nottingham college was notorious for the lack of support from local industry, and in the absence of wealthy supporters it was, unlike most 'civic' colleges, dependent directly on the town council. It had a reputation as a 'people's university', and an unusually high proportion of working-class students.[24] Lack of autonomy and dependence on sub-degree work stood in the way of obtaining a charter, and the principal's 'Christian Socialist' views did not help to win over business opinion. In 1910 the principal and registrar were forced to resign after errors were found in the college's returns to the Board of Education.[25] It was not until the 1920s that Nottingham was put on a sound footing by 'the noble loot / derived from shrewd cash-chemistry / by good Sir Jesse Boot',[26] and it had to wait until 1948 for its charter.

More successful was Birmingham. In 1870, the steel-pen manufacturer Josiah Mason decided to endow a college 'specially adapted to the practical, mechanical, and artistic requirements of the manufactures and industrial pursuits of the Midland district ... to the exclusion of mere literary education and instruction'; theology was banned.[27] The 'Mason Science College' did not open until 1880, Mason himself still being alive. Its opening was marked by a speech from Huxley, hailing the event as a triumph for the scientific cause, and endorsing Mason's hostility to the classics and theology. 'Within these walls,' he hoped, 'the future employer and the future artisan may sojourn together for a while, and carry, through all their lives, the stamp of the influences then brought to bear upon them.'[28] In the event, like other colleges, Mason College developed a range of liberal and vocational subjects, and squeezed out the artisans. In 1892 'Science' was dropped from the title, and the college took over a medical school dating from 1828. Work in arts expanded with a Day Training College, and in 1898 a charter was obtained as 'Mason University College'. The university cause was then taken up by Joseph Chamberlain. A wealthy businessman, a famous civic leader, and by this time a leading national politician and advocate of imperialism, Chamberlain launched a campaign which resulted in Birmingham becoming the first civic university with full degree powers in 1900. Chamberlain also led a large fundraising effort, which along with his own contributions allowed the university to move from the city centre to a spacious suburban site at Edgbaston.

Chamberlain wanted Birmingham to be 'a first-class University, inferior to none in the world', yet did not seek to compete directly with Oxford and Cambridge. The university should train the 'captains of industry', by which he meant specifically not the generals or colonels, but the middling ranks, the technicians and managers. Wealthy employers preferred Oxbridge, and it was local professional and business families who were the core clientele of all the civic colleges.[29] They found there a cheap, practical and non-denominational education. The non-denominational aspect was important in the early years, and Mason was not the only founder who excluded theology. Beyond that, the colleges can be seen as culturally distinct, both as expressions of a provincial ethos striving for self-assertion against the metropolis, and as 'community service stations', embodiments of a modern, utilitarian, scientific spirit which had its own historical roots.[30]

The colleges were undoubtedly an expression of civic pride, and while some stressed their industrial and scientific character, as at Sheffield or

Leeds (where the original title was the Yorkshire College of Science), others were symbols of cultural prestige, like museums or town halls, which proved that the provincial bourgeoisie were as civilized and cultured as their London counterparts. This was part of Owens' purpose at Manchester, and the Liverpool charter of 1881 defined that college's aim as 'to provide such instruction in all the branches of a liberal education as may enable residents in the City of Liverpool and the neighbourhood thereof to qualify for Degrees in Arts, Science, and other subjects ... and at the same time to give such technical instruction as may be of immediate service to professional and commercial life'. While Mason College had Huxley, Liverpool invited Matthew Arnold to speak at the opening of its 1882 session, and when the Victoria Building designed by Alfred Waterhouse opened in 1892 (it was the original 'redbrick' building), the slogan carved into its facade was 'For advancement of learning and ennoblement of life'.[31]

Some historians have seen in this drift away from the colleges' original scientific and technical emphasis a betrayal of their purpose, and another symptom of the decline of the entrepreneurial spirit. They were 'colonized' by Oxbridge, which provided most of their staff and inspired their curricula, and in deferring to the values of liberal education they contributed to the downgrading of practical and vocational studies which has marred British education.[32] It is certainly true that the civic colleges formed a second tier in the English university system, that few of their graduates broke through to positions in the national elite, and that charters and state grants formalized a proto-binary line, distinguishing true university education from the more open and flexible forms embodied in the technical sector.

But was a radical alternative vision strangled in its cradle? It seems an exaggeration to say that the civic universities surrendered to Oxbridge values, and there is plenty of evidence of self-confident belief in their own ethos.[33] The development of arts teaching was a natural response to local needs for professional training, including the demand for teachers. The balance between subjects remained very different from that at Oxbridge, and there was no reluctance to teach applied science or to cater for local specialities like mining (Newcastle), brewing (Birmingham), metallurgy and glass technology (Sheffield) or textiles (Leeds). The real problem often lay with industry itself, which showed limited interest in employing technically qualified graduates or applying the results of basic research. Even at Leeds, the Drapers' Company, a London livery company in search of a useful purpose for its wealth, contributed as much money as the local textile industry. It was rare for local industries to give consistent corporate support. More commonly, money came from the private fortunes of benefactors who might have their own philanthropic vision or cultural enthusiasms – at one point Liverpool had four chairs of archaeology, financed by local magnates but of dubious value to the city's economy.[34] Nor did local businesses show much interest in the faculties and degrees in commerce to which some universities, notably Birmingham, devoted elaborate efforts.[35] It is worth remembering that before 1914 all universities together were serving barely one per cent of the population, at a time when the 'middle classes', broadly defined, formed a fifth or a sixth of it.[36] In 1910 the three counties of Lancashire, Cheshire and Yorkshire, one of the wealthiest and most industrialized regions in the world, with a population of nearly ten million, had just 3246 students in their four universities.[37] However dynamic, modern and scientific the new universities might be – and recent judgements of this are mostly positive – their influence on everyday business life was necessarily limited.

Their community roots were reflected in the student body – in 1908 three-quarters of the students were local, and it was still 60 per cent in 1948 – and in their government, which was normally by a lay council of local notables and businessmen.[38] In the early years, professors were simple employees with no security of tenure, but even when they improved their status lay chairmen and treasurers remained powerful figures in making policy, and in directing the financial appeals, sometimes successful and sometimes not, on which the colleges relied for new buildings or chairs. This was seen as a mechanism of public accountability, as was the influence of graduates through Convocations or similar bodies; this idea started with the reform of London University in 1858, and was derived from Oxbridge and from rather hazy medieval precedents. In practice Convocations were run by small groups of activists, representing the local business and professional community. Thus the civic universities were national in status and ambition – and this was seen as one of the criteria for awarding charters – yet still strongly embedded in their urban and regional context.

The intervention of the state in university policy is often identified with dependence on state finance, and traced only to 1919, when the University Grants Committee was founded. This is a very Oxbridge view, since it was only in 1923 that state grants were extended to the ancient universities. But the state's general interest in universities was much older, and its financial interest, as we have seen, went back to 1889 in England, and further in Scotland and Ireland. It is true that Britain had no bureaucratic machinery on continental lines for intervening continuously in university affairs, but it did have a long tradition of parliamentary inquiries and legislation, and a significant change of gear can be seen around 1900.[39] Between 1900 and 1910, the number of students in Great Britain rose from 20,249 to 27,728, including 3284 women in 1900 and 5654 in 1910.[40] The 1910 total corresponded to around 1.3 per cent of the age-group in England, 1.9 in Scotland, figures not out of line with European norms; in the 1860s, when England had undoubtedly lagged behind other countries, it had been 0.3 per cent there, 1.4 in Scotland.[41]

New public interest in universities and scientific research reflected renewed concern for Britain's great power status and economic competitiveness. The so-called 'national efficiency' movement, supported by important political figures like the Unionist Chamberlain and the group of 'liberal imperialists' around Lord Rosebery, took up older complaints about the backwardness of British scientific and technical education and the need for more expertise in government, and added a new emphasis on human resources. The Boer War of 1899–1902 underlined both the defects of ruling-class amateurism, and the poor physical state of the working class. New attention was given to primary education, and also to the barriers which an educational system divided by class and privilege put in the way of talent. This was wasteful to the nation's efficiency and narrowed the base of its elite. A modern state needed to mobilize its latent intellectual reserves, and the metaphor of the 'ladder' of opportunity for individuals became a commonplace, reinforced in the 1900s by advances in psychology which promised that intelligence could be measured scientifically, particularly for selecting 'bright' children to pass from elementary into secondary schools with scholarships or free places. The 'Oxford and the Working Class' movement reflected the same concerns, though with a different emphasis, and the term 'equality of opportunity' began to come into use.

One mark of this more vigorous approach was the creation in 1899 of the Board of Education, a unified ministry for England and Wales, headed in its early years by a dynamic administrator, Robert Morant. It did not have direct responsibility for universities, but absorbed the Science and Art Department and its technical education work. In Scotland, the existing Education Department acquired the same responsibilities and began to concentrate higher technical education in 'central institutions'. The next step south of the border was the 1902 Education Act, which gave control of all levels of education short of universities to county and borough councils. These were required to provide systematically for secondary education. The gaps left by the previously haphazard reform of endowed schools were now filled by state grammar schools, for boys and girls, whose curriculum was quite closely prescribed by the Board, and emphasized academic subjects. The 1902 Act was intended, in the words of the prime minister, A. J. Balfour, to create 'a really national system of education', with a 'rational or organic connection' between primary and secondary schools, 'and through the system of secondary education, with the University education which crowns the whole educational edifice'.[42] The new grammar schools allowed the universities to insist on higher entrance standards, and an honours degree became in practice a prerequisite for secondary teaching. No measure did more to fill the arts and science faculties of the civic universities, and to loosen their dependence on immediate local needs. For women graduates, from old and new universities alike, teaching became the main career. The day training college system for elementary teachers was also reformed, and from 1911 students who promised to enter teaching (the 'pledge', which lasted until the Second World War) received a state grant allowing them to take a degree followed by a year of professional training. By the 1930s the universities were training about 1600 teachers a year, compared with 5000 emerging from two-year courses in the eighty or so training colleges run by the churches and local authorities.[43] The 1902 Act also allowed local authorities to offer university scholarships, and by 1911 there were about

1400 of these.[44] Thus even before 1914 a significant number of students were supported, directly or indirectly, by the state.

According to the *Westminster Gazette* in 1907, 'We seem ... to be threatened with a complete division of the educational system of the country into two parts – the expensive schools with the older Universities in one department, and the modern Council schools with the newer Universities in the other.'[45] In practice the division was not so rigid, for the new grammar schools began to score successes in the Oxbridge college scholarships which became the token of a school's prestige. But the relationship between 'council schools' and civic universities was real, and it was now that the latter came of age. They still had many financial problems, and were tempted to take on work of all levels to bring in the cash, but now had a regular student body, both male and female, able to study for full-time degrees. State grants and royal charters made them less dependent on local pressures, and introduced various features of traditional university status as understood in Germany or Scotland, including a new emphasis on research, organization into faculties and departments, and academic freedom for professors. The creation of a Senate or academic council was the guarantee of this freedom, though non-professorial staff, still not very numerous, had little security or voice in university government. Another symptom of the new order was the emergence of the vice-chancellor as a commanding figure. Men like Michael Sadler at Leeds, one of many idealist thinkers from the Oxford extension stable, were educational experts of national stature. Another man of vision was Principal W. C. Childs of Reading, who was determined to raise University College at Reading from a local institution specializing in agriculture into a national one. At a time when most provincial students were locally recruited, and lived at home or in lodgings, Reading pioneered the hall of residence: the halls were to be named after Saints George, Andrew, David and Patrick to symbolize this national mission.[46] Childs successfully cultivated local benefactors, and his ultimate aim – not gained until 1926 – was a full charter. His recollections betray an obsession with the trappings of university status – coats of arms, maces, gowns and hoods, the title of vice-chancellor itself – of a kind not unknown in more recent bids for promotion.

The term 'civic universities' was popularized by R. B. Haldane, another of the politicians whose involvement in university affairs illustrated their new national importance. Haldane was Liberal minister of war between 1905 and 1912, but was already involved, as a member of commissions or an influence behind the scenes, in university policy in Wales, Ireland, and London – though not in his native Scotland. Haldane was an Edinburgh graduate who had also been deeply influenced by study in Germany. Admiration of Germany's universities and 'technical high schools' was a standard motif of the national efficiency lobby, as of the scientific pressure groups in a previous generation, and this was sharpened by the emergence of Germany as Britain's main commercial and naval competitor. To this Haldane added an Arnoldian admiration for the cultural role of the state and the spiritual mission of universities. He believed each civic university should stand at the apex of a regional educational hierarchy: 'I do not believe any system of education will ever be satisfactory which does not link together the primary, the secondary, and tertiary system, and make the tertiary the head, with a University dominating the whole edifice with what the Germans call *Geist* – a spirit of intelligence.'[47] This meant 'the recognition of the double function of our educational institutions, the imparting of culture for culture's sake on the one hand, and the application of science to the training of our captains of industry on the other'.[48] Haldane told the Edinburgh students who elected him rector in 1905 that it was the 'ideal work of the Universities to produce men of the widest minds – men who are fit to lead as well as merely to organize'; they must 'make themselves accepted leaders; so only can they aspire to form part of that priesthood of humanity to whose commands the world will yield obedience'.[49]

Haldane was particularly important in the reorganization of the University of London, the result of a long and controversial campaign to turn it from an examining into a teaching university, in order to strengthen its constituent parts and actively promote higher education in the capital. This was achieved by legislation in 1899, with a complex federal constitution. The London colleges had shared the travails of the early provincial colleges, and had become a 'virtual dependency of Oxbridge', recruiting their staff there and sending their best students on rather than using the London degree.[50] In the 1890s King's College was so impoverished that it considered closing down, but as part of the new university (which required abandoning its Anglican restrictions) the college found a new purpose and enjoyed a large influx of degree students.[51]

The new University of London owed much to Sidney Webb, chairman of London County Council's technical education board, as well as Haldane. Webb was a notable product of the evening class and open examination tradition, attending no university but passing civil service examinations. Sidney and Beatrice Webb became the moving spirits of the Fabian Society, which promoted a state-socialist version of national efficiency. Its greatest achievement was the foundation from private funds in 1895 of the London School of Economics and Political Science (the LSE). Intended to be a school of scientific administration, in both public and business spheres, the LSE became the chief powerhouse of British social science. It was followed by the Imperial College of Science and Technology, formed in 1907 from the existing science and technical schools in South Kensington, with the joint support of Webb's committee and of Morant at the Board of Education. In effect this was a state foundation, unlike the older London colleges, and deliberately modelled on the German technical high schools. In a short period, therefore, higher education in London was transformed, permanently shifting the balance of the English system.

As the title of Imperial College implied, London was intended to be 'a university fit for the metropolis of the Empire', a theme much stressed by Haldane and others.[52] The LSE and other London colleges were to have a strong influence on the training of Indian and colonial elites and (though this was hardly the original intention) on anti-colonial nationalism. The creation of Imperial College also showed the state's growing acceptance of the need to support scientific research, and it has been argued that this breakthrough, like the change in the public attitude to universities, had occurred before the 1914 war, and that Britain was well on its way to catching up with Germany.[53] Lloyd George's National Insurance Act of 1911, which provided medical insurance for workers, included funds for a Medical Research Committee (later Council), the forerunner of a mighty research empire. Once the war broke out, the deficiencies revealed in Britain's scientific and manufacturing base led to the creation of the Department of Scientific and Industrial Research (1916), which with the MRC became the main channel for state aid to research, until replaced by a set of more specialized research councils in the 1960s.

The general grant to English university colleges, which started at £15,000 in 1889, was periodically increased. Paid by the Treasury, it was at first supervised by a series of ad hoc advisory committees, and there were regular inspections of the colleges, usually by Oxbridge dons. In 1906, after a report by a committee under Haldane, the advisory committee was given permanent status. There was then a battle of influence between the Treasury and the Board of Education, which was also a source of university finance through its grants for technical education and teacher training. By 1911, at £150,000, these approximately equalled the Treasury grants, and in that year the administration of the latter was taken over by the Board's 'universities branch'.[54] The Board had a more intrusive approach than the Treasury, demanding statistics on staff teaching hours: 'Nothing so ungentlemanly has been done by the Government since they actually insisted on knowing at what time Foreign Office clerks arrive at Whitehall', complained the vice-chancellor of Sheffield.[55] This particular demand was dropped, but inspections and reports became more frequent. When the Treasury took control again after the war, and delegated its powers to the University Grants Committee, universities gained a sixty-year remission from ungentlemanly absorption into the bureaucratic state.

The new English and Welsh universities also had significant income from local authorities, through direct aid from the rates as well as technical education grants. At Sheffield in the 1900s, 40 per cent of the university's income came from the city (using the profits of its tramways) and from other Yorkshire authorities, a quarter from central government, and only a sixth from student fees.[56] This was an unusually high local contribution, but it was normal for the Treasury grant to provide between a quarter and a third of the universities' income, student fees less than half. Local authority contributions continued until the 1960s. They did not exist in Scotland, but here state grants accounted in 1907 for between 27 and 37 per cent of income, student fees between 17 per cent (St Andrews) and 50 (Edinburgh); the Scottish universities had more endowments to fill the gap than the newer English ones.[57] By 1914, therefore, when the Treasury grant had risen to £185,000, all British universities except Oxford and Cambridge already depended on the state, and if local authority contributions are included about half their income came from public funds.[58] Put another way, students paid less than half the true cost of their education. Oxbridge finances were more opaque, but wartime inflation was to end their self-sufficiency.

A final development before the war was a new concern for equality of opportunity, especially once the Liberals were in power after 1905. The 'new liberalism' of the 1900s stressed social solidarity, and the need to move from unbridled individualism to a more active role for the state. Welfare measures would help to integrate the working class into society, and to retain their loyalty as Liberal voters, and this meant satisfying the social ambitions which were burgeoning as elementary education matured and school leaving ages moved upwards. From 1907, state-aided secondary schools were required to provide 25 per cent of their places free to pupils from elementary schools, and on the eve of war the government was considering, through a committee chaired by the inevitable Haldane, how equality of opportunity might be further extended. Radicalism had its limits, however: Haldane saw the recruitment of clever boys into the elite as a safety-valve for social unrest, and a royal commission on recruitment into the civil service, reporting in 1914, found existing scholarship systems broadly satisfactory.[59]

These initiatives were absorbed into general plans for post-war reconstruction, as social reform came to be seen as the necessary reward for the unprecedented involvement of citizens in the national effort. One outcome was the Education Acts of 1918, one for England and Wales, another for Scotland. The former was the work of Herbert Fisher, appointed by Lloyd George as President of the Board of Education in 1916, and notable as the first academic to hold such a post – he was an Oxford historian who had been vice-chancellor of Sheffield. But Fisher's views were quite conservative, and the 1918 Act was essentially the work of his civil servants, based on proposals which had been evolving since before the war.[60] As in other fields of reform, postwar policies expressed shifts which were accelerated by the conflict, but already well under way.

6

National Identities

The nineteenth century was the age of the nation state, and historians and theorists of nationalism have emphasized the importance of education in integrating modern nations and forming their identity.[1] Social cohesion required a common culture and an elite imbued with common national values. In Germany, the universities were central to the creation of national consciousness, and this was one reason for their influence throughout Europe, as universities became a symbol of national aspirations. But even in established states like Britain, the advent of democracy and the strains and complexities of an industrialized society led to a new and conscious concern with the training of leaders and experts. The reform of the ancient English universities fits into this pattern, but the formation of elites was complicated by the overlap between English, British and 'greater British' identities, and by the existence of subordinate national identities and educational systems. In Scotland, the universities were among the distinctive institutions prized by local patriots. In Wales, which had no higher education until 1872, a national university movement produced three colleges and a federal university by the 1890s. In both Scotland and Wales, cultural nationalism was compatible with British political loyalties, but in Ireland university education failed to promote national unity, becoming instead a focus for religious and cultural divisions.

In some ways, the Scottish universities changed less than other British ones in the nineteenth century. There was no real need for new foundations – University College at Dundee, opened on the English civic model in 1883, became affiliated after a few years to neighbouring St Andrews, not regaining full independence until 1967. Student enrolments, already high, grew fast between the 1860s and the 1880s, but more slowly thereafter. Even so, the need was felt for legislation, in 1858 and 1889, to modernize constitutions and curricula. The 1858 Act removed Edinburgh from the control of the town council, and brought about the fusion of the two colleges at Aberdeen. There were several striking features of these reforms. Nobody challenged the right of the state to carry them out, not least because it was already supporting Scottish universities financially. Most professors were paid small official salaries, which they supplemented with student fees, and these and other payments were consolidated and increased by the two Acts. After 1892, the universities received £72,000 a year – twelve times as much in relation to population as the English ones. In the 1880s there had been a proposal to privatize the universities by converting annual grants to a once-for-all endowment, but this had been strongly resisted by Scottish opinion. For James Donaldson, principal of St Andrews, 'The Scottish Universities are not private corporations – they are national seats of learning, existing for the nation, and controlled by the Parliament of the nation. And the Universities have no wish to become independent of the State, or to be removed from the control of the State.'[2] The country's distinctive educational system and its public character were an important element in national identity, and were held to have been guaranteed by the Act of Union.[3]

The national significance of the universities was further demonstrated by the strict uniformity imposed on them in 1858 and 1889. Constitutions were identical, as far as local conditions allowed, and so were the curricula, prescribed in considerable detail. No university could make major changes without consulting all the others, and the inflexibility which this caused was one reason why legislation became necessary again in the 1880s. Constitutionally, Scottish universities were answerable to public opinion mainly through their General Councils, created in 1858 to represent graduates, and similar to the London Convocation. They allowed local professional men to take an active part in university affairs, often in ways unwelcome to the professorate, which ran academic affairs through the Senate. The General Council elected members to the Court, which was to control appointments and (from 1889) finance. But most existing chairs had been created by the state, which usually retained the right of appointment: in 1858 there were nearly a hundred professors, and the crown appointed forty-three of them; only gradually, as new chairs were created, did the balance shift to the Court, and in practice to the Senate as academic criteria came to outweigh political or religious ones.

The Scottish curriculum came to be characterized not only by uniformity between universities but by lack of choice for students. In the early nineteenth century, however, conditions approximated to German *Lernfreiheit*. There was a common arts curriculum required by the church from students for the ministry, but other students were free to choose from the lectures on offer. Few graduated formally, and certificates of attendance at lectures replaced traditional oral examinations. As the 1826 royal commission described it, 'all persons may attend any of the classes, in whatever order or manner may suit their different views and prospects'. This flexibility helped to attract a very diverse clientele, and first-year classes were at an elementary level to allow for the deficiencies of the schools. The commission claimed that 'the attempt to introduce into the Scotch Universities any system of government or instruction similar to that which subsists in the English Universities, would be inconsiderate and hurtful'.[4] But they wanted a more systematic and demanding curriculum for 'regular' students, and their report was the beginning of a reform movement designed to encourage graduation, to restore a uniform arts degree, and to raise both standards and the age of entry. Written examinations appeared, and after 1858 a common degree structure was imposed. Under the uniform curriculum devised then, all students for the MA had to study classics, philosophy, and mathematics, and it was claimed that each part of this tripartite system had its own virtues in training the intellect – not to mention the 'special and most beneficial influence on the national character' of the Scottish philosophical tradition.[5] It became possible to take honours degrees (complete with the Oxbridge classification system), but only after the full MA programme had been completed, and the natural sciences had no real foothold in the system; the universities got round this by creating separate BSc degrees on the London pattern. The uniform MA survived the assaults of the royal commission of 1876, but its inflexibility, the elementary level at which subjects had to be taught when they were compulsory for all, and the exclusion of new subjects, even non-scientific ones like history and modern languages which were now established in secondary schools and needed graduates to teach them, led to further reform in the 1890s and again in the early twentieth century.

By then nearly all students came to university after a full secondary schooling, and followed a regular curriculum culminating in graduation

– whereas as late as the 1870s only one in five or six of arts students had left with a degree.[6] The reformed system lasted in essence until the 1960s. All students started together, but diverged after one or two years into either 'ordinary' (general) or honours degrees; new disciplines were admitted to the academic circle, and no single subject was now compulsory, but the curriculum was structured around groups of courses, among which the old categories of languages, philosophy and mathematics were still visible, so that every student was exposed to a variety of intellectual disciplines.

The growth of honours teaching allowed professors to develop advanced work more clearly related to their research, and improvements in secondary education meant higher entry standards: a compulsory entrance examination, long a bone of contention, was introduced in 1892 and was equivalent to the national school Leaving Certificate set up by the Scottish Education Department in 1888. The standard entry age rose from fifteen or sixteen in the early nineteenth century to seventeen or eighteen by its end.[7] The higher entrance standard also meant that the elementary first year of the traditional four-year curriculum could be abolished, and since only about a quarter of students took honours, the majority of arts students stayed for three rather than four years, and it was common to take an ordinary degree before going on to degrees in law and divinity, though not in medicine. This distinctive system operated until the later twentieth century, when the pressures of specialization made the four-year honours degree the norm for most subjects, while squeezing out liberal education as a preparation for professional degrees.

The characteristic ethos of the Scottish universities is often described by the term 'the democratic intellect', which covers various features: the idea of the universities as a national system, organically linked with schools, and open to all rather than based on social class; wide social recruitment, drawing on this egalitarian thinking; and a broad and unspecialized curriculum, emphasizing a general philosophical approach and allied with 'metaphysical' traits of the Scottish mind derived from the Calvinist inheritance. Much of this is based on an implicit contrast with England, and part of an argument about the 'anglicization' of the university curriculum as a result of nineteenth-century reform.[8] Some of it is based on sentimental assumptions, notably about the classlessness of Scottish society, which do not stand up to close examination.

As far as the curriculum is concerned, it seems clear that the compromise arrived at in the 1890s still required breadth of study and retained a distinctively Scottish educational ethos. Besides, scoticization of the English universities was as significant a movement as the reverse. The London University arts degree was for many years based on compulsory subjects in the Scottish style, though with a stronger scientific content, and the civic universities followed the same mix of general and specialized degrees when they acquired their own degree powers.

The real spur to reform was the advance of professionalization and the career demands of the Scottish middle classes, who had to keep up with their English counterparts, especially Oxbridge graduates, in the new world of competitive examinations. Scotland was a large exporter of ministers of religion, teachers, doctors and engineers, to the British empire as well as other parts of Britain. In the late nineteenth century, only about half of Aberdeen's graduates stayed in Scotland, and this was probably typical.[9] These patterns help to explain why Scottish cultural identity was so easily combined in the middle classes with British political loyalty. The Scottish universities were far more angled to the professions and public service than the English civic ones, and integrated into local professional rather than business communities. Both divinity and law developed academically after 1858, and medicine even more so: between 1860 and 1914 medical students were generally 40 or 50 per cent of the total at Edinburgh, a quarter to a third at Glasgow and Aberdeen.[10]

This professional character was reinforced by the lack of pressure to develop technical subjects, as these were accommodated elsewhere. In Glasgow, 'Anderson's University' was founded in 1796 under the will of the scientist John Anderson; it later dropped the university title, but was a centre of scientific and technical education, as was the School of Arts founded at Edinburgh in 1821. These institutions were expanded and remodelled in the 1880s as, respectively, the Glasgow and West of Scotland Technical College (later Royal Technical College) and Heriot-Watt College. Similar colleges appeared at Aberdeen and Dundee, and were among the predominantly vocational 'central institutions' (including colleges of art, domestic economy, agriculture and navigation) which the Scottish Education Department developed after 1900. At Glasgow and Edinburgh at least, the Department liked to claim that the colleges were 'industrial universities', on a level with the German technical high schools.[11] In England the distinction between university and technical education was blurred, but in Scotland a stronger central authority created a sharper separation of missions.

The claim that the Scottish universities were open in principle to all and drew their students from the poor as well as the rich can be traced back at least to the early nineteenth century, and became a national myth of which the scientist Lyon Playfair was one of the chief propagators. In the 1890s, the term 'lad o' pairts' came into use to describe the poor student, with a rural or small-town background and modest social origins, who used his intellect to climb the ladder of ambition. This became a favourite theme of sentimental literature, reflecting nostalgia for a rural Scotland that was disappearing, and for the ancient parish schools which were giving way to a modern, stratified system.[12] This aspect of the 'democratic intellect' can be tested against historical data, which show both that it corresponded to a certain reality, and that opportunities for poor children did not decline as a result of university modernization. In the 1860s, about a third of Scottish students came from professional families, but at the other end of the social spectrum a fifth could be described as 'working class' – which usually meant the sons of artisans and tradesmen rather than the really poor. In the 1900s, their share was much the same, though it was now a working class which included the skilled workers of the shipyards and engineering works.[13] One reason was that Scottish secondary education was cheap and relatively open, university bursaries were numerous, and from 1901 the Carnegie Trust, founded by the eponymous Scottish-American millionaire, paid the university fees of any Scottish-born student who applied. Another reason was a stronger tradition of graduate schoolteachers in Scotland than in England. The traditional lad o' pairts set his eyes on the church, but teaching now became the classic upwardly mobile career. The prestige of teaching was one reason for the higher proportion of women students in Scotland – once women had been belatedly admitted in 1892.

In Scotland, universities created national identity not just through the experiences which the elite took away from their student years, but because they had a place in the national psyche as part of a myth (in the sense of an idealized reality) about the democratic superiority of the national educational tradition. In Wales, a similar myth was created from scratch at the end of the nineteenth century. The development of university education in Wales was partly a response to rapid industrialization, but also reflected the distinctiveness of Welsh religious and linguistic culture, particularly the dominance of Nonconformism. The first new foundation was the Anglican St David's College at Lampeter, founded in 1827 to train priests who could not afford Oxford or Cambridge, in order to strengthen a church which was losing the allegiance of the Welsh people. In the 1850s it acquired the power to award its own degrees, but otherwise differed little from theological colleges founded at this time in England, both by the Nonconformist churches and by many Anglican bishops unhappy with the lack of real theological education at Oxford and Cambridge.

Lampeter's Anglicanism excluded it from the Welsh university movement, which started in the 1850s with support among the Welsh community in London as well as within Wales. It was not until 1872 that a university college opened at Aberystwyth. According to the organizing committee in 1870, 'the object which they are charged to carry out is one intimately connected with the advancement of learning in the Principality and the social elevation of its young men of the middle class'.[14] The college struggled at first, but a public campaign for state support led to the appointment of the Aberdare Committee by Gladstone's 1880 government. Its report in 1881, starting from the premise that 'the existence ... of a distinct Welsh nationality is ... a reason for securing within the limits of Wales itself a system of intermediate and higher education in harmony with the distinctive peculiarities of the country', recommended the foundation of additional colleges, teaching scientific and modern subjects to meet 'the requirements of commercial or professional life', together with a Welsh university to conduct examinations and award degrees.[15] Colleges were founded at Cardiff in 1883 (after a contest with its rival Swansea) and Bangor in 1884, and all three colleges were given state grants. The federal University of Wales received its charter in 1893. An equally important result of the Aberdare Report was a system of intermediate or 'county' schools, secondary schools serving the local middle class but also giving university access to poorer children; these were created in 1889, before anything similar in England.

The Aberdare Committee hoped that the university would bring higher education 'more closely home to the daily life and thoughts of the people', and 'might, under favourable circumstances, tend to develop new forms of culture in affinity with some of the distinctive character-istics of the Welsh people'.[16] At Cardiff, serving a booming industrial area, the college resembled the English civic colleges. Bangor and Aber-ystwyth were in Welsh-speaking areas and spread their roots in rural culture. Socially, they drew on the world of ministers, farmers, shop-keepers and small professional men, with a significant presence of the children of miners and quarrymen.[17] But the relation of the university to the Welsh language was ambiguous: by 1900 just half the population spoke it, there was no teaching in Welsh at the new colleges, and it was only after 1914 that demands to use the language in the university were heard.[18] The university was a classic expression of cultural nationalism (along with the National Museum and National Library, both founded in the 1900s) and it helped to form a distinctive Welsh literary and political intelligentsia, but for many graduates the aim was to get jobs outside Wales, and Wales became an exporter of teachers.[19] The focus on an academic education turning out pastors and teachers made the university of limited interest to Welsh industry and commerce, which did little to help finance it, and Wales has been cited as a prize exhibit in the charge that education reinforced anti-entrepreneurial values.[20]

Two vigorous Welsh myths of higher education soon arose. One was that Wales was an ancient land of learning, the second and more plausible that higher education was democratically accessible, as in Scot-land.[21] The university movement was described in 1905 as 'a movement which brings into strong relief the peculiar national characteristics of an ancient people ... the history of learning in Wales ... is the history of the nation itself'. It was 'the embodiment of the genius of a race, and the final expression of a national tradition of learning which has sur-vived the vicissitudes of centuries'; for had not St Illtyd, in the days of Celtic Christianity, founded at Llantwit Major 'a great school of learn-ing which was in every sense of the word a university long before Oxford or Cambridge became famous'? The new university was thus 'the cre-ation not of sovereigns and statesmen, but of the people themselves'.[22]

There was substance to this claim, as Aberystwyth and Bangor were both sustained in their early years by the 'pennies of the poor' – public collections at chapel services and elsewhere, to which working men were generous contributors.[23]

'It is in the Universities, with their power over the mind ... that we see how the soul of a people at its highest mirrors itself', R. B. Haldane told Aberystwyth students in 1910.[24] Irish nationalists would have agreed. But whereas in Wales the university was a force for unity, binding together north and south, rural and industrial regions, in Ireland the university question was bitterly divisive, reflecting relations between the religious communities and cultures in the island, and between them and the British state. At Trinity College, Dublin (TCD) religious tests for students were abolished in 1794, but scholarships and teaching posts remained closed to non-Anglicans until 1873. The semi-colonial status of Ireland allowed the British government to impose solutions as it could not on the mainland, but it was constrained by strong hostility at Westminster to any public subsidy for denominational Catholic education. The Catholic seminary at Maynooth, funded by the state from 1795 in an attempt at equitable treatment, was always controversial. When governments returned to the problem after the emancipation of Roman Catholics in 1829, Peel legislated in 1845 for three strictly non-denominational Queen's Colleges at Belfast, Cork and Galway. These opened in 1849, as non-residential colleges organized on professorial lines, including faculties of law and medicine (the latter proving their most successful branch). The state paid generously for buildings and chairs, and in 1850 created the Queen's University to award degrees, on the model of London in 1836. Peel's aim had been to win over 'the great body of wealthy and intelligent Roman Catholics', and it was hoped that a new Irish elite free of clerical control and sympathetic to British rule would emerge.[25] But the official Catholic view, similar to that of Anglican conservatives in England, and reinforced by the ultramontane policies of Pope Pius IX, was that secular and religious education were inseparable, and that Catholics and Protestants must not be educated together. The 'godless colleges' were condemned, and the Irish hierarchy forbade Catholics to attend them. Thus while Queen's College at Belfast was successful, the colleges at Cork and

Galway were only half-effective, all three together attracting fewer students than TCD.[26]

The episcopal boycott of the Queen's University was crucial in the growing identification of Catholicism with Irish nationalism. The bishops' riposte to the secular colleges was to found a Catholic University at Dublin, on the model of Louvain in Belgium. J. H. Newman was appointed as rector, and the lectures which he gave in Dublin leading up to the university's opening in 1854 were the basis of the book later known as *The Idea of a University*. There Newman put forward a high ideal of liberal education, but as rector he aimed to provide a full range of scientific and professional training, to give the Catholic upper and middle classes 'that commanding position in society, which an educated intellect and the reputation for mental attainments are the means of securing'.[27] The early years were difficult: there were no degree-awarding powers, standards suffered from the inadequacy of Irish secondary schools, Newman's ideas on the purpose of the university differed from those of the bishops, and he resigned in 1858. Only in the 1880s, when it was renamed University College Dublin (UCD) and taken over by the Jesuits, did it begin to flourish. Besides meeting the demands of the Catholic middle class, the college fostered the Gaelic cultural movement, and was the seedbed of a new nationalist intelligentsia, the poet and schoolteacher Patrick Pearse being a characteristic product.

The rival institution in Dublin, TCD, was a conservative but relatively efficient and economical institution; a royal commission appointed in 1851 in parallel with those on Oxford and Cambridge made only minor criticisms. The curriculum was more like Cambridge than Scotland, with an emphasis on mathematics and science as well as classics, and in the course of the nineteenth century it was adapted to include modern and professional subjects. Dublin graduates competed on the British level in the civil service and for posts in the empire. But TCD hardly widened its social recruitment, and its ethos, though in its way intensely Irish in character, was not welcoming either to the growing Catholic middle class, urban and rural, or to the Presbyterian farmers and small bourgeois of the industrializing north. The rise of the Queen's Colleges diminished Trinity's national role and made it more than ever the domain of the Dublin professional classes, a bastion of Unionism and 'the central institution of the Dublin Protestant world'.[28] Although the surviving religious tests were abolished in 1873, this only led to Rome extending the attendance ban to TCD, a godless college being worse than an Anglican one, and as nationalists and Home Rule politicians came to identify with Catholic educational demands, TCD was marked out as 'anti-national'.[29]

Meanwhile, a new attempt to solve the Irish university question was made by Gladstone, following his disestablishment of the Irish Anglican church in 1869, but a national framework which could somehow accommodate all religious allegiances proved elusive. The Irish university question was as insoluble as the Irish question itself. The Catholic Church opposed any solution which did not 'endow' the fully Catholic institutions demanded by the majority of the people. A government Bill in 1873 was defeated, causing a serious political crisis. The compromise eventually arrived at in 1879 was to convert the Queen's University into the Royal University of Ireland, another examining university, but one which unlike the older body was open to candidates wherever they were educated. This opened the path to degrees for Catholic students. The Royal University had salaried fellowships held by college professors, and since these were distributed equally between Catholics and Protestants, UCD benefited indirectly from state subsidy. The Royal University examinations were also open to women, allowing them to obtain degrees outside the college structure: for Dublin Protestants Alexandra College, founded in 1869, combined secondary and higher education, and Victoria College had a similar role in Belfast. For Catholic girls, convent education was dominant, and some convents offered higher education courses. The Queen's Colleges opened to women in the 1880s, UCD rather later, and Trinity, conservative to the last, in 1904.

Irish higher education now developed more rapidly – by the 1900s the percentage of the population using it was higher than in England.[30] Religious divisions did not prevent the colleges from serving expanding professional needs, and Ireland exported doctors as Wales did teachers. But politically the 1880s compromise satisfied few. Four royal commissions probed the question, and the eventual outcome was the Irish Universities Act of 1908, which gave the system its modern shape. Trinity College remained independent and received no state funding; the Queen's College at Belfast became an independent institution as Queen's University; and the Royal University was replaced by the

National University of Ireland, a federal rather than a simple examining university, comprising UCD and the colleges at Cork and Galway. The National University was officially secular, but in spirit Catholic and nationalist, and it demonstrated its nationalist credentials (controversially) by making a knowledge of the Irish language a condition of admission.

The tripartite university structure of 1908, representing the three cultural and religious traditions of Ireland, marked the end of attempts to create a genuinely 'national' Irish university and foreshadowed partition in 1921.[31] The historic loser was Trinity College, which became the university of a beleaguered rather than a dominant minority. In 1908, however, it had seemed likely that the National University would take its place within a Home Rule Ireland, as one more complexity of a 'British' university system which had to take account of subordinate cultures and nationalisms. For the nineteenth century, the history of Irish universities cannot be separated from problems on the mainland. Issues like religious tests and denominationalism, or examining versus teaching universities, linked Irish and British university politics, not least in the mind of Gladstone when he wrestled with these problems in the 1870s. More broadly, the failure to integrate the educated classes of Ireland into a single elite shows by contrast how successfully the other universities, notably in Scotland, helped to form a British and imperial identity which came to be taken for granted.

7

Ideas of the University

The Idea of a University Defined and Illustrated was the title given by John Henry Newman to the 1873 edition of a set of lectures and essays which originated in 1852, when Newman lectured in Dublin on his hopes for the new Catholic university. A previous version, in 1859, was called *The Scope and Nature of University Education*. Newman's book has come to be regarded as a classic statement of the ideal of liberal education and of the university as a place for the disinterested pursuit of truth and the cultivation of the mind. Its central principles are that knowledge is 'its own end', and that academic specialization and vocational training, while not bad things in themselves, should be subordinated to the universality of knowledge and the interdependence of different branches of learning. A liberal education should be one which develops a 'philosophical habit', relating the individual's studies to the 'pure and clear atmosphere of thought' fostered by the university as a community of learning: a habit of mind 'which lasts through life, of which the attributes are freedom, equitableness, calmness, moderation, and wisdom'. Such a training teaches the student 'to see things as they are, to go right to the point, to disentangle a skein of thought, to detect what is sophistical, and to discard what is irrelevant. It prepares him to fill any post with credit, and to master any subject with facility.'[1] The English ideal of the gentlemanly generalist is partly rooted in Newman; he did not exactly equate the cultured intellect with the qualities of the gentleman, but he did use the latter concept in a way which made his ideal seem more socially restricted than it really was.

Newman argued that the pursuit of knowledge did not need external justification: it was its own end and its own reward, and 'liberal Education, viewed in itself, is simply the cultivation of the intellect, as such, and its object is nothing more or less than intellectual excellence'.[2] The 'pursuit of excellence' is a concept much appealed to by modern

university pundits, but it is anachronistic to imply that Newman anticipated the modern research ideal. For him, the university 'is a place of
teaching universal *knowledge.* This implies that its object is, on the one
hand, intellectual, not moral; and, on the other, that it is the diffusion
and extension of knowledge rather than the advancement. If its object
were scientific and philosophical discovery, I do not see why a University should have students; if religious training, I do not see how it can
be the seat of literature and science.' The simple advancement of science
was better pursued in academies and research institutions, for 'to dis-
cover and to teach are distinct functions; they are also distinct gifts, and
are not commonly found united in the same person'.[3] Newman was thus
not endorsing the Humboldtian union of teaching and research, but his
belief in scholarship as an ennobling pursuit and a means of bringing
the human personality to full development had parallels with German
Bildung.

In seeing the university's primary task as teaching, not religious training, Newman was defying pressures from his superiors in the church.
Yet he was much concerned, in a way which may disconcert the modern reader, with theology as a branch of knowledge, and with
reconciling the search for truth with Catholic authority. In other
respects he remained faithful to the ideal which he had developed as an
Oxford tutor, with its emphasis on the pastoral influence of the teacher
– a relationship quite different from the German idea of scientific master and apprentice. In justifying classics as the core of liberal education
Newman reproduced the arguments of the Copleston era, which were
already old-fashioned, and he made no special effort to relate them to
contemporary controversies (over the place of science in education, for
example), or to define the purpose of university education in social
terms. The timeless nature of his thought has perhaps been its attraction
in recent times, as a weapon against utilitarian and instrumentalist views
of the university; indeed, it seems that Newman was rather seldom read
or cited in his own day, and that his fame was a twentieth-century development. He has also been more venerated, and given more scholarly
attention, in the United States than in Britain.

The lack of intellectual connection between Newman and the poet
and critic Matthew Arnold is particularly striking. The two men are

often seen as the twin apostles of English humanistic culture, yet they seem to have had little interest in each other's writings. Arnold was a fellow of Oriel twenty years after Newman, but was brought up in the liberal, broad church traditions of his father Thomas Arnold, which were anathema to Newman. Matthew Arnold did not become a don, spending his professional career as a school inspector, but came to be seen as a representative of the Oxford spirit, a celebrant of the city, its river and its countryside. It was Arnold who spoke of Oxford's 'dreaming spires', and of the city 'spreading her gardens to the moonlight, and whispering from her towers the last enchantments of the Middle Age ... home of lost causes, and forsaken beliefs, and unpopular names, and impossible loyalties'.[4] But there was an element of irony or self-parody in this, and Arnold was far from being a simple nostalgist. His thought engaged with contemporary social and cultural problems as Newman's did not, and not only had more direct influence, but drew on an existing tradition of thinking about the 'clerisy' and the role of the state in education.

This tradition derived chiefly from S. T. Coleridge, whose *On the Constitution of the Church and State* (1830) argued that the traditional partnership of the state and the national church should be extended by reclaiming the national 'patrimony' alienated when Henry VIII dissolved the monasteries, in order to endow a secular clerisy. Coleridge seems to have seen the clerisy primarily as a force of parish schoolmasters, supplementing the efforts of the clergy itself. But part of the national endowment would support the men of learning in the universities who trained both clergy and teachers and stood 'at the fountain heads of the humanities'. The function of the whole system would be 'to preserve the stores, to guard the treasures, of past civilization, and thus to bind the present with the past', and 'to perfect and add to the same, and thus to connect the present with the future'.[5] The clerisy would provide continuity and cultural leadership in a society fragmented by industrialization and corroded by the 'mechanico-corpuscular' philosophy which ran from Locke to Bentham. The Benthamite London University of 1828, a mere 'lecture bazaar' dependent on the market, was a particular target of Coleridge. The clerisy idea was thus in part an argument for state support of universities, to allow their members to do their work properly as spiritual and cultural agents.

This argument was a familiar one in Scotland, where both William Hamilton and the influential religious leader and political economist Thomas Chalmers argued that the free market would not support learning and culture any more than it supported religion, and extended the principle of state establishment to universities in the same way as Coleridge. For Chalmers in 1827, the aim was to support 'an aristocracy of letters ... by which to qualify and to soften the vulgar aristocracy of mere rank and power'. Later, Coleridge's idea of the clerisy directly influenced Scottish figures like the lawyer and university reformer James Lorimer, who argued in the 1850s that the state should endow a 'learned class' on a lavish scale.[6] Scottish intellectuals were impressed by the role of the state in France and Germany, just as Coleridge was an important channel for the transmission of German ideas to Britain.

The continental model of the state as a positive cultural force was taken up by Arnold, whose enthusiasm for it was reinforced both by his first-hand study of other educational systems and by admiration for the work of Humboldt. In Germany, 'the idea of culture' embodied in universities was 'a living power', balancing the dangers of 'industrialism'.[7] So too the British state should be the 'organ of the national reason', through which the community expressed its collective higher interests.[8] The urgent task in the 1860s was to organize secondary and higher education for the middle classes, at a time when the cultural leadership of the upper classes was flagging: the latter had been diverted, in public schools and ancient universities, by the cult of games, and now showed 'a torpor of intellectual life, a dearth of ideas, an indifference to fine culture or disbelief in its necessity, spreading through the bulk of our highest class, and influencing its rising generation'.[9] Vitality had passed to the middle classes, yet their culture was equally underdeveloped. An upper stratum was seduced into the public schools and upper-class ways, to its detriment, while the bulk of the business class had a 'philistine' outlook. This group needed to be given a new and solid culture, by the creation of state secondary schools (here Arnold's campaigns were unsuccessful) and new provincial universities. In his report on continental education in 1868, Arnold concluded that the reform of Oxbridge was not the first priority.

> We must plant faculties in the eight or ten principal seats of population, and let the students follow lectures there from their own homes, or with

whatever arrangements for their living they and their parents choose. It would be everything for the great seats of population to be thus made intellectual centres as well as mere places of business; for the want of this at present, Liverpool and Leeds are mere overgrown provincial towns, while Strasbourg and Lyons are European cities.

These new faculties would be more suitable centres for medicine and other practical studies than Oxbridge. Arnold thus had a more radical vision of university extension than the one which actually prevailed: Oxbridge chairs and financial resources should be transferred elsewhere, so helping 'in the happiest manner to inaugurate a truly national system of superior instruction'. London University should also be radically reformed, turning it into a teaching institution worthy of the capital.[10]

It is therefore misleading to see Arnold simply as a spokesman for effete public-school and Oxbridge ideals, though his vision of culture was certainly a conservative one, which emphasized the ethical and civilizing role of literature. One of the great defects of the English middle class was its 'Hebraism' – narrowness of views derived from Protestantism, and especially from the Nonconformity of which Arnold was a severe critic. This should be corrected by a dose of Hellenism, and Arnold's deep belief in the study of Greek civilization had German as well as English roots. The contrast of Hebraism and Hellenism, and the prescription of culture as a source of 'sweetness and light', were central themes of Arnold's *Culture and Anarchy* (1869). There he defined culture as 'a pursuit of our total perfection by means of getting to know, on all the matters which most concern us, the best which has been thought and said in the world'; in this, and in seeking to teach men to 'see life steadily and see it whole', he was not so far from Newman.[11] But for Arnold salvation lay in modern as well as classical literature. English literature was only beginning to establish its academic credentials at this time – it had footholds in London and Scotland, but was only introduced at Oxford and Cambridge, against considerable resistance, in the 1880s. Perhaps it is unsurprising that Arnold was to have his greatest admirers in English departments.

Coleridge had assumed that the Church of England could still be the national church, and that the clerisy would strengthen its role. By the 1860s the loss of faith which so preoccupied Arnold (not least as a theme of his poetry) made this an unattainable ideal, but Arnoldian culture could be seen as a secularized Anglicanism, an ideological correlate of the leadership ideal of Jowett and Green.[12] Like other religion-substitutes of the late Victorian age, it sought to provide an alternative source of authority and a focus for morality and idealism. The concept also had political implications in the troubling aftermath of the extension of the vote in 1867, another of Arnold's worries. More radical liberals welcomed the dawn of a new democratic age in which intellectuals would lead the people forward to progress – an 'alliance of brains and numbers' against aristocratic privilege.[13] Arnold wished rather to shape an intellectual aristocracy blending new and old elites, urban modernity and aristocratic tradition, to resist the tyranny of the majority and stabilize the disruptive forces of industrialism. And while Coleridge's clerisy was to be chiefly a body of religious and secular teachers supported by the state, Arnold's vision was that culture should permeate the whole of the professional and business middle classes. It was a 'cultured, liberalised, ennobled, transformed middle class' which would lead the working class down the path of civilization.[14]

Arnold's programme of national cultural renewal under the aegis of the state may have been utopian, but it was not disconnected from contemporary debates on university reform. Mark Pattison, whose *Suggestions on Academical Organization* of 1868 sought to graft German academic rigour onto Oxford tradition, shared many of Arnold's ideas.[15] For Pattison too, the middle classes needed to be taught that 'the highest form of education is culture for culture's sake ... that intellectual and moral nourishment for want of which we are in danger of starving in the midst of all our gold'.[16] Both men contrasted true liberal education with the sterility of the 'mental training' and examination culture of Jowett's Oxford: Pattison thought that the 'examination screw ... has become an instrument of mere torture which has made education impossible and crushed the very desire of learning'; and Arnold cited the views of continental observers who dismissed the English universities as overgrown secondary schools dispensing social status rather than learning.[17] For Arnold, literature (or 'poetry') should be the basis of general culture, but within universities it was German *Wissenschaft*, knowledge acquired by strenuous and systematic pursuit of the truth, which exemplified the serious intellectual effort on which culture should rest. University education was in the opinion of the best judges, the weakest part of our whole educational system ... The want of the idea of science, of systematic knowledge, is ... the capital want, at this moment, of English education and of English life; it is the university, or the superior school, which ought to foster this idea. The university or the superior school ought to provide facilities, after the general education is finished, for the young man to go on in the line where his special aptitudes lead him, be it that of languages and literature, of mathematics, of the natural sciences, of the application of these sciences, or any other line, and follow the studies of this line systematically under first-rate teaching. Our great universities, Oxford and Cambridge, do next to nothing towards this end.[18]

Arnold was speaking here as an official, and his private attitudes to science and specialization may have been less sympathetic. But his concept of a humane, liberal education was not narrowly tied to the classical tradition. The true aim of education was 'to develop the powers of our mind and to give us access to vital knowledge', and the circle of knowledge was wide: 'the idea of a general, liberal training is, to carry us to a knowledge of ourselves and the world'. The humanities teach us to know ourselves, natural science to know the world. Both should be part of 'the beginnings of a liberal culture' shared by all – preferably in secondary schools, as in Germany – before passing to those more specialized studies suited to the individual's aptitudes.[19]

The earlier English ideal of liberal education exalted the unique liberalizing virtues of classics or mathematics, while the Scottish encyclopedic ideal tried to bring all subjects within its philosophical compass. The expansion of knowledge and the growth of professional specialization eventually made both ideals untenable. The relations between science and the humanities, and between general and specialized education, were fought out in a public debate on the purposes of university education which extended from the 1860s to the 1880s.[20] Arnold and Huxley, friends in private life, were often seen as rival symbols of the 'two cultures' of literature and science. Champions of science had to contend with two prejudices. One was that science was philosophically 'materialist', and hence hostile to religion. Even after the controversies over Darwin's *Origin of Species* (1859) died down, the 'scientific naturalism' to which most scientists subscribed (this is the term favoured by British historians of science: 'positivism' was the broader European term) seemed dangerous to many because of its determinism. The humanities had higher claims, it was argued, because they expressed 'the work of the human spirit itself', the operations of free will and human agency, while the sciences studied the operation of non-human forces, the realm of 'human limitation and passivity'.[21] The second prejudice was that science was too practical, too closely tied to the vulgar world of industry, technology and money-making. To counter this, Huxley distanced himself from the kind of crude utilitarianism and scientism represented at the time by Herbert Spencer, and argued strongly that science had an educational value independent of its practical applications; in the nineteenth century it should be an indispensable element of 'culture', and hence of liberal education, for the decision-making elite just as much as for manufacturers or technical experts.

John Stuart Mill also contributed to this debate in a much-noted rectorial address at St Andrews University in 1867, to which Huxley in turn replied when elected rector at Aberdeen in 1874. If scientific spokesmen were nervous about too close an association with vocationalism, Mill went further. He not only declared at St Andrews that 'an University ought to be a place of free speculation', whose members 'seek for truth at all hazards', but claimed, with echoes of Newman, that 'there is a tolerably general agreement about what an University is not. It is not a place of professional education. Universities are not intended to teach the knowledge required to fit men for some special mode of gaining their livelihood. Their object is not to make skilful lawyers, or physicians, or engineers, but capable and cultivated human beings ... Men are men before they are lawyers, or physicians, or merchants, or manufacturers; and if you make them capable and sensible men, they will make themselves capable and sensible lawyers or physicians.' Professional training might be given under the university's roof for convenience, but could equally well be given elsewhere.[22] Perhaps Mill was only seeking to distinguish core functions from optional ones, but his dismissal of professional education was a startling one in the Scottish context, and also ignored centuries of university history, as Hastings Rashdall would point out.

'To comment upon the course of education at the Scottish Universities', Mill claimed, 'is to pass in review every essential department of general culture.'[23] But in Scotland as elsewhere, disciplinary specialization advanced inexorably. Behind it lay the general development of the various branches of knowledge, but also two more specific changes: the professionalization of intellectual life, and the acceptance of research as an essential function of the university, if not necessarily the dominant one. Subjects which had once been the province of amateurs, accessible to a wider educated public through the serious quarterly and monthly journals, became more technical and demanding. The characteristic modern apparatus of professional associations, conferences and learned journals began to appear. Science led the way in this movement, but was followed quite closely by subjects like classics and history, both fields where German scholarship had great prestige. Academic culture based on expertise and professionalism became distinct from the broader literary and artistic culture which still flourished in London and in the press, even if some individual academics managed to straddle the two.

The 1870s and 1880s seem to have been the crucial period for the rise of the research university – the 'reception of the Humboldtian ideal' in historians' jargon. The ability to make original contributions to the subject became an essential criterion for appointing to chairs, or to the junior lectureships which were beginning to proliferate and to make possible lifetime academic careers. Loyalty to the discipline rather than the institution was one result, as was a national market in jobs based on a common academic culture. In Scotland arts and science professors were almost all Scots until the 1880s, but there was then a large English influx, and after 1900 Scots-born professors were a minority.[24] Oxford and Cambridge continued to recruit from their own graduates, and there the demands of research conflicted with a teaching ethos which was still very strong, especially in the humanities subjects traditionally associated with the education of the governing elite. But college fellows were now essentially professional scholars and scientists, and frustration at the limitations of Oxbridge was often a motive for seeking chairs in Scotland, London or the English provinces, as in these professorial universities it was easier to apply the research model.

Research was still seen more as a personal obligation of the teacher, to be pursued according to an individual judgement of where the frontiers of the discipline lay, than as a collective activity of the university. In the 1890s the term 'postgraduate' began to be used, but Britain was slow to adopt formal research training. Those who wished to pursue a scholarly career had to find money and opportunities where they could, and in many fields, especially in science and medicine, a spell in Germany or France was almost de rigueur. (Germany had the magnetic appeal for ambitious academics which the United States was to assume after 1945.) At home advanced scholarships or research grants were scarce: they usually came not from the state, nor to any large extent from industry, but from college resources at Oxbridge or from individual endowments. In Scotland, the Carnegie Trust acted effectively as the first British research foundation. Various types of doctorate were created towards the end of the century, usually of a lengthy and demanding kind, but the shorter, standardized PhD was not adopted in Britain until 1919; even then, it was originally meant to attract young Americans, diverted from the German universities discredited by the war, rather than to train British academics.[25]

German ideas often reached Britain at second hand from the United States, where research universities were now developing. But patterns in the two countries remained different, and the 'graduate school' failed to emerge in Britain. Perhaps this was because modernization of the curriculum at Oxford and Cambridge had made the single-subject degree standard, so that in England professional degrees in subjects like law, medicine or theology became first degrees. It may also be that secondary schools reached higher (if narrower) standards in Britain than in America, making it easier to introduce specialization in undergraduate degrees, while in America the 'liberal arts' university tradition remained strong. These national differences have persisted.

In British undergraduate education, a research-based or 'training of scholars' model now became accepted. Once past the elementary stage, students should become familiar with the latest developments in their discipline, and should receive at least an elementary initiation into research techniques and the tools of the academic trade. Students in science and medicine were expected to work at the laboratory bench, in arts to read widely for themselves in the libraries which were (as it became a cliché to point out) the laboratories of the arts. To provide the necessary buildings, equipment and books was expensive, which was one reason why the civic universities turned to the state in the 1880s. Only a minority of students were likely to enter academic life, but in an elite system enough of them were entering professions to which university science and scholarship were intellectually relevant (including schoolteaching) to make this initiation into academic ways of thinking a meaningful and long-lasting experience. The union of teaching and research, and the university as a 'community of scholars' devoted to the pursuit of truth and critical thinking, became rather more than rhetoric (though there was plenty of that) and fed the self-esteem of the new academic profession.

Thus the objective pursuit of science and scholarship, even in specialized fields, could be seen as a modern form of the old ideal of mental training. Any subject could be an instrument of general education if it was studied in a liberal, disinterested spirit, 'for its own sake' rather than purely for its usefulness. The practical legacy of Newman, Arnold and Mill was to provide a principled rationale for non-vocational education. Here the humanities and science could find common ground, and the rivalries of the Arnold–Huxley era died away; the division was in any case blurred by the growth of the social sciences (economics being the pioneer), whose subject matter was human behaviour but whose pursuit of general laws shared the spirit of natural science. By the early twentieth century, indeed, the prestige of science was such that a positivist model of knowledge spread to disciplines like history and literature. There was, however, one caveat: purely vocational or technical subjects could not share in the liberal spirit, unless they could be presented in the clothing of a profession. A profession required mastery of a body of fundamental theory as well as practical knowledge, and an ethical commitment to ideas of impartiality and public service, instilling which was the university's speciality. There had always been a useful elision between the 'liberal' professions of law, medicine and theology and 'liberal' education, between social status and learning. This notion could now be extended to university training as a whole – provided that pure 'training' as opposed to 'education' was excluded. Hence the pressure on the civic colleges to drop these more vulgar activities if they were to receive charters and grants – pressures which were never entirely successful. Hence also the resistance at Oxbridge, from a higher level of intellectual and social self-confidence, even to some well-established and professionalized branches of knowledge which had a taint of practicality.

If academics came to agree on the unity of teaching and research, they disagreed in the nineteenth century about the unity of teaching and examining. London University, the Victoria University of 1880, and the examining universities in Wales and Ireland represented the principle of separating the two, as indeed did Oxford and Cambridge, where colleges taught and the university examined. The idea of examining as an external process had strong support, and was seen by outsiders as a specifically English tradition.[26] In the controversies in the 1880s and 1890s over converting London from an examining to a teaching university, there were many who opposed integrating the existing colleges into the university because teachers would then be examining their own students.[27] It was only in Scotland that professors insisted that these functions could not be separated, and even there some reformers in 1858 (led by Gladstone, with Irish parallels in mind) wanted to set up a national Scottish university of which the four old universities would become mere colleges. This was defeated, but the price paid was the acceptance of external examiners to monitor degree standards, apparently the origin of this uniquely British institution.

The examining university was part of a wider Victorian passion for examinations as a meritocratic device. The argument in its favour was that it secured objective standards; the arguments against, that it froze innovation because it could not adjust to the constant evolution of research which teaching should embody and that it defined university education as a collection of examinable knowledge, not a search for originality or truth. Robert Lowe, the right-wing Liberal politician who as minister responsible for education in the 1860s introduced 'payment by results' in elementary schools, and who was accordingly at the head of Arnold's list of philistines, once said that 'what I mean by an University is an examining board'.[28] After 1900 the Scottish conception generally prevailed in other universities, and the old arguments were forgotten. Yet external examination remained orthodox in secondary and technical education, and enjoyed a revival in the 1960s when the Council for National Academic Awards served to provide common standards for the new polytechnics as London University had done for the fledgling civic universities. This was abolished in 1992, since when the integrated, degree-awarding, unitary university has again become the norm, creating tension between university and colleges in those federal universities which survive, London and Wales.

Lowe was a champion of the free market, hostile to state provision of education for the middle classes, and the Victorian examination system could be seen as embodying an open conception of knowledge, available to adults, to part-time students, and to men and women of all classes, free of the monopolistic grip of chartered universities.[29] Academic orthodoxy, however, moved in the other direction, not just to a belief that universities should be communities of scholars, but to one that they should be communities in the fuller sense, where students learnt as much outside the classroom from their shared social life as within it. Student 'corporate life' did not necessarily entail residence, and from the 1880s it developed strongly in Scotland, where students lived at home or in lodgings: student unions, newspapers, political clubs, debating societies and athletics were all part of the Scottish model, and spread from there to the English civic universities. The American campus was another influence, as American universities became better known in Britain; Chamberlain's university in the Birmingham suburbs was one result. The communal ideal had some roots in Newman's pastoral vision, and in the (Thomas) Arnoldian public school, but probably owed most simply to the irresistible prestige of Oxford and Cambridge, and to the intensified social and athletic life of their reformed college system. In the twentieth century the ideal of socialization through living in a residential community spread downwards in diluted form until it was seen as central to the English (and eventually even the Scottish) university ethos.

Disciplinary specialization, personal relations between teacher and taught, the university as a community: these ideals became engrained in the British academic mind. Higher education inspired by notions of humane, liberal culture, aiming to develop the whole personality, and feeding graduates into the professions and public services, marginalized those conceptions of knowledge as a practical, examinable, market-driven, utilitarian affair which had also been characteristic of Victorian Britain, but which now went underground, or were relegated to the inferior and fragmentary technical sector. University education proper came to be defined by its institutional context, whose boundaries were carefully patrolled and whose ideology was attuned to the formation of a leadership elite. This was to be the dominant note of university development in the early twentieth century, but it confronted serious problems of adaptation when the elite university began to turn into the mass university, whose objectives were defined by the state, in social and economic terms, rather than by the autonomous and self-directing scholars of the Humboldtian dream.

8

Interwar Conservatism

The far-reaching effect of the two world wars on British life makes them natural chronological turning-points. But for university history a broader period makes sense, from the consolidation of a national system around 1900 until the 1960s, when the foundation of new 'greenfield' universities and the Robbins Report of 1963 marked the beginnings of the transition from elite to mass higher education. Within that period, the essential social and intellectual character of British universities remained the same. The First World War aroused hopes for greater democracy and individual opportunity, but these were largely disappointed, and much of the dynamism apparent in the decade before 1914 was dissipated. The interwar years saw only modest numerical expansion, and there was no step forward in scientific and technical education to regenerate the British economy. But the Second World War generated urgent new demands, and created longer-term pressures for social change which transformed the educational system. These pressures confronted a university culture which in the 1940s and 1950s remained conservative, combining a characteristic complacency about British institutions with a vigorous reassertion of the liberal and idealist educational tradition. The 'two cultures' debate featuring the scientist and novelist C. P. Snow and the Cambridge literary critic F. R. Leavis, which coincided with the deliberations of the Robbins Committee, brings this period to an end.

The formation of the University Grants Committee (UGC) in 1919 was seen at the time as a piece of administrative tidying-up rather than a significant new departure.[1] Wartime inflation, a bulge in student numbers as servicemen returned, and a new appreciation of the importance of science and technology together required a substantial increase in state finance (to about a million pounds a year), and the opportunity was taken to amalgamate and rationalize the English, Scottish, Welsh and Irish grants. Since the Board of Education had authority only in England and Wales, the UGC was put directly under the Treasury. From its foundation until the 1970s, the UGC maintained an 'arm's length' relationship with the government. In its own dealings with the universities it scrupulously rejected any kind of detailed direction or earmarking of funds which might entrench on their autonomy, and sought to protect them from other external pressures. 'The greatest service a university can render to the nation as a whole is to remain true to itself', said the UGC in 1930.[2] Under a system of quinquennial planning which went back to the prewar system, the universities put forward detailed needs, but the block grant which they then received for the next five years could be spent as they wished, and there were no penalties for failing to conform to the original guidelines.

This autonomy seems remarkable in retrospect. It has various possible explanations. The sums involved were quite small as a proportion of government expenditure, university education was an elite affair affecting only a small segment of society, and university questions did not arouse much controversy or political interest. According to Eric Ashby, a leading university figure of the 1950s and 1960s, the success of the system ('the envy of other countries') came from the fellow feeling between dons and Oxbridge-educated civil servants, the latter 'as much at home in the intellectual world as ... in the political world ... The civil servant who is at the same time fellow of All Souls is the best guarantee one could have for the autonomy of British universities.'[3] The Treasury came to see its role as a source of prestige in Whitehall, and was proud of its amicable relationship with its protégés. Civil servants recruited from the Oxbridge elite shared the ethos of the dons: in 1939, negotiating on wartime finance, one UGC official sought the support of a Treasury colleague on the grounds that 'the Universities stood for Civilisation with a capital C and appealed to him as an Oxford man. I think this somewhat immoral shaft went home.'[4] The extension of state grants to Oxford and Cambridge made this fellow-feeling a powerful defence of autonomy, just as the mid-Victorian reform of these universities had been limited by the presence of their alumni in Parliament and public life. Now the other universities could shelter behind their protection. But apart from all these reasons, politicians and bureaucrats belonged to a political culture which was suspicious of the power of the state, and really did believe that the independence of universities was an important liberal value, a tradition to be cherished, and that they worked best when left to determine their own policies.

If the UGC's role as a buffer between state and universities was an unintended development, it soon came to be seen as a unique British contribution to public administration. For the American observer Abraham Flexner in 1930, it was 'a gentle, but powerful influence for good. In the absence of control by an education ministry, it has assisted what is good and quietly ignored all else.'[5] For the historian Charles Grant Robertson, former vice-chancellor of Birmingham, writing in 1944, it 'has won the complete confidence of the universities by the tact and sympathy with which it has exercised its powers'.[6] For the historian of a civic university in 1955, it was 'that remarkable body that now serves so well to interpret the needs of the universities to the Government and the needs of the nation to the universities'.[7] For Lionel Robbins, whose report in 1963 fervently endorsed the block grant and the UGC's role, 'we in this country have hit upon an administrative device of immense value: it is certainly the object of great admiration and envy abroad'.[8] It became a rhetorical commonplace that the UGC was the envy of the world, though few countries outside the British Commonwealth seem to have taken the hint and copied the model.

Until the Second World War, members of the UGC could not be active in university affairs, which led to the appointment of retired academics and administrators, and an average age of seventy. In 1937, five of the eight members were over eighty and only one, the chairman, was under sixty.[9] This certainly enhanced the buffer function of the UGC, but was hardly a recipe for dynamic policy-making. The committee's influence was also limited since its grants, as before 1914, only accounted for about a third of university income. With some minor exceptions it gave only annual grants and did not fund capital expenditure, leaving the universities to rely on private benefactors or public appeals for new chairs or buildings. Yet if the UGC was not a planning body, it was certainly able to guide developments in approved directions and to block undesirable ones. In its annual reports, and in periodic wider surveys, it made clear what these were. It worked closely with the university heads, themselves organized since 1919 as the Committee of Vice-Chancellors and Principals (CVCP), and much was decided (critics alleged, and surely not incorrectly) in informal meetings at the Athenaeum Club. Each university received a 'quinquennial visitation' from the UGC, which was more gentlemanly than an inspection, but still a source of information and influence.

A fundamental power of the UGC, and of the state which it represented, was recognition of which institutions would be subsidized: in a sense, autonomy was only made possible by a rigid definition of what a university was and what it should be doing. The UGC concentrated on maintaining and improving standards in the existing universities rather than extending the system.[10] Oxbridge and London absorbed a large proportion of the grants. Even more than before 1914, purely vocational or technical subjects were discouraged – though liberal adult education of the WEA type was supported. W. C. Childs' Reading finally achieved its charter in 1926, a college at Swansea was added in 1920 to the University of Wales, and Exeter was admitted to the grant list. But grants were refused to new university colleges at Hull and Leicester until 1946, and while the Royal College of Science and Technology in Glasgow was given a grant, its Edinburgh equivalent Heriot-Watt College was turned down. In England and Wales, technical colleges remained under the control of local authorities answering to the Board of Education. The boundaries of the university sector were thus closely guarded, and the proto-binary system emerging before 1914 was confirmed.

In theory, perhaps, a vigorous policy of modernizing university (and secondary) education would have helped Britain recover from the economic problems of the interwar years. But in reality, lack of dynamism in policy reflected a very limited demand for university education, which was still seen as tied to the professions, teaching or the civil service, at home and in the empire; there was some development of 'commerce' as a university subject between the wars, but only a few large firms were interested in recruiting graduates as managers. The result was that, after a postwar boom, numbers settled at a higher plateau but did not expand much thereafter. In the 1920s, the British total settled at 47–48,000, then rose slightly in the 1930s, to 50,002 in 1938–39, corresponding to less than 2 per cent of the age-group. But most of this increase was in England: Scotland and Wales both had fewer university students in 1938 than in 1920 or 1930, reflecting the impact of the depression. For some observers this decline was a desir-able response, for in many continental countries unemployed graduates were a breeding-ground for fascism. There is some evidence that the economic crisis actually boosted enrolments, by making the security and prestige of the professions more attractive than careers in business, and that they fell again when the economy recovered.[11] But one major graduate outlet, teaching, suffered after 1931 from cuts in government spending, and this especially affected women: in all three countries, the percentage of women students reached a peak around 1930, then declined. Twenty per cent of British students were women in 1910, 27 per cent in 1930, but only 23 per cent in 1938.[12] At Sheffield, hard hit by the depression, the number of women students halved in ten years.[13]

These figures exclude Northern Ireland. When the UGC was created, its remit briefly extended to the whole of Ireland, but after partition Queen's University Belfast was directly financed by the Northern Ireland Parliament. It operated much like an English civic university, and university policy hardly diverged from that on the mainland. But the UGC's statistics did not include Northern Ireland, and in the 1960s it was excluded from both the remit and the abundant statistical inquiries of the Robbins Committee – a good example of how, despite its loyalty to the British connection, the province was marginalized in British consciousness.

Enrolment statistics thus do not suggest any expansionist dynamic developing in the 1930s and waiting to be released by war. Because of the relative stagnation of numbers, the system continued to be domi-nated by Oxford, Cambridge and London, which together with Scotland accounted for three-quarters of all students in 1937, and since they also supplied the civic universities with most of their teachers their ethos was pervasive.[14] The civic universities generally enjoyed a modest prosperity, but remained quite small, and in northern England as in Scotland and Wales the collapse of staple industries between the wars affected both the civic pride and self-confidence so apparent before 1914 and the busi-ness fortunes which might have provided new endowments. Stability was also apparent in the distribution of students between subjects: in 1938–39, in a pattern typical of the interwar years, 45 per cent were in arts, 15 per cent in pure science, 27 per cent in medicine, and 13 per cent in technology and agriculture.[15]

Universities did not grow as fast as secondary schools, where the 1914–18 war saw significant growth which continued in peacetime. Between 1920 and 1937/38, enrolments in state secondary schools rose by 53 per cent in England and Wales and 50 per cent in Scotland. The free places introduced in England and Wales to encourage children from elementary schools covered 34 per cent of pupils in 1914, and this rose to 46 per cent by 1938 (44 per cent in England, but 64 per cent in Wales), while in Scotland fees in most secondary schools were abolished in 1918.[16] But these changes failed to feed through into university enrolments. One reason was that secondary schools still only reached a minority of the population: most children either left school at fourteen or continued in various types of school which were post-elementary rather than truly secondary. On both sides of the border, the Education Acts of 1918 disappointed democrats like R. H. Tawney who advocated 'secondary education for all'. A series of later reports and reorganizations moved towards this ideal, but it had not been achieved in 1939. The last of the prewar English reports, the Spens Report of 1938, pointed towards the tripartite system adopted after 1944, in which only a selective 'grammar' sector would prepare pupils for university entrance. Even in the supposedly academic prewar grammar schools, the majority of pupils left early, or went into business at seventeen or eighteen. The social barriers guarding secondary schools combined with the restrictive definition of the purpose of university education to choke off new demand.

Nevertheless, there was now a narrow path for scholarship children. State scholarships for universities were introduced in England and Wales in 1920, paying both fees and maintenance, and divided equally between men and women. Initially there were only 200, which rose to 360 in 1936, but they were significant as the state's first direct intervention in student funding, apart from grants for prospective teachers. The state scholarships, most of which were held at Oxford or Cambridge, were complemented by the expansion of scholarships from local authorities. In the 1930s the UGC found that over half the students in civic universities had started their education in elementary schools, and half had grants or scholarships.[17] Oxford and Cambridge also saw a small but real shift in recruitment. Scholarships were everywhere highly competitive, and probably more generous in cities than in rural counties. The historian A. L. Rowse, from a poor working-class background, went to Oxford in the 1920s with a Cornwall county scholarship – but there was only one such scholarship a year, and Rowse could not take it up without additional private help.[18] Significant numbers of lower middle- and working-class students did go to university between the wars, but much depended on chance and motivation: scholarships were haphazard and usually needed to be supplemented from other resources, and there was no automatic path of social mobility.[19] A key part of this mechanism was the School Certificate, standardized in England and Wales in 1917. Its higher level, taken at seventeen or eighteen, qualified for entry to an honours degree. The Board of Education encouraged grammar schools to develop appropriate advanced courses to 'stretch' their pupils, and it is to the 1920s that the tradition of sixth-form specialization can be traced. The golden age of the grammar schools lasted until the 1960s, and the sociologist A. H. Halsey, another scholarship boy from a poor rural background, has underlined both the solid education and opportunities which they offered to provincial society, and their severe limitations as instruments of social mobility.[20] Prewar grammar schools, like universities, were not really selective: anyone who could pay was admitted if they met a minimal standard, and it was only those in search of scholarships who had to compete with each other. A fee-paying middle-class clientele coexisted with a narrow path of social mobility for talented children from the classes below.

Still, that path did exist, and there was some social change between the wars. The social functions of university education can be investigated in two ways: by analysing the social backgrounds of students, and by analysing the university backgrounds of selected elite groups, such as civil servants, judges, or company directors. The evidence varies in quality and scope – surprisingly little is known, for example, about students at the London colleges – and this is not the place to enter into detailed discussion of a complex question.[21] The point to emphasize is that although universities were elite institutions, this did not mean that they only served the topmost stratum of British society. In the late twentieth century, university education became the almost universal mode of access to well-paid careers and positions of influence; but in earlier years it was associated chiefly with the professions and public services, both sectors which were growing, but stood apart from the great mass of middle-class jobs in commerce and industry. The universities filled the higher ranks in law, politics and intellectual life, but also trained the rank and file in the clergy, the medical profession and secondary schoolteaching. There were opportunities for students from relatively modest backgrounds, and the social profile of the universities, where it can be discovered, was more diverse, even before 1914, than might be supposed. One important study of successive cohorts of elite members between 1880 and 1970 argues that meritocracy became a reality. The dominance of Oxford and Cambridge graduates, with a small leaven of London and Scottish ones, hardly diminished, but their school and social backgrounds broadened. Among top civil servants, for example, a comparison of the generations of 1880–99 and 1940–59 showed that, while the proportion educated at Oxbridge actually rose from 44 to 61 per cent, those educated at public schools fell from 58 to 46 per cent, those with 'elite origins' (an index based on family connection with the old upper class) fell from 51 to 8 per cent, and those with lower middle- or working-class origins rose from 2 to 16 per cent.[22] The key changes seem to have been first a broadening of middle-class recruitment to Oxford and Cambridge through the lesser public schools and grammar schools, then the advent of scholarship-holders from the lower middle and working classes. At Oxford, 5.6 per cent of male students were the sons of clerks, shopkeepers or workers in 1900–13, 10 per cent in 1920–39, and 19 per cent in 1946–67.[23]

When state grants were extended to Oxford and Cambridge, they were conditional on an inquiry headed by Asquith, but this made no radical recommendations; the main complaint of prewar critics, compulsory Greek, had already been abolished. No pressure was put on these universities to expand their social base or their recruitment of women. The popular image of Oxford and Cambridge between the wars is very much an upper-class and public-school one, encouraged on the one hand by the flood of novels and memoirs from the self-admiring Oxford of Evelyn Waugh, Anthony Powell, John Betjeman and so many others, on the other by the 1930s contingent, stronger at Cambridge than Oxford, of left-wing scientists and communist activists, mostly also

from public-school rather than working-class backgrounds. Nevertheless, the establishment of a grammar-school elite at Oxbridge was the
work of the interwar years, preceding the 1944 Education Act: Harold
Wilson, Edward Heath, Roy Jenkins and Margaret Thatcher were all
Oxford scholars from the provincial grammar schools of the 1930s. Once
such students arrived at Oxford or Cambridge they were under strong
pressure to conform socially, and particularly to abandon their native
accents – just as, indeed, the Waughs and the Betjemans, from professional or business families, sought to blend into the more aristocratic
scene.

It is a weakness of elite studies that they largely exclude women,
whose cause made less progress, as we have seen, between the wars.
When the German feminist Helena Lange had visited Girton College in
1888, she found 'fresh young women of blooming colour and energetic
movements. The extraordinarily liberal supply of food in the college
adds undoubtedly to the looks and disposition of the inmates', dinner
consisting of 'nutritious meats, vegetables, and puddings', followed by
tea, coffee or cocoa.[24] Forty years later, Virginia Woolf was famously less
impressed by Cambridge women's food: 'gravy soup', beef, greens and
potatoes, prunes and custard, cheese and biscuits. The contrast between
the poverty of the women's colleges and the opulence and privilege of
the men's ones was the starting-point of A Room of One's Own, which
argued that despite women's admission to the universities they were still
excluded from the potentialities of independent intellectual life.[25]

As long as schoolteaching was the only important outlet for women
graduates, it was perhaps inevitable that wealthier families would not be
very interested in a university education for their daughters. Further
progress depended on women breaking into a wider range of careers.
But it was also the case that universities felt little need to adapt their
ways to the presence of women, and that equality in the lecture-room
proved quite compatible with the maintenance of gendered ways of
thinking and separate patterns of social life, and with barriers against
women advancing professionally in the academic world.[26] One expression of women's separate sphere, though also a field where they could
carve out their own careers, was the teaching of domestic science within
universities, originally as a branch of teacher training, and reflecting
'national efficiency' concern for healthy families. When King's College

London developed courses for women from the 1870s onwards, they were situated in genteel Kensington, away from the dangers of the Strand, and in 1908 classes in domestic science became a speciality. When other subjects moved to the main college in 1915, the 'household and social science' department remained behind, eventually in 1953 becoming the independent Queen Elizabeth College, still specializing in nutrition and household science (it was absorbed back into King's in 1985). Cardiff and Bristol were other universities which developed this specialism, while in Scotland domestic science was taught in separate colleges in Edinburgh and Glasgow, which have evolved into modern universities.[27]

Such university expansion as there was between the wars was due as much to a widening of the concept of graduate careers as to a broadening of the social base of recruitment. Neither went far enough to change the fundamental idea that universities were elite institutions whose purpose was to produce the leaders of society; if anything, this was intensified by greater emphasis on the university as a community. The halls of residence movement started at Reading was encouraged by the UGC, which commended 'the traditional British belief that education consists in the development of the whole man, and not merely of the intellect'.[28] By 1939 even the Scottish universities had opened a few halls of residence. The corporate life of students enjoyed more official support, and sporting activities developed beyond team games to embrace the kind of outdoor activities – camping, hiking, climbing, sailing – which were in vogue in the 1930s. From 1937 there were government grants for new sporting facilities, channelled to universities through the UGC.[29] It became the accepted view that students learnt as much from their social lives as in the classroom, and the 'nine-to-five' university was condemned. This became a central theme of university thinking from the 1940s to the 1960s.

In many fields of social policy, such as health and town planning, or indeed secondary education, the foundations for postwar advance were laid in the 1930s. This can hardly be said about universities. There were no prewar commissions of inquiry to set a new agenda. While some studies using the new techniques of sociological investigation underlined the steepness of the scholarship ladder and called for improved methods of selection, there were few who called for radical expansion or democratization. Books and pamphlets on universities in the 1930s and 1940s were often critical of current trends, but generally from the viewpoint of the liberal tradition. The Committee of Vice-Chancellors remained a club or discreet pressure-group rather than seeking to influence public opinion, though the Association of University Teachers, founded in 1919 primarily to defend professional interests, began to pronounce on wider issues in the 1930s. Its views were mildly progressive, but many felt, in the words of one contributor to its journal in 1931, that universities were sinking under the 'sheer weight of the mediocrities who have diluted and deteriorated the universities they have so copiously invaded'.[30] The National Union of Students, founded in 1922, espoused left-wing politics in the late 1930s and its Communist president in 1939–40 Brian Simon (later a distinguished historian of British education) set out its wartime demands for democratization in 1943.[31] While criticizing unimaginative teaching methods, the NUS supported the consensus in calling for improved social and corporate facilities, but had its own take on specialization, seen as designed to produce cogs for the capitalist machine.[32] Criticism of excessive specialization was an issue which united left and right, radicals along with academics nostalgic for a golden age of liberal education.

The prevailing tone was not critical but complacent and celebratory. Grant Robertson, in a standard survey first published in 1930, anticipated that historians in the twenty-first century 'will unquestionably find in the university movement of the nineteenth century one of the most striking and enduring achievements of British nationalism'. By this he meant the British genius for 'empirical pragmatism' and peaceful adaptation of inherited institutions exemplified by the reform of Oxbridge: 'to the uninitiated the result remains, like the British Constitution [on which Robertson was an expert], almost irrational because it is inexplicable'. The parallel reforms in Scotland showed 'the ineffaceable force of Scottish national character and sentiment', while the creation of the civic universities was a triumph of individualism and private enterprise; the princely gifts of Owens, Mason, and others matched those of the medieval university donors. British universities were thus the work of 'the private citizen inspired by public spirit', and 'the creation of the British nation, not of the British State'.[33] Hector

Hetherington, vice-chancellor of Liverpool, also saw the founding of the civic universities by private benefactors as a romantic and inspiring tale.[34] Such interpretations, no doubt intended to drop hints to the wealthy, considerably underestimated the actual role of the state and its financial contributions.

Traditional views were reinforced by outside observers like Abraham Flexner, an American expert on medical education who published a widely read book in 1930. For Flexner, British education was already too utilitarian, and his judgements on this point were severe: medical training was amateurish, dominated by the practical demands of the hospitals and not by medical science. Flexner put forward a German-inspired view of the university's strictly non-vocational function. Its essential mission was science and scholarship. The fundamental purpose of university teaching should be to train the next generation of scholars, but in Britain research and postgraduate provision were neglected. 'The splendid English amateur has had his day in industry and in politics; graduate schools must convert him into a professional.' Law and medicine were appropriate university subjects because these were 'learned' professions with 'their roots deep in cultural and idealistic soil'. But most of the applied science teaching which Flexner found in the provincial universities was condemned, and Oxford and Cambridge were praised for holding out against utilitarian trends, despite the lack of research orientation in their teaching (here Flexner echoed an old debate). For Flexner, universities should be 'wholesome and creative influences in shaping society towards rational ends', and 'must at times give society, not what society wants, but what it needs'. Conservatism was justified if it was based on a 'sense of values', not on mere inertia.[35] Flexner's critique may have encouraged more intellectual rigour in British universities, but it reinforced the elite conception of their role, and the values of disinterested *Wissenschaft* were probably strengthened by the influx of German and Austrian refugees from Hitler, who brought much stimulus to British scholarship and cultural creativity.

Advocacy of a research culture and of the university as a community were combined in the most influential university treatise of the 1940s, *Red Brick University* by 'Bruce Truscot'. This was the pseudonym, successfully maintained, of E. Allison Peers, professor of Spanish at

Liverpool; his book was published in two parts in 1943 and 1945, and as a single work in 1951. It popularized the term 'redbrick', and was very widely read. It dealt in passing with many contemporary university problems, and dwelt on the poverty and limited ambitions of the redbricks. Truscot's idea was that they should be raised to equal status with Oxbridge, abolishing the hierarchy of prestige – which would also mean reducing Oxford and Cambridge from a national to a regional role. Truscot asserted the need to combine research and teaching, but saw research, 'the search after knowledge for the sake of its intrinsic value', as the university's 'nobler' and more fundamental task.[36] He was scathing about its neglect by redbrick professors. Truscot also saw the university as a school of character, and thought the redbricks must develop community and residential life, escaping from their cramped urban context. His book seemed to reject the original inspiration of the civic universities, which was urban and provincial, but it influenced the new universities of the 1960s. Truscot did not himself see the need for much expansion: at a time when most opinion thought the prewar total of 50,000 students should rise by at least half, he thought an extra 10,000 would be ample, for stringent selection should keep out all those who did not 'give evidence of sufficient scholarliness of mind' to be suitable recipients of academic teaching. If England had sixteen universities with an average size of 3000, 'all reasonable demands would be met for a long time to come'.[37]

As part of the revival of communal life, Truscot wanted to see official sponsorship of religious worship. A departure from the strict secularism of Liverpool and other civic universities in their early years, this was only a small part of Truscot's scheme, but the religious basis of much university debate in the 1940s is striking. The Student Christian Movement and other bodies of an evangelical kind were active in organizing conferences and publishing pamphlets. It was from this milieu that another much-noticed book appeared, *The Crisis in the University*, by Walter Moberly (1949). A philosopher and former vice-chancellor of Manchester, Moberly had been the first full-time chairman of the UGC from 1934 until his retirement, and was a prominent Anglican layman, moving in circles influenced by T. S. Eliot, whose own *Notes Towards the Definition of Culture* (1948) argued that the preservation of culture depended on elite educational institutions. Moberly's book did not have this restrictive social implication; it ranged as widely over general university problems as Truscot's, and rather more profoundly.

As its title indicated, Moberly's book did not breathe a spirit of post-war optimism, but argued that the world faced a spiritual crisis, to which universities had a duty to respond. The war had been fought to defend civilization against barbarism, yet the collusion of the German universities with Hitler, the discovery of the Nazi death camps, and Hiroshima all undermined the certainties of liberal humanism; so did Soviet totalitarianism, and as the Cold War intensified liberal education could be seen as a weapon of cultural rearmament. In the first of a series of 'university pamphlets' launched by the SCM in 1946, the Edinburgh theologian John Baillie set the tone. 'Never in any culture has intellectual life so much lacked a sense of direction as in the Western world during the last several generations.' With the rise of science, 'questions of ultimate conviction are regarded as taboo', and universities had abdicated from 'their ancient function of guiding the public mind in its quest of ultimate truth'. To this end, Baillie defined university education in idealist fashion as a 'community of seekers after truth' where students were 'undergoing initiation into the spirit of research', and he cited the reforming public-school headmaster, Sanderson of Oundle, on education as 'the escorting of a soul to the frontiers of knowledge'.[38] Richard Livingstone, a classicist and former vice-chancellor of Oxford, took a similar line. He thought specialization generally bad, but especially bad in science, which had cut itself off from human values: his remedy was that everyone should read Plato.[39] As for Moberly, he defined the university as 'a community in pursuit of truth', based on the active and critical life of the mind: he thought that the cult of research and 'objectivity' had led the universities to withdraw from their proper social obligations, and hoped that Christian activists would lead them back to engage with the problems of postwar society.[40]

University thinkers of this period all adhered to the idea of a community of scholars, but emphasized the educational and moral influence of the research ethic on students rather than the practical value of research for national needs. There was a new (or neo-Arnoldian) stress on the university's role as transmitter and defender of culture. When Routledge published a volume on universities in their influential 'International Library of Sociology and Social Reconstruction', it was a translation of the Spanish philosopher Ortega y Gasset's *Mission of the University*. First published in 1930, this was an attack on the sterility of the German research ideal, and a defence of general culture. 'The trend towards a university dominated by "inquiry" has been disastrous. It has led to the elimination of the prime concern: culture', and 'professionalism and specialism ... have smashed the European man in pieces'.[41] British critics of specialization were also influenced by a similar debate in America, and particularly by the Harvard report of 1945, *General Education in a Free Society*.

Grant Robertson in 1944 identified 'the increasing danger of breeding a really illiterate, and de-humanized race of specialized scientists', and hoped that in an age when 'the advance in knowledge is demonstrably outstripping the advance in moral power, the universities can make themselves the central arsenals of a true humanism' and 'real laboratories and power-houses of spiritual and moral efficiency'.[42] Those who praised general education and attacked specialization usually wrote from an arts point of view, suspicious of science, and positively hostile to technology, seen as an intruder into the sacred precincts. Since science and technology enjoyed immense prestige after the Second World War, and promoting them was the main feature of an expansionist higher education policy, much of British academic culture appeared backward-looking, snobbish, and alarmingly out of touch with contemporary needs. One response to this was Eric Ashby's *Technology and the Academics* of 1958, a pioneering essay on modern university history which was well informed about the Humboldtian ideal, though it idealized the autonomy of British universities and played down the role of the state. Ashby criticized the 'mischievous' antithesis between science and humanism and the 'unprofitable debates on specialisation versus a liberal education'. He argued that the civic universities had successfully embraced the nineteenth-century scientific revolution – they 'absorbed German *Wissenschaft* in their very foundation stones' (a questionable assertion); universities should now extend the same welcome to technology, the creator of material progress and social welfare, on which a new humanism could be built.[43]

A similar impatience with academic conservatism led Charles Snow, Cambridge scientist, former civil servant and novelist, to formulate the idea of the 'two cultures' which became a commonplace of debate around 1960. Its main statement was in a lecture of 1959.[44] Snow diagnosed the split between literary and scientific cultures as a longstanding feature of the British scene. Like Huxley, he deplored the undoubted fact that nearly all the administrative and political elite had an arts education. Snow admitted that the narrow outlooks of scientists could be equally damaging, but it was for them that he spoke. Scientists were the 'new men' who had won the war for Britain, were creating progress and prosperity, and had 'the future in their bones'. *The New Men* was the title of a volume in Snow's ponderous cycle of novels, the best-known of which (including *The Affair* of 1960) purported to give an inside view of Cambridge and its academic politics.

This in turn irritated the embattled Cambridge literary critic F. R. Leavis, and the 'two cultures' debate is now best remembered for the highly personalized attack which Leavis launched in 1962 on Snow's thesis and his literary reputation.[45] Leavis had published his own contribution to the university debate in 1943, but it had not attracted the attention given to Truscot or Moberly. In *Education and the University*, he claimed that the study of literature was essential to the preservation of British identity and culture, because it alone provided organic continuity with the age before social relationships were disrupted by the industrial revolution. English provided a 'humane centre' in which specialism could be anchored, and gave a training in values, discrimination and sensitivity which would allow the elite to respond to the problems of the modern world, reconstituting the kind of educated public which had existed (so Leavis claimed) in the Victorian period when culture was not degraded by commercialism.[46] Leavis saw himself in the critical tradition of Coleridge and Arnold, a tradition recently restored to visibility in Raymond Williams's *Culture and Society 1780–1950* (1958). Just as Coleridge had attacked the 'mechanico-corpuscular' philosophy, for Leavis the enemies were 'technologico-benthamism', the affluent but rootless society which it was creating, and the 'progressive' metropolitan intelligentsia which presided over it. Only 'the university, conceived as a creative centre of civilization' could counter these forces.[47] His practical proposals were for an interdisciplinary curriculum spanning literature and history, of a kind often introduced in the new universities of the 1960s, on which Leavis, like Truscot, had a real influence. For he was a prophet who inspired disciples, many of whom became teachers in grammar schools, and in turn sent their best sixth-formers to study under the master. This kind of influence was only possible in the closed university world which was vanishing, and it was not surprising that Leavis turned in the late 1960s to denouncing university expansion and comprehensive education. His unabashed belief in the virtues of an elite and his affinities with an Eliot-style defence of cultural continuity (though without the religion) seemed conservative, yet his moralism and puritanism made him temperamentally a figure of the left.

Contemporaries sometimes saw the Snow–Leavis debate as a rerun of Huxley versus Arnold. Leavis's 1962 lecture included a brief restatement of his 1943 proposals, and was only indirectly a contribution to the university debate. But it took place while the Robbins Committee was deliberating, and it is a reminder that the Robbins proposals for expansion, however inevitable they may seem in retrospect, were launched on a conservative university world which in some ways was little changed since 1914.[48] It still seemed natural to think that what was taught in universities mattered because it was forming the values of an identifiable leadership elite, that universities were there to provide spiritual guidance for society, and that two cultures were a bad thing because, somehow, the nation might still have a single culture. The Robbins Report deferred to some of these ideas, but became the symbol of transition from privilege to meritocracy, and from a still deferential and hierarchical society to a democracy of multiple and divergent values.

9

Postwar Revolution

The Robbins Report of 1963, the work of a committee set up by Harold Macmillan in 1961, has become the symbol of postwar university expansion. The report proclaimed the 'Robbins principle', that higher education places should be provided for 'all those who are qualified by ability and attainment to pursue them and who wish to do so', and it provided formidable statistical backing for a decisive growth of higher education.[1] That expansion has continued, with only intermittent pauses: the percentage of the age-group in higher education was 8.5 in 1962, but forty years later was projected to reach 50 per cent. Thus it is natural to see Robbins as a decisive turning-point. Yet in many ways it only endorsed what was happening already. Student numbers and state spending were expanded as soon as the war was over, eight or nine new universities were planned and in some cases opened before 1963, and it was the earlier Anderson Committee, reporting in 1960, which led to universal student grants.

In the long run, the Second World War unleashed social ambitions which could only be satisfied by the breaking down of traditional barriers, but its immediate effect was to strengthen political consensus and social solidarity. Victory seemed to reinforce the prestige of centralized planning, of science and expertise, and of the state as an agent of progress. Britain's university-educated public servants had known their finest hour. Postwar expansion did not at first break with tradition: the benefits of university education were extended without changing its essential nature, and the UGC pursued its policies of gentle guidance with enhanced authority. Even the introduction of free secondary education for all in 1944, one of the most far-reaching pieces of wartime legislation, entrenched the position of the grammar schools while building on the modest democratizing role which they were already performing in the 1930s. The position of the public schools was left untouched, despite the Fleming Report of 1942 which had proposed closer relations with the state. As the previous chapter has suggested, British academic life remained conservative, and the new claims of science and technology were resisted. The American political scientist Edward Shils, who established himself in Britain in the 1950s, was struck by the complacency and parochialism of British culture.[2] His response was to found the journal *Minerva* (1962) to promote and defend science and scholarship, one way of doing so being to publish some key texts by Humboldt.[3]

The 1944 Act affected higher education only indirectly. Secondary education became free and universal, and was normally organized on the 'tripartite' system, not prescribed by the Act, but recommended by the Norwood Report of 1943. Children with academic ambitions were selected for grammar schools at the age of eleven, and these schools were effectively the only ones which led to the universities. Secondary modern schools did not take children beyond fifteen or sixteen, and the third tripartite type, secondary technical schools, remained underdeveloped or non-existent. The failure of the state to encourage a strong technical sector, with secondary schools leading on to advanced colleges of technology, has often been seen as one of the lost opportunities of British education, killed off by the anti-utilitarian prejudices of the liberal tradition. That tradition flourished in the grammar schools, which typically took only 20 or 25 per cent of the children in their areas. When university education was a minority interest, this was not too restrictive, as most grammar-school pupils still went into apprenticeships or offices direct from school. But expansion after 1944 encouraged more to stay until eighteen and qualify for university entry, and it was this trend, combined with a high postwar birth rate and the extension of graduate occupations, which by the 1960s created the pressures on entry to which Robbins responded.

Greater opportunities for women were part of this educational shift, but the barriers of gender did not crumble rapidly: despite the contributions of women to the war effort, it was not until the 1960s that they began to break into a wider range of professional and business careers, and that their presence in higher education rose decisively above prewar levels (it was 27 per cent in 1930, 24 per cent in 1958).[4] In the 1940s, after the war had underlined the deficiencies of British technical and scientific education, and the urgency of returning to this long-identified but neglected problem, discussion focused on the shortage of scientific and technological 'manpower', the subject of a series of inquiries. The emphasis in thinking about science in this period was on the need to produce more graduates rather than on the economic value of research. The Percy Report of 1945 on 'higher technological education' accepted the division between university and technical work, but recommended building up selected technical institutions to prepare for degree-level qualifications. It laid down basic lines of development taken up in the Barlow Report of 1946, which called for a doubling of graduates in science and technology and a new technological university. Barlow foreshadowed Robbins in deploring the social barriers which kept potential talent out of the universities, arguing that there was a wider 'pool of ability' than conservatives supposed.[5]

But even before these reports, when thoughts turned to postwar reconstruction there was wide agreement that university enrolments needed to be raised permanently by 50 per cent, and after the war the necessary funds were provided. The UGC's recurrent grant, two million pounds before the war, was raised to five million in 1945, and had reached twenty million by 1952; capital grants, rare before the war, now supported large building programmes.[6] The UGC encouraged a host of new initiatives, but at this stage it thought expansion could be accommodated in the existing universities and was opposed to new foundations. By 1949 university numbers had risen to 85,000 (from 50,000 in 1938), and the proportion of science and technology students had also grown significantly (26 per cent in 1938, 33 per cent in 1949).[7] But the total then stabilized until the mid-fifties, and it seemed that, as after 1918, there would be consolidation at the new level rather than continuing growth. By 1948 the UGC was worrying about graduate unemployment,[8] and standard works of the period on British universities contained little hint of any impending shift to mass higher education.[9]

It was a common view, based on continuing belief in residential communities, that a university should have no more than 3000 students.[10] Most civic universities in the 1950s were smaller than this, and the redbrick campus novels of the period such as Kingsley Amis's *Lucky Jim* (1954) and Malcolm Bradbury's *Eating People is Wrong* (1959) depict intimate provincial communities, where staff and students attend the same dances and drink in the same pubs. Both were based on Leicester, where Amis's friend Philip Larkin worked for a time (Amis himself taught at Swansea).[11] In the mid-1950s University College, Leicester had about 700 students.

In the 1950s, the main debate was over the expansion of technical education: should it find a place within the universities, or remain in a separate sector? The technical colleges of the prewar era were subsumed into what was now called 'further' education, where work at degree level (for London degrees), or for the vocational Higher National Diploma dating from the 1920s, was mixed up with a mass of sub-degree work, for adults or adolescents, much of it in evening classes. The sector's lack of prestige seemed to inhibit higher developments. Administrative rivalries were also involved, for the Ministry of Education (as the Board had become) had its own agenda for developing a technical education sector, while the UGC was prepared to absorb technology into the universities only if it met stringent criteria for degree-level studies. Despite a powerful technological lobby, supported by industrialists, scientists and some politicians, postwar governments were slow to act. The proposal for a new technological university was defeated in 1952, when the UGC argued that the same needs could be met by building up Imperial College. It was the Conservative White Paper of 1956 which eventually led to action. Twenty or so 'regional' technical colleges were identified and given special support (the nucleus of the polytechnics of the 1960s), and eight colleges (later ten) were designated as Colleges of Advanced Technology; three were former London polytechnics.[12] In 1961 the CATs passed from local authority control to direct-grant status under the ministry. They specialized in degree-level work, sanctioned by a new qualification, the Diploma in Technology – not called a degree, as the universities fought to keep that name for themselves. The dualism identifiable even before 1914 thus continued, and the postwar growth of technical education, though vigorous, was subordinated to the existing status hierarchy and not permitted to challenge it.[13] This division was one of the problems which the Robbins Committee was to address.

Behind these developments lay a decisive shift of balance. Before the war, universities were certainly seen as national institutions, but derived only a third of their income from the state (36 per cent in 1938). Now the initiative in policy moved to the state, and universities came to be seen as a public service with a strong element of autonomy rather than a collection of independent institutions receiving state support. One symbol of this was the introduction of a national salary scale for academics in 1949, a longstanding aim of the AUT. The parliamentary grant rose to 70 per cent of university income by 1953, and reached nearly 80 per cent in the mid-1960s. Local authority grants were phased out, endowment income became insignificant for most universities, and the contribution of student fees fell from 30 per cent in 1938 to 7 per cent in the 1960s, by which time they were mostly paid by the state in any case; no attempt was made to keep fees in line with actual costs.[14] This dependence on a single source of funding seems a danger in retrospect, but at the time confidence in the UGC as a buffer was undiminished, and the principle of the block grant remained sacrosanct: there was 'earmarked' funding for a few years in some specialized fields of national importance, but this was seen as a temporary and undesirable expedient.

In 1946 the UGC's remit was enlarged, and it was now expected to advise on 'national needs' and to ensure that the universities met them. The restrictions on membership of the UGC were also removed, and it became a sphere of action for some powerful university figures, including several serving or former vice-chancellors, who were keen to exploit the climate of expansion to raise the status and national prestige of the redbrick universities, as advocated by Truscot.[15] The collaboration of existing universities in the rapid growth of student numbers was an important achievement in itself, even if there was much dispute over priorities, and sometimes fears of a dilution of character and regional identity.[16] But there were limits to how far this process could go, given the now orthodox emphasis on residence and personalized teaching, which seemed to dictate a maximum size.

Though the UGC was initially against creating new universities, the University College of North Staffordshire (University of Keele from 1962) slipped through the net in 1949. This was a late offshoot of Oxford idealism, inspired by the philosopher A. D. Lindsay, master of Balliol, whose Scottish academic background and passion for adult education were other influences. Lindsay worked with local civic leaders, building on a tradition which went back to Tawney's tutorial classes at Longton. Tawney himself was a member of the UGC between 1943 and 1948, and Lindsay's project was helped by his contacts in the Labour government. Unlike earlier university colleges, North Staffordshire was allowed to award degrees from the start, under academic supervision from existing universities, a device taken over for the new universities of the 1960s. Keele offered a deliberately broad curriculum, with an interdisciplinary 'foundation year', as a corrective to sixth-form specialization and the research-based single-subject degree. For Lindsay, as for Moberly and so many others, graduates should not be mere specialists or experts, but should give the country intellectual and moral leadership in an age of spiritual crisis.[17]

Under the chairmanship of the Scottish economist Keith Murray (1952–63), the UGC was converted to expansionism, and created eight new universities on greenfield sites (the term 'plateglass' sometimes used at the time did not catch on: brutalist concrete was anyway more characteristic). These were at Sussex (the first, opened in 1961), York, East Anglia, Essex, Lancaster, Warwick, Canterbury (Kent), and Stirling in Scotland. The New University of Ulster at Coleraine (1969), though outside the UGC's territory, was part of the same pattern. Like Keele these universities were able to award degrees from the start, and unlike the older civic universities, the CATs, or the new universities designated in 1992, they did not grow organically out of existing local colleges.

When Anthony Sampson wrote the first of his *Anatomy of Britain* series in 1962, a gossipy guide to British institutions, his chapter on universities emphasized the slow pace of change and the dominance of Oxbridge. The 'rift' between redbrick and Oxbridge 'cuts right through this book', though the new universities 'seem to offer a real chance of breaking the social monopoly of Oxbridge'. The next edition in 1965 retained the passage on the redbrick rift, but reported the social success and glamour of Sussex and East Anglia. In 1971 the tone was still positive – though Sampson also noted a revival of redbrick, where expansion was now concentrated, and anatomized the new polytechnics. By 1982, he had decided that the new universities 'seemed daring innovations at the time, but each of them was modelled on Oxbridge, cloistered and consciously stylish, each run by a vice-chancellor from Oxbridge'.

Oxford and Cambridge themselves were still the real 'nursery of power', he concluded, their only rival being the LSE.[18]

The new universities were all on residential campuses. This was not the original intention – some were deliberately sited near seaside resorts (Sussex, Essex, Lancaster) so that they could make use of out-of-season lodgings. But the UGC insisted on a single site with a minimum of 200 acres, and these were impossible to find except outside towns. Besides, the reaction against the 'nine-to-five' ethos was so strong at the time that campuses were difficult to resist. A UGC committee on halls of residence had reported in their favour in 1957, and the prevailing orthodoxy was that the university should be 'a community, whose members, young and old, can live together and play together and wrestle with the fundamental problems of life together, as well as pursue their intellectual tasks together. Spiritual and moral power can be generated to the full only through complete living.'[19] Several of the new universities adopted college systems, and encouraged staff to live on site and fraternize socially with students. The maximum size of the new universities was fixed at 4500 – Albert Sloman, vice-chancellor of Essex, whose BBC Reith lectures in 1963 sought to define the philosophy of the new university movement, was out on a limb in setting a target (never reached) of 10,000. Critics claimed that growth could easily have been accommodated in the existing universities if it were not for the pseudo-Oxbridge residential ideal. But the campus universities were not true clones of Oxbridge, where most fellows had long since ceased to live in their colleges, and the strains of institutional life were tempered by integration into the urban fabric, with its shops, pubs, cafes, bookshops and cinemas. It is not surprising that some of the isolated, half-built campuses of the new universities became focuses of student rebellion. (As did the very urban LSE, so this is only one explanation.)

The choice of sites came after bids from local campaigning groups, usually including prominent business and local government figures, who saw a university as a source of cultural prestige and economic regeneration. But while the Victorian university colleges were founded with local money, it was now the state which had the financial muscle. The lay governing councils were less powerful than those of the civic universities, and it was the academics, working with the UGC, who determined priorities and curriculum. This caused considerable friction, as the UGC refused to sanction vocational subjects which might serve local industries, or links with existing technical colleges. Engineering was everywhere discouraged, in view of the recent expansion of technical education and the creation of the CATs. At East Anglia, agriculture was ruled out; at Coventry, the rejection of plans to integrate Warwick University with the local authority's technical college caused much bitterness.[20] West Midlands business interests, which not unreasonably thought that the new university should help to modernize the motor industry, then at the heart of the British economy, came into conflict a few years later with the anti-capitalist idealism of campus radicals.[21] Nor did the new universities have strong links with local schools and communities, despite generous contributions from the ratepayers. At East Anglia in the early 1970s, only 4 per cent of the students came from the region.[22] But this delocalization had some advantages too. The universities were seen from the start as national, and could present themselves as fresh and intellectually exciting alternatives to Oxford and Cambridge for a middle-class clientele. Early media attention gave them a glamour which, for a time at least, overshadowed solid but old-fashioned universities like Manchester, with their gloomy Victorian settings, despotic professorial control, limited student life and – not least – their traditional, lecture-based curricula.[23] Socially, this meant that the new universities were meeting an expanded demand from the middle classes; unlike the new or expanding technical colleges, they did not express their mission in terms of widening access or extending higher education down the social scale, and their lack of local roots made them ill-adapted to part-time or adult students.

Innovation in teaching was seen as the most notable feature of the new universities: their introduction of 'new maps of learning' was celebrated by the historian Asa Briggs, an influential member of the UGC in the 1960s, and a founding father of Sussex.[24] Tutorials and seminars were preferred to lectures, a trend strongly reinforced by the report of another UGC committee, the Hale Committee on teaching methods, in 1964. This, of course, required low staff–student ratios: one to eight was accepted as the norm at this time, and was achieved and more or less maintained until the 1980s.[25] The older civic and Scottish universities went along the same road, requiring the recruitment of many new staff. While combining teaching with research in a way which distinguished them from technical colleges, the new universities also tried to respond to contemporary criticisms of specialization and the single-subject degree. The Keele foundation year was not replicated, as it required a four-year degree, but teaching was often through interdisciplinary schools rather than traditional departments, and sought to bridge the two cultures. Many of the new universities' staff came from Oxbridge, and like the dons who migrated to chairs in the Victorian university colleges, they welcomed the chance to break away from the old routines. As the first generation of teachers retired, however, there was a tendency to drift back to single departments and disciplines, especially perhaps in science, but the new universities did have a stimulating effect on British teaching practices and were notable for new departures in both the natural and the social sciences.[26]

One reason why the new universities could be 'national' from the start was the system of student finance introduced in 1962, following the report of the Anderson Committee in 1960. This committee rationalized the 'jungle' of competitive student awards – state scholarships, local authority awards, scholarships and bursaries given by universities and colleges. There would now be a standard entitlement for every student who qualified for university entry, administered by local authorities (the Education Department in Scotland) but effectively national. The state paid the fees of students, and gave a maintenance grant to cover the expenses of living and studying away from home; the argument used to justify this was that students had the right to choose freely between institutions. Though there was a means-tested parental contribution (against the Anderson Committee's majority recommendation), for most students higher education was now in practice free, and for a whole generation financial problems became a minor concern of university life. This decision pre-empted any full discussion of student finance by Robbins, though both committees considered the alternative of student loans, anticipating many of the arguments heard forty years later. Anderson was against them, Robbins more divided. Robbins himself summarized the debate: 'On the one side is the contention that a free education to the full extent of ability to profit is the legitimate expectation of the citizen of the enlightened and humane society. On the other, is the contention that since the higher education of the individual involves an increase in his earning power, to finance him by grants out-right is contrary to the principle of equality', and might subsidize the rich at the expense of the poor. Robbins found the loans argument 'ulti-mately very difficult to resist', but accepted that they would be a deterrent to working-class attendance while the habit of going to uni-versity was a new one. He predicted that the issue would revive once 'the advantages of higher education are more generally perceived and the burdens of financing its expansion are more severely felt'.[27]

The Anderson Report was seen as a piece of tidying-up, yet its impli-cations were as profound as those of Robbins. In 1960 there seemed little sense of impending expansion. The Anderson Report devoted only three pages to the cost of its proposals, and estimated that growth over 'the next few years' would double this from £17 million (for 65,422 award holders) to £34 million (for 107,000).[28] Robbins was soon to make such figures obsolete, but from 1962 government expenditure was tied directly to student numbers. Setting numerical targets became the main policy decision, and once large-scale expansion was decided on, fund-ing had to follow; if the quality of the university experience was to be maintained, implying low staff–student ratios as well as halls of resi-dence, the UGC block grant would have to keep pace with student grants.

Tying finance to individual student careers also gave the state a strong incentive to keep university education short. Three years remained the norm, which was out of line with both American and continental prac-tice. In Scotland four-year honours degrees were protected by a rather lower level of school-leaving qualifications, as well as by national senti-ment, and in fact became more common as the prestige of the three-year general or ordinary degree declined; but such four-year degrees as existed in England came under pressure. The increasing com-plexity of professional and intellectual demands might have led to a natural lengthening of university education, but instead the response was to increase specialization, to squeeze out what remained of liberal preparatory education, to teach medicine and law as first degrees (com-pare the American graduate school), and to divert more advanced demands to postgraduate courses, where mandatory grants did not apply and the old system of competition for limited funds survived. Finally, the grant system favoured full-time students and school-leavers, and inhibited flexibility and openness: in many countries, intermittent attendance was a common way of building up qualifications, but in Britain students who did not stay the course were defined (and still are) as 'drop-outs' wasting public money. Fortunately the Open University planned by Harold Wilson's government, which took its first students in 1971, offered adults an alternative path outside the grant and selection system, while establishing an academic rigour which put its degrees on a level with those of the conventional universities.

A further consequence of the new grant system, once studying away from home was fully funded, was to break the close local connections of the civic universities. Even in 1947, a history of Birmingham University could take it for granted that 'it exists for Birmingham and the Midlands', crowning the regional educational edifice in the way recommended by Haldane. Yet the same historians believed that 'the final patina of a university education is only acquired by residence', and endorsed Truscot's view that a period in halls should be compulsory for all students.[29] A trend to studying away from home had appeared well before the Anderson Report, and all the civics embarked on the building of halls, initially with grants from the UGC, though these stopped in the late 1960s. The movement spread to Wales and Scotland. Before 1939, nearly all University of Wales students had been Welsh, but they were down to 63 per cent by 1960, and were a minority after 1964.[30] This provoked both protests from Welsh-speaking students, and a movement for 'defederation' as the university ceased to be a national symbol, though the first defection, Cardiff, was not until 2004. In Scotland delocalization was slower, due both to a strong counter-tradition and to a non-university sector which was much larger than in Wales and continued to recruit locally, but 'anglicization' became an issue there too. It is a paradox that the creation of separate university funding councils for Scotland and Wales in 1992, and legislative devolution in 1999, have coincided with a loss of genuine national identity in their universities, and seem unlikely to restore it against the tide of national and global homogenization.

The British path from elite to mass education would be an expensive one compared with the two alternative models, American and European. The American model was of a decentralized university system, containing great diversity of types and standards, with a mixture of public and private funding, in which students could find their own place through choice and the operation of the market. The state had its part to play in America, at both federal and state levels, but there was no attempt to guide the system as a whole. In Britain, however, university education since the beginning of the twentieth century had been defined in terms of common standards, with a high degree of homogeneity imposed by the Treasury and the UGC as gatekeepers. By the 1960s, the university system was seen as a single, national, essentially public structure. Yet it differed from continental European systems in having a hierarchy of prestige which was the legacy of historical development. In most European countries, students had a right of university entry if they passed the standard school-leaving examination, and fees were low or nominal, with no general right to maintenance grants. Universities were more or less equal in prestige, and it remained normal to attend the one nearest to the student's home, even if those in capitals like Paris, Rome or Madrid had a national attraction. Universities were open, not selective, and the result could be massive overcrowding of lecture-halls, laboratories and libraries, with a high rate of attrition in the early years of study – one reason for the troubles in France, Germany and elsewhere in 1968. The British system was more personal and intensive, and less wasteful since a high proportion of those selected eventually graduated, but selection at eighteen closed off democratic opportunities which continental systems left open.

The fact that Oxford and Cambridge were not only at the top of the hierarchy, but also collegiate universities whose inherent character depended on limitation of numbers, ruled out any policy of open university access. Control of admissions came in Britain to seem one of the essential attributes of university autonomy, which was not the case elsewhere in Europe. There was a further reason why competitive selection was necessary. The expansion of the universities after the war, and the Anderson and Robbins reports, were expressions of the welfare state or 'postwar settlement'. Higher education should no longer be a privilege but a right for all who could benefit from it. The idea of a ladder to be climbed by individual scholarship children became obsolete. The principle of the welfare state was that social rights derived from citizenship, not from wealth or the market. In most cases, including secondary education since 1944, the benefits conferred were universal, and financed by taxes which all paid according to their ability. Higher education could not be a universal benefit, but the taxpayer's support for universities and a universal right to individual student support could be accepted as fair and legitimate as long as selection was rigorously meritocratic. A democratic state could not use any overt criteria except intellectual ability. The result was, in effect, a national system of selection, an eighteen-plus analogous to the eleven-plus which was necessary for the same reasons when state secondary education had similar gradations of prestige. According to the philosopher of the welfare state, T. H. Marshall, there was a 'natural right to be educated according to one's capacities', but 'the right of the citizen in this process of selection and mobility is the right to equality of opportunity ... In essence it is the equal right to display and develop differences, or inequalities; the equal right to be recognised as unequal.'[31]

Various consequences followed. One was to give the eighteen-plus examination, 'Highers' in Scotland and A Levels elsewhere, the central role in selection. These examinations were reformed just at this time, moving from the balanced curriculum required by the older school certificates, in which subjects had to be chosen from a number of groups, to greater specialization, requiring only two or three subjects for university entry. Early specialization was often deplored, not least by Robbins, but in vain as policy moved in the other direction. Moreover, the need for impartiality and comparability of standards meant that these examinations remained strictly external, when this practice was discredited at university level. The creation of this sacred cow in the early 1960s still weighs heavily on British education.

A second consequence was the setting-up in 1961 of the Universities Central Council on Admissions (today the Universities and Colleges Admission Service). This rationalized another jungle, of admissions procedures, and eventually became the channel for nearly all applications to higher education. Bypassing this system through feepaying (or through such devices, common in the American system, as preference for the children of alumni) was now unacceptable. But there the analogy with secondary education broke down: for eleven-plus failures, private education was an alternative, but the cost of higher education and the state's monopoly of awarding degrees ruled this out for the eighteen-plus. Universities, unlike secondary schools, could claim to stand above social class, and higher education was the only form of social benefit 'for which no private substitute is available ... and which no amount of money can buy'.[32] As Sydney Caine, director of the LSE, put it in 1969, 'rationing of university places by the purse has been replaced by rationing by A level grades and interviewing boards'.[33] This meritocratic revolution was a far-reaching piece of postwar social engineering, acutely analysed in 1958 by Michael Young: in Young's dystopian vision the reign of the examination and the intelligence test would create not a classless society, but a new privileged caste based on intellectual ability alone.[34]

Underlying this tighter bond between education, merit and power was the extension of graduate status to an ever-wider range of occupations. The professions and public service were the traditional outlets for graduates, and the interest of middle-class families in higher education had been selective. Now there were new professions, and expanding ones like teaching, many of which had the national or local state as their main employer, a factor much increased by the creation of the National Health Service, to which university medical education became an annexe. The tendency of industry and commerce to recruit managers, scientists or engineers from the universities, already growing between the wars, now accelerated. One result was to transfer the costs of professional training from employers and employees themselves to the state – as when solicitors or accountants, for example, took degrees instead of being trained through articles. Another was that higher education ceased to be a relatively marginal concern for the middle classes, and became, by the end of the twentieth century, the essential badge of middle-class status itself. This made the examination system and university selection an even more fraught process. It also meant that the expansion of student numbers, both before and after Robbins, was about extending middle-class just as much as working-class opportunities. The rhetoric of democratization concealed a surprising stability in the social groups from which students were recruited.

There were thus clear if complex connections between the historically conditioned hierarchy of British universities, the state's decisions on funding, the ideals of equality of opportunity and the welfare state, the tradition of short but intensive degree courses, and the distinctly English ideal of the university as a community. The fundamental decisions which guided development for the rest of the twentieth century were already in place before the Robbins Committee started work, but it was to add to the mix a determination that university expansion should give a new generation of students the same quality of experience, intellectual and social, as their predecessors.

10

The Robbins Era

Public debate on university expansion was in full swing even before the Robbins Committee was appointed. It was in 1960 that Kingsley Amis attacked the 'university numbers racket', and declared that 'more will mean worse' (not 'more means worse' as usually cited). From his experience at Swansea, he assured the readers of *Encounter* that universities were 'already taking almost everyone who can read and write', and that it was a delusion to suppose that any young people capable of benefiting from university education were missing out. 'University graduates ... are like poems or bottles of hock, and unlike cars or tins of salmon, in that you cannot *decide* to have more good ones. All you can decide to have is more.'[1] This brief squib, part of a diatribe against contemporary trends, has been remembered when the more serious writings of the period have been forgotten. Even in 2003 the White Paper on higher education felt the need to reassure the public that more did not mean worse, though quality was now characteristically defined not in terms of cultural standards, but by the claim that the 'salary premium' of graduates had not declined while the participation rate had risen from 6 to 43 per cent.[2]

Amis was reflecting views expressed with rather more sophistication by T. S. Eliot or by the conservative philosopher Michael Oakeshott. Oakeshott defined the university in essentialist terms as a place where scholars engaged in the pursuit of learning, a cooperative activity concerned with understanding the world and human nature. Undergraduates were there to join in this 'conversation', but could not do so unless they were 'in tune' with university culture. Such persons were already in short supply, and 'anyone who has worked in a contemporary overcrowded university knows it to be an illusion that there was any large untapped reserve of men and women who could make use of this kind of university but who never had the opportunity of doing so'.

Oakeshott simply denied that universities had any social function or even spiritual mission beyond being true to their nature (he was a strong critic of Moberly), and thus avoided having to engage in any real argument about how they should be supported or where students would come from.[3] More practical conservatives relied on the 'pool of ability' (or 'reservoir of brains') theory: the number of students truly capable of benefiting from a university education was small, and the existing mechanisms of selection were already efficiently identifying them.[4] For critics of Robbins like the *Times*, the only result of expansion would be a decline of 'standards'; these arguments were often closely allied, as in Amis's case, with a defence of 'humane' values against the barbarisms of technology, as represented by Snow and Robbins. Even Eric Ashby, spokesman for science and technology, thought in terms of a 'thin clear stream of excellence', a natural elite which the nation should (expensively) nurture.[5]

Robbins used a formidable array of statistics to invalidate the 'pool of ability' argument, particularly by underlining the social differentials of university access. In the higher professional classes, 45 per cent went on to full-time higher education, but in the skilled manual classes only 4 per cent, and among semi- and unskilled workers only 2 per cent. There were those who argued that genetic factors counted as well as environmental ones in determining fitness for university study, and authority was lent to this when Karl Jaspers' classic *Idea of the University* was translated in 1960. Jaspers argued that 'innate differences of ability between sociological classes with a long unbroken tradition are entirely conceivable ... Children from families who for generations have kept alive a cultural tradition are intrinsically different from other children.'[6] The counter-argument, today associated especially with the French sociologist Pierre Bourdieu (writing later), was that the 'cultural capital' of middle-class families did indeed give their children an inbuilt advantage and allowed them to move with ease into the world of higher education, but this advantage was not innate and could and should be reduced by egalitarian educational policies.

For Robbins, the 'pool' was of untapped talent lost to the nation, and the committee saw no risk that expansion would lead to any decline of standards.[7] The argument was analogous to that over the eleven-plus and comprehensive education, but Robbins did not enter into that debate, and the report's projections for 1980 were conceived within the framework of selective secondary schooling. Grammar schools were already creating a new demand from below, and it was on this that the central Robbins principle rested. More and more young people were meeting the test of fitness for university entry (two A Levels, not a high requirement), therefore they had the same right as their predecessors to a university education of the existing type. It would have been quite legitimate to concede that the expansion of higher education was driven by the needs of the economy and the labour market, and would necessarily draw on different and probably lower levels of qualification and ability, but Robbins preferred to stress the argument from individual rights and opportunities. In practical terms, a shortage of places was already appearing, and parental pressure for equal chances, which progressively increased as more and more parents were themselves university graduates, was already, and was to remain, an electoral force which no political party could ignore.

The Robbins recommendations were readily accepted because they rested on a sociocultural critique which had been building up since the 1950s. The British school of sociologists focused on social class and stratification, and their work showed how inadequate the existing mechanisms of social mobility were. Despite formal equality of access to grammar schools, working-class children, however clever, had to contend with psychological tensions arising from conflict between the values of home and school, and to accept the latter if they were to succeed. While defenders of grammar schools pointed to their success as incubators for working-class talent, critics saw their academic culture as a barrier to recruitment. Richard Hoggart's *The Uses of Literacy* (1957) was an early, autobiographical essay on this theme, and was reinforced by surveys like Brian Jackson and Dennis Marsden's *Education and the Working Class* (1962), and the statistical and theoretical work of A. H. Halsey, Jean Floud, Basil Bernstein and others. The American Ralph Turner took Britain as an example of 'sponsored mobility', with an educational system designed not to encourage individual opportunity but to weed out at successive stages all but a small minority, and to assimilate them to the dominant culture.[8] From a different angle, all studies of British elites emphasized the grip of Oxford and Cambridge as well as the public schools. Criticism of the 'establishment' and the 'old school tie' became common political currency in the 1960s, a theme combined with belief in the 'white heat of technology' in the electoral programme of Harold Wilson. When elected in 1964, Wilson not only endorsed the Robbins targets, but symbolically appointed C. P. Snow as House of Lords spokesman for the new Ministry of Technology.

The statistics collected by Robbins were also used to argue that Britain was falling behind other countries, especially the United States, where one in five went to university, and the Soviet Union, then seen as a major scientific competitor. Comparisons with west European countries did not give such a clear message, but the committee claimed that other countries had much more vigorous plans for expansion, making action in Britain urgent if parity in 'general cultural standards and in competitive intellectual power' was to be maintained.[9] Arguments in favour of science backed up by international comparisons had, of course, been familiar since the 1860s. The basic Robbins projection was for 507,000 students (558,000 including overseas students) in all types of higher education by 1980, which implied a participation ratio of 17 per cent. Within the overall figures, there should be a shift to science and technology, from 39 per cent of students in 1962 to 47 per cent. This 'massive expansion' would be 'the dawn of a new era in British higher education'. If the country was to 'hold its own in the modern world', there was a need for 'a greatly increased stock of highly educated people', for 'even if there were not the spur of international standards, it would still be true that to realise the aspirations of a modern community as regards both wealth and culture a fully educated population is necessary'.[10]

The committee defined four objectives for a higher education system. The first was 'instruction in skills', which should not be seen as inferior to the tasks of general education. Nevertheless, the second aim was that 'what is taught should be taught in such a way as to promote the general powers of the mind. The aim should be to produce not mere specialists but rather cultivated men and women.' Third came 'the advancement of learning': though the balance between teaching and research might vary, 'the search for truth is an essential function of institutions of higher education and the process of education is itself most vital when it partakes of the nature of discovery'. Finally, there was 'the transmission of a common culture and common standards of citizenship ... to provide in partnership with the family that background of culture and social habit upon which a healthy society depends', perhaps especially needed in an age when higher education was drawing on new social strata. Under this heading was also placed the contribution of universities to the cultural life of their local communities.[11] The committee did not expand on what 'common culture' and 'citizenship' were – perhaps this seemed obvious so soon after the victory of 1945. Nor, despite the appearance of the adjective 'spiritual' from time to time, did they use the language of mission, leadership and religious renewal so common in university writings since the 1940s. Their vision was a secular and scientific one. It is also worth noting that, while taking the ideal of equality of opportunity as a given, Robbins did not put social justice or social mobility among the explicit functions of universities: the emphasis was still the traditional one of self-development to the limit of each individual's capacity.

To achieve these objectives, Robbins endorsed the British university model, seeking to extend the best of its features to a new clientele rather than devising any scheme for cut-price expansion, or rethinking the nature of the university. They did not seek simply to extend Oxbridge values (indeed, they ventured some badly received criticism of the collegiate system and the ancient universities' inability to adapt to national priorities),[12] but they did sing the advantages of communal life and personal relations between teacher and taught, and criticized old-fashioned lecture methods. Belief in the residential ideal had become 'an unexamined article of faith', putting an unnecessary curb on expansion, commented the American sociologist Martin Trow.[13]

Most of this found a receptive audience among academics, for whom the Robbins era opened up new professional vistas, but one important element in the committee's thinking fell on deaf ears. They deplored the way in which pressure for university entry, especially for Oxbridge, had increased A-Level specialization; by the sixth form, the gap between arts and science had become impassable. Broader courses would be preferable for many students, and the committee suggested experimenting with different selection methods, including the Scholastic Aptitude Tests used in America.[14] Lionel Robbins himself declared his 'absence of sympathy with the whole sixth form ideology', where specialization was 'almost without parallel in the rest of the civilized world', and deplored the way in which 'the single subject honour specialization has spread so widely in the last fifty years'.[15] His committee recommended a return to breadth in degree courses, claiming to have received complaints from many quarters about over-specialization, whereas the aim of the first degree 'should be to teach the student how to think'. The committee did not revive the old concept of a liberal education based on privileged or compulsory subjects, but they did advocate more combined and inter-disciplinary degrees, commending the Scottish general degree, at that time still taken by the majority of students in arts. Pressure on the first degree should also be relieved by expanding postgraduate study, from 20 per cent of all students to 30 per cent, a policy recommended in any case as part of the upgrading of science and technology.[16] Postgraduate expansion did take place, but only in proportion to general growth, and was still around 20 per cent in the early twenty-first century. The effect of concentrating student support on undergraduate degrees was, as we have seen, to inhibit the lengthening of university education, and to pile on the pressure for specialization: even in Scotland, despite George Davie's influential restatement of the traditions of the 'democratic intellect' in 1961, the honours degree was eventually to displace the general one.

The Robbins remit was 'to review the pattern of full-time higher education in Great Britain' and to advise 'on what principles its long-term development should be based' in the light of national needs and resources.[17] The committee was concerned as much with the structure of higher education as with student numbers, but here its recommendations were less effective. The 'binary' policy of 1965 set higher education on a different path, along which expansion was channelled down to the 1990s. In considering the structure of 'higher education' (and this overall concept was itself a novelty), Robbins had to include not only technical colleges but teacher training colleges, an expanding third sector soon to be renamed colleges of education. Between 1938 and 1962 university numbers had risen from 50,000 to 118,000, but in technical education they had risen from 6000 to 43,000 and in teacher training from 13,000 to 55,000; the participation ratio in 1962 was 4 per cent for universities alone, but 8.5 per cent for all of higher education.[18] This expansion, the result of decisions taken in the 1940s and 1950s, reinforced a duality which the Robbins Report sought to bridge but not to abolish.

For there was a second Robbins principle – 'equal academic awards for equal performance'; qualifications gained should be related to the attainment of the individual, not the status of the institution. There was certainly 'a need for a variety of institutions whose functions differ', but the difference should be genuinely functional rather than a matter of tradition and prestige, and there should be 'no freezing of institutions into established hierarchies', but rather 'recognition and encouragement of excellence wherever it exists and wherever it appears'.[19] Thus technical colleges should come into closer association with universities, which would give degrees to their advanced students, and as standards rose individual colleges should be promoted to university status. The colleges of education should remain separate, but become linked with their regional university through Schools of Education.

The university sector would thus expand: its share of total enrolments should be about the same in 1980 as in 1962, growing to 346,000.[20] Since the committee saw research as a necessity in all institutions with a university title, and insisted on the need to preserve teaching quality and the 'unit of resource' (expenditure per student), this was an expensive recipe for growth, and made the committee's structural recommendations less politically acceptable than their expansion targets.

Those recommendations were complex. Higher technological education was to be given full university status, as part of the shift of student numbers towards science and technology. The CATs should be designated as technological universities and transferred to the UGC, and there should be five high-powered SISTERS (Special Institutions for Scientific and Technological Education and Research), with a strong research and postgraduate emphasis; the Massachusetts Institute of Technology was one of the models. Three of these would be existing colleges in London (Imperial College), Manchester, and Glasgow, one would be an existing but unspecified CAT, and one would be new. Robbins favoured big cities as the site for new foundations, implicitly criticizing the UGC's own recent policy, and saw no objection to expanding universities to 8000 or even 10,000 students. Even so, five completely new universities would be needed, and 'some ten' technical colleges and colleges of education should be allowed to gain university status by 1980, either independently or through mergers.[21]

In the committee's view it was natural, even desirable, that there should be concentrations of research and scholarship, and different levels of state subvention. Thus higher education would continue to have three sectors, with universities distinguished by their research commitment and the higher funding which this entailed, but the boundaries would be permeable. In arguing that technology should be fully embraced by the university sector, and that the existing barriers should be broken down, Robbins was challenging the traditions of the UGC. But in other respects it endorsed that body's work, and accepted unreservedly the buffer principle, the block grant and university autonomy. It regarded the Ministry of Education as an unsuitable supervisory body, for research and the guardianship of higher culture made universities fundamentally different from schools. The UGC should therefore be answerable to a new ministry for arts and science, which would also supervise those other exemplars of hands-off administration, the research councils, the BBC and the Arts Council. The government rejected this, and responsibility for the UGC and its grants was transferred instead to the Department of Education and Science, as the ministry became. Robbins' structural proposals were not calculated to win the sympathy of the department, which would have faced a progressive loss of control of its empire, as would local authorities. It was particularly determined to maintain control of teacher supply, and hence of the colleges of education, absorption of whose funding into the UGC block grant would make national planning impossible. These were legitimate interests, and it was hardly surprising that this aspect of Robbins ran into trouble. The result, two years after its report, was the binary policy.

There was never much chance of the Robbins proposals being accepted as a package. The transfer of the CATs to university status and UGC funding was carried out, but there were to be no SISTERS, and the colleges of education remained under direct ministry control. The Labour government decided that no new universities would be designated for at least ten years – and in the event none were until 1992. The centrepiece of the binary policy was the creation of thirty polytechnics in England and Wales, in most cases by merging smaller colleges.[22] These remained under local authority control, and were neither given access to university degrees, nor allowed to award their own. Qualifications and standards were regulated by the Council for National Academic Awards, created in 1964: itself a Robbins recommendation, the CNAA was a reincarnation of the nineteenth-century examining university. In Scotland, policy followed similar lines. The term 'polytechnic' was not used there, but the equivalent 'central institutions', some of them general colleges, others monotechnics like art colleges, were directly controlled by the Scottish Education Department, which used its powers to hold them to a vocational mission. Scotland had larger and fewer colleges of education than England, and these too remained under central control and separate from the universities. Northern Ireland followed the polytechnic policy, but was also the first to abandon it by the 'trans-binary' merger in 1984 of the New University of Ulster and the Ulster Polytechnic.

The binary policy was announced in a speech at Woolwich in 1965 by Anthony Crosland, who took over the Department of Education in that year. As the author of *The Future of Socialism* (1956), Crosland was the leading ideologist of modern Labour. But that book said nothing about university policy: its egalitarian hopes focused on comprehensive secondary education, enacted by Labour in 1965, which was expected to expand educational opportunity by allowing advanced courses leading to A Levels to be offered to all pupils instead of only to the grammar-school minority selected at eleven. Recent historical work has confirmed that Crosland came to office without any fixed views on the binary policy, and adopted the response to Robbins already worked out by his department, particularly its head of further education, Toby Weaver. This policy was partly a defence of administrative territory, but also rested on arguments which appealed to a technocratic minister. If made part of the university sphere, the best colleges would be tempted to abandon their practical, vocational orientation, and as Weaver argued in a memorandum of 1964, 'a unitary system would lead to lower status for the senior technical colleges and would accentuate the distinction between "U" and "non-U" institutions' (a catchphrase of the time). Instead of a moving frontier, the boundary between the two sectors must be stabilized so that colleges 'will settle down to their most important task of becoming comprehensive communities organized to serve their wide range of students and the growing needs of industry'.

Criticism of universities as elitist, and of the Robbins Committee's snobbery in seeing them as the only 'pukka' form of higher education (Weaver's phrase again), struck a chord with Crosland.[23] The binary policy also reflected the political clout of the largely Labour urban education authorities. But it could also appeal to conservatives, by protecting the university sector from a new irruption of technical colleges and working-class students; it had the support of the UGC, and attracted bipartisan political backing. Comprehensive secondary schools were controversial because they threatened the middle classes, who had been well served by state grammar schools and by the 'direct grant' schools which were now forced to move from the public to the fee-paying sector; the binary policy was not, because it preserved the privileges of the universities which were the middle-class preference. There was also the practical argument, attractive to all parties, that if higher education was to be expanded, it could be done more cheaply through the polytechnics than through universities with their expensive research and residential requirements. University policy, after a few years in the political limelight, now disappeared as a contentious issue until the 1980s.

Robbins himself saw the binary policy as a betrayal, and pointed out the irony that the government which was abolishing the eleven-plus seemed at the eighteen-plus level to be introducing 'an educational caste system more rigid and hierarchical than before'.[24] One answer to this criticism, made by Crosland in the 1966 White Paper which formalized the policy, was that polytechnics were themselves 'comprehensive academic communities' offering degree work among a range of options.[25] Another was that a new clientele for higher education would be more effectively served by a 'public sector' (as the polytechnics became known, though the term was misleading as universities were hardly less public) which was responsive to local pressures, linked with schools and further education, flexible in its curricula, and sympathetic to ideals of social mobility and to the needs of adult and part-time students and those who might be deterred by the mysteries of university culture. This conflicted with the older left-wing policy of giving working-class students 'nothing but the best', but in an age of mass higher education perhaps this needed rethinking.

The binary policy claimed that universities and polytechnics would enjoy 'parity of esteem'; their functions would be different, but equally valuable. Critics argued that to corral vocational education in a non-university sector would condemn it to permanent inferiority; but against that Weaver and Crosland argued that the Robbins proposals would debilitate the technical sector by the progressive transfer of its strongest members, dilute its practical values, and divert it from its true mission, a phenomenon later dubbed 'academic drift'. This argument, however, was undermined by the conversion of the CATs into universities. A parallel technological sector with prestigious elite institutions at its head might have corrected ancient British prejudices, but the policy adopted cut the head off the body. The division became, as Robbins had feared, one of prestige and social clientele rather than function.

When the polytechnics gained full university status in 1992, their emancipation from the binary system was welcomed, and it has since been a standard condemnation of government policies to say that they threaten a return to binarism. This obscures the fact that when the system was in operation it was celebrated by many spokesmen for the polytechnics, who saw them as representing a distinct tradition with its own historical roots; the title 'polytechnic' was rapidly jettisoned after 1992, but for some it had been a badge of honour. North-East London Polytechnic, under its director George Brosan, was seen as a flagship for the binary policy. Brosan developed a 'polytechnic philosophy',[26] and the college produced other evangelists for the polytechnic ideal like Eric Robinson and Tyrrell Burgess. Looking back in 1995, Burgess and authors associated with him argued that Britain has two traditions of higher education, the 'autonomous' and the 'service' traditions. The former prizes its detachment from society, and is 'aloof, academic, conservative and exclusive'; the latter 'explicitly expects higher education to serve individuals and society and justifies it in those terms', and is 'responsive, vocational, innovating and open'. The autonomous tradition values research and the pursuit of truth wherever it may lead; the service tradition 'does not, on the whole, claim to pursue knowledge for its own sake', but uses it to serve society and solve practical problems. Polytechnics 'are typically teaching institutions, devoted to helping students towards some qualification'. They were people's universities, the heirs (often through a direct institutional chain) of the mechanics' institutes and the art and technical colleges of the nineteenth century;

the civic universities had also been founded in this tradition ('community service stations') but had drifted away from it. In this view, the binary policy had the specific virtue of resisting academic drift and bolstering the service tradition. The Robbins Report, by contrast, was 'the high water mark of the autonomous tradition ... the Robbins vision of higher education was a kind of club, with the universities as full members, the colleges of education as associate members and a few further education colleges always on a gratifying waiting list. The Robbins Committee proposed to institutionalize academic drift.'[27] For the polytechnics, it was essential (though difficult) to carry on resisting this drift; the leaders of the movement were hostile to assimilation to the university sector, though also keen to get more autonomy of their own from the local authorities, seen as bureaucratic and interventionist, an aspiration with which the Department of Education sympathized.

For most of the 1970s, the growth of student numbers followed the Robbins projections fairly closely, though they tailed off at the end of the decade, and the total for 1980 fell short – 524,000 compared to the projected 558,000, giving a participation ratio of about 13 per cent. The polytechnics took a disproportionate part of the strains of expansion, though not perhaps to the extent anticipated in 1965: the percentage of students in universities proper fell from 60 in 1962 to 57 in 1980. More significantly, while Robbins had hoped for a shift to science and technology, there was actually a fall, from 39 per cent of students in 1962 to 34 per cent in 1980, and the UGC accepted that the targets were unattainable.[28] There were various explanations of this shortfall. One was a factor not really anticipated by Robbins, a significant breakthrough of women into higher education, related to wider changes in the labour market. The percentage of women students in universities rose from about 25 per cent in the early 1960s to 38 per cent in 1980, and went on rising, passing 40 per cent in 1984.[29] Women were more likely to choose arts and social sciences than science or (especially) technology. The rise of the social sciences, including business studies, was another development only partly anticipated by Robbins, which worked in the postwar tradition of identifying national economic needs with science and the demands of manufacturing industry; British higher education may have fallen down in that sector, but arguably it responded well to the shift of the economy towards finance and services. Humanities and social science were cheaper to teach than science or engineering, and the polytechnics expanded into this field; for having devised the binary policy, the Department of Education did little to keep colleges to their supposedly more practical mission, any more than the UGC did for the now autonomous CATs. These failures, however, reflected problems of demand as much as supply, since university policy was not accompanied by any reform in secondary schools to strengthen science or attack early specialization.[30]

If places in higher education were to be more than doubled by 1980, at a time when universities had come to depend on the state for three-quarters of their income (and the public sector for nearly all of it), governments were committing themselves to heavy expenditure, which had to compete with other priorities. In the 1970s, when student disturbances alienated public opinion and the new universities had lost their early glamour, higher education was no longer a fashionable cause, and it was hardly surprising that politicians sought ways of trimming expenditure without compromising quality. One was to require universities to charge realistic fees to overseas students, enforced as early as 1966 by Crosland, but strongly resisted by the universities on idealistic grounds. Another was the set of proposals by Shirley Williams, when minister of state at the department in 1969, known as the 'thirteen points'. Some of these have since become policy, notably a shift from student grants to loans; others were more gimmicky. The universities' almost contemptuous dismissal of the thirteen points did not help their cause in political circles.[31] Even so, the bipartisan approach to expansion survived, and under Edward Heath's government the White Paper *A Framework for Expansion*, presented in 1972 by Margaret Thatcher as Secretary for State, revised the targets upwards: there were to be 750,000 places by 1981, corresponding to a participation ratio of 22 per cent. These figures were 'adopted as the basis for the Government's longer-term planning in higher education'.[32]

But the White Paper also sought to reduce expenditure per student, and such planning was soon thrown into chaos by the oil-related economic crisis of 1973–74, which marked the end of the post-Robbins bonanza. Pressure for cuts in public expenditure became continuous, and was exacerbated by the strong inflation of that period, which made planning difficult (the UGC abandoned the quinquennial system in 1974–75) and allowed cuts to be enforced simply by not compensating for rising prices. It was now that a long-term decline in the comparative value of academic salaries set in. The UGC proved less adept at handling decline than expansion of resources. It gave priority to preserving academic standards as it understood them, and on the whole did so (the staff–student ratio was still one to nine in 1980),[33] but achieved this by holding back student numbers and by a policy of 'equal misery' which left the universities to take the painful decisions.[34] A more interventionist role would have required the UGC to define priorities and to plan in a positive way, which it was still reluctant to do. There was a particularly severe set of cuts in 1977. By 1979 many politicians had decided that the management of universities, at both institutional and UGC levels, lacked the imagination and flexibility needed to respond to Britain's real needs. The universities were 'already ripe for the chopper' in 1979, reported Anthony Sampson, and the traditions of autonomy established since 1919 faced their nemesis.[35]

At the beginning of the twenty-first century, the Robbins era is often looked back to with nostalgia as an Indian summer of the liberal university. It was certainly one expression, like the new campus universities, of the energy, optimism and generous vision characteristic of the 1960s. Some critics have seen its stress on the economic benefits of higher education as the beginning of a disastrous trend away from liberal humanist principles.[36] A more common criticism, in some ways the reverse of this, was that Robbins espoused expansion without attempting to rethink the nature or purpose of university education, and simply endorsed the existing university model, creating financial commitments for the state which were ultimately unsustainable. The sociologists Halsey and Trow noted in 1971 that so far 'the expansion of the 1960s has been strongly contained within the English idea of a university', and they maintained this criticism in later years.[37] The tension between a uniform elite model derived from Oxbridge and the diverse needs of mass higher education in an industrialized society was never resolved. This argument was linked with the historical view that, as before with the civic universities, the Oxbridge model overwhelmed all alternatives, a view which underestimates both the un-Oxbridge-like emphasis of the Robbins Report on social science and technology as well as science – Robbins himself was, after all, an LSE economist – and the continuing diversity of British university traditions.

Champions of the polytechnics, as we have seen, claimed to represent just such an alternative tradition, which suggests a more positive appraisal of the binary policy than has become customary. After all, it did not replace an existing 'unitary' policy. The division between the university sector and the technical one was longstanding: the question was to what extent, and through what institutional relationships, parts of the latter should be given higher status and encouraged to develop university-level work. Robbins anticipated the creation of about fifteen new universities by 1980, the binary policy produced thirty in 1992. It fitted into a well-established tradition whereby existing colleges with local roots were nurtured, under external academic tutelage, until they were ready for full university status: the civic universities had followed that path, as had the CATs; the new universities of the 1960s, as brand-new creations, were exceptional.

Whatever Crosland's original intentions in 1965, it is unlikely that the binary division could have become permanent. One reason is that, in financing if not in prestige, parity of esteem was a reality. The polytechnics' staff–student ratios were no higher than those of the universities themselves, and they were not much cheaper for the state to run than universities. They developed ambitions to offer a wider range of subjects, to invest in research, and to repudiate local control. Some might deplore this as a manifestation of academic drift. Noel Annan offered a different view of the same phenomenon in 1986. Expansion had been 'wrecked by the notion of parity of esteem', because the power of the liberal tradition encouraged the illusion that every part of the higher education system could meet the same standards. The aim was 'Rolls-Royce higher education' for all, but no country other than Britain adopted such a policy. 'No country could afford within a decade to double the number of university institutions, create thirty-two polytechnics, upgrade the colleges and finance the expansion on the principle of parity of esteem. No country could afford to run all its major institutions with staff–student ratios of 1:10 or lower. No country could afford centres of excellence ... *and* declare that all other comparable institutions were to be given equal status.'[38] Annan's prescription, a significant one from a pillar of the liberal academic establishment, was an American-style market in which shorter and cheaper forms of higher education could flourish alongside elite ones. In 1992, the binary line was abolished. But the illusion of parity of esteem was not, and the system has since struggled with the contradictions which this created. Even in the 1980s, however, it was suffering from the state's unwillingness either to continue funding universities at the Rolls-Royce level, or to discriminate between them when applying financial cuts; parity of esteem had turned negative, dragging universities down instead of levelling them up.

11

State or Market?

'The Party is the first to recognize and honour the traditional autonomy of British universities', announced a Conservative Party document in the 1950s, and the American political scientist Robert Berdahl testified to the sincerity of this belief.[1] Conservative thinkers like T. S. Eliot or Michael Oakeshott saw themselves as defenders of cultural standards against the irruption of the masses, and the preservation of elite education seemed a natural conservative cause. But traditionalist conservatism was a victim of the remodelling of the Conservative Party by Margaret Thatcher, whose advent to power in 1979 marked a return of universities to the political agenda. The reasons for this were not narrowly political, as the 1980s saw the breakup of the postwar consensus on social reform and the role of the state, the decline of deference towards traditional authority and institutions which embodied it, the extension of consumerist demands to public and professional services, and the worldwide advance of neoliberal belief in market mechanisms. The sociologist Martin Trow saw a university participation rate of 15 per cent as the point where a system tipped from elite to mass higher education, and it was in the 1980s that this point was reached in Britain.[2] The strains created by the Robbins style of expansion would eventually have imposed a reassessment of policy on any government. Moreover, no one denied that universities had a duty to serve national needs and to be socially accountable, and it was not only Conservative politicians who thought that they had become unresponsive and unwilling to modify their traditional ideals.

But the Thatcher government also had a particular set of views and prejudices, nourished by the right-wing press, which made universities and their values natural targets. The student troubles of the 1960s were more than a recent memory: even in the 1980s, government ministers met violent receptions on their university visits.[3] The teachers did not have a much better image, as a prime example of a feather-bedded producer interest committed to the corrupting values of the 1960s. There was to be an end to what A. H. Halsey called 'donnish dominion'. Halsey himself, as a socialist and sociologist, represented much of what the new ideology objected to, and the Thatcher governments had a prejudice against the social sciences which led to direct intervention in the academic sphere of a kind which was sometimes petty, as in the renaming of the Social Science Research Council (as 'Economic and Social'), and sometimes serious, as with cuts in research funding. Another sociologist, Ralf Dahrendorf, director of the LSE from 1974 to 1984, was to ask: 'When has there ever been such a wave of destruction of successful institutions, with the authors of the destruction gleefully viewing their work?'[4]

This reflected a general breakdown, perhaps inevitable as the university system expanded, of the comfortable consensus between establishment culture and the academic world.[5] There is also a narrower sociological explanation. The old Conservative Party still represented a patrician, professional and even landed elite, familiar with Oxbridge values. The new one drew more on the business and managerial middle class, and at the end of the twentieth century it represented this class nationally, while Labour was the party of the public-service professionals, who were more likely to be graduates. Criticism of parasitic and privileged universities, it has been argued, tapped a rich vein of envy and resentment among middle-class Conservative voters.[6] However this may be, belief in business values and economic utility was certainly a feature of the 1980s. Once the heirs of the organic conservatism of Coleridge and of aristocratic, paternalist traditions of elite culture, the Tories now seemed to be the new technologico-benthamites, heirs of Arnold's philistines. The Thatcherite appeal to 'Victorian values' was historically shallow, but neoliberalism had authentic precursors in figures like Robert Lowe. In this utilitarian perspective, not only were the universities turning out the wrong sort of graduates for a modern economy – there was nothing new in that criticism – but their corporate and collegiate practices needed an infusion of managerial efficiency and market reality. This emphasis on economic functionality and business methods was boosted by two ideological influences, one being a historical critique of British education as anti-entrepreneurial, the other the appearance of a cluster of educationists who departed radically from the statist consensus: the creators of the 'Black Papers' of the 1970s and of the experiment with a private university at Buckingham.

One of the central arguments of Robbins had been that the expansion of higher education, especially of science and technology, would transform Britain's economy and restore her position as a leading industrial power. By the mid-1970s this promise did not seem to have been fulfilled, and the issue fed into the wider declinist 'state of Britain' debate, which blamed cultural factors for long-term problems of economic performance: entrepreneurial dynamism was undermined by the gentlemanly, anti-industrial, anti-urban values which had captured the middle classes. As we have seen, this debate on the 'English disease' had a historical dimension which looked back to the alleged failures of the Victorian state and the civic universities, and economic and educational historians were to be found on both sides of it. The most influential contribution politically was Martin Wiener's elegant essay on *English Culture and the Decline of the Industrial Spirit, 1850–1980*, which appeared in 1981, well timed to influence a government pledged to reverse that decline; Keith Joseph was said to have made all his civil servants read it when Secretary of State for Industry. Also influential was *The Collapse of British Power* by the military historian Correlli Barnett, which had appeared in 1972. Barnett argued that the British governing class had abandoned a hard-headed concern for national interests because of the idealist influence of evangelicalism, the Victorian public schools and the Jowett tradition of public service. They had pursued imperialist chimeras and neglected the realities of military power, with fatal results in the 1930s. Resources had been diverted to foreign ambitions which should have been spent on modernizing the economy. In a sequel, *The Audit of War* (1986: the second of what became a series of four), Barnett showed how the Second World War exposed the disastrous weaknesses of British industry, and blamed the Attlee government for pouring money into the welfare state instead of into industrial investment. Belief in the 'new Jerusalem', which made 1945 a 'lost victory', was again attributed by Barnett in large part to the idealist educational tradition, and this element in his work chimed with the Thatcherite view of the recent past.

But the politicians read these books very selectively. Central to Barnett's thesis was the view that British pursuit of great-power status was an illusion in the contemporary world, and that a powerful state should intervene directly in modernizing the economy. Such views had no more Thatcher appeal than his argument that it was a long-term mistake to make Britain 'the principal partner in world affairs of the United States'.[7] Neither Barnett nor Wiener actually said much about universities. Barnett focused on the failings of technical education at a lower level, and both authors were highly critical of the public schools. The latter criticism, however valid historically, was becoming less applicable as these schools rebranded themselves as 'independent', and carried out a fundamental shift from athleticism, classics and character formation to the cultivation of examination success. In the age of competitive university entrance, the ability of the public schools to produce high A-Level grades for their middle-class clientele became their special selling-point. Their social exclusivism remained (a royal commission set up by the Wilson government in 1965 came to nothing), and combined with their independence from the state and their harmony with business values to make them politically untouchable. It was much easier to divert the attack towards the universities, without putting forward any evidence that they were failing the nation. In reality, more university students in Britain at this time studied science and technology, and fewer studied arts and social science, than in other advanced countries, including the USA, Japan and Germany.[8]

If the educational system was indeed failing to respond to economic needs, some attributed this to state direction. Between 1968 and 1970 three 'Black Papers' were published by the journal *Critical Quarterly*.[9] They were a rallying-point for critics of comprehensive education, 'progressive' trends in schools, and what would later be called political correctness. They also inveighed against the student unrest of the time and the threats, from outside and within, to traditional academic standards. The *Black Paper* authors included some well-known champions of selection by intelligence testing, who believed in the heritability of intelligence, but to describe them as 'the Ku Klux Klan in mortar boards' is a little unfair.[10] It is more apposite to see the *Black Papers* as the revenge on Robbins of the 'more means worse' brigade, and Kingsley

Amis contributed to all of them.[11] But, as several critics have pointed out, the standards which these 'right-wing scholarship boys' were defending were essentially those of the meritocracy created by the grammar school and university selection system since 1944, and not traditional at all.[12] To regard university education as a privilege open only to the clever was a new idea, which would have surprised the nineteenth-century dons who struggled with passmen and 'almost idiots'. It was the very state which the *Black Papers* condemned which had rescued the universities from penurious dependence on an unintellectual upper-class clientele, and allowed British academics to cultivate scholarly standards in a climate of strenuous intellectual endeavour.[13]

The *Black Papers* included articles by Conservative MPs as well as dons and headmasters, and represented an influential position within the party. Several of the authors had links with the foundation of the private University of Buckingham, along with activists in the Institute of Economic Affairs, a free-market pressure-group. The figure most associated with Buckingham, and its first head, was the Oxford historian Max Beloff. In 1967 Beloff had warned readers of *Minerva* of the danger of universities depending on the 'public purse', and he contributed an article on egalitarian threats to Oxford to the second *Black Paper*.[14] The idea of a private university was now launched, with Sydney Caine, retired director of the LSE, as another heavyweight supporter.[15] The argument was by no means purely elitist or traditionalist: the Institute of Economic Affairs endorsed university expansion, but argued that it was throttled by dependence on the 'public feeding-trough', which also hampered experiment and innovation. Only a direct connection through the market with the career demands of students would restore vigour and accountability. Endowments from industry or wealthy sympathizers as well as student fees would be needed to secure independence, and these pioneers looked forward to a 'British Stanford', a university of the highest international calibre with at least 3500 students, which would be a pilot for reforming the whole British system. The university (whose siting in the small town of Buckingham was capricious, and probably damaged its potential) was opened in 1976 by Margaret Thatcher, then leader of the opposition, but failed to develop in the way hoped, or to inspire any imitators. It found a niche as a small private university teaching law and business studies, relying mainly on overseas students, and with little research activity. It seems unlikely that this was what Beloff, a champion of traditional liberal education and intellectual excellence, had intended. While Lindsay's Keele had been a success and a model for new foundations, Beloff's Buckingham, in some ways a comparable venture, failed to take off. The fundamental reason was no doubt that to dispense with state finance was now a quixotic enterprise: economic fees could only work if there was some system of student loans – and who but the state would provide them? But the experiment kept the desirability of a diversity of funding on the agenda.

Keith Joseph, secretary of state for education between 1981 and 1986, and the longest-serving such minister since Fisher, was seen as the mind behind 'Thatcherism' and was a longstanding supporter of the Institute of Economic Affairs. Yet the Thatcher government did not adopt free-market solutions to university problems. Nor did it particularly favour elite universities, as Oxford's refusal of an honorary degree to the prime minister in 1985 testifies. It chose rather to manage the state system in a more interventionist and intrusive way, coupled with a squeeze on resources. It was part of monetarist economic doctrine that public expenditure should be reduced to make room for private investment and lower taxes. Universities must bear their share of this, all the more so since demographic projections at the end of the 1970s predicted long-term stability in student demand. A government discussion document published in 1978 calculated that numbers in higher education would rise from 522,000 in 1977 to 604,000 in 1985, but would then fall steadily back to 520,000 in 1995; even so, because the eighteen-year-old age-group would decline, the age participation ratio would rise from 14 per cent in 1977 to 18 per cent in 1995.[16] The bulge of numbers in the early 1980s, it was argued, could be coped with by 'tunnelling through' this peak, maintaining the existing level of funding at the cost of temporary austerity.

   These predictions proved wrong. University numbers actually fell until 1984, but then started to grow again, and as in the 1960s governments had little choice but to respond to social pressures. This was a dilemma for a party hostile in principle to increasing public expenditure, and there were two outcomes. The first was a harsh reduction in expenditure per student, which fell by over 40 per cent in the twenty years down to 1997, with a direct impact on teaching: at East Anglia the staff–student ratio was around one in eight until 1980, but worsened to 1:26 by 2000 (1:18 was then the official national figure).[17] Secondly, there was intense pressure to save money through greater 'efficiency' and stronger, more businesslike management. The universities had to keep on tunnelling.

In the 1970s, cuts in university finance were the outcome of international economic crisis. Now the motives were internal, political and ideological, and the cuts which materialized in 1981 were more savage than any that had gone before. They posed a dilemma for the UGC, already struggling to cope with adaptation to declining resources. Under new leaders, the committee abandoned 'equal misery' for a more active planning role, which was intended to preserve the 'unit of resource', and hence the quality of the academic experience. The UGC limited student intakes (contrary to the government's intentions), discriminated between universities in the allocation of funds, and imposed the closure or amalgamation of departments, balanced by funding for 'new blood' posts.[18] There were advantages in this attempt to take a national view, and one well-informed commentator thinks that the UGC rose to the occasion quite effectively.[19] But the criteria on which unpopular decisions were based were far from clear: the technological universities (the former CATs) suffered particularly from the cuts, despite the government's emphasis on the needs of industry and business. The UGC lost the confidence of the universities and the academic profession, without really gaining that of its political masters. Even so, while Keith Joseph was minister there seemed to be no intention of abolishing the UGC, nor was that the recommendation of an inquiry into its role which reported in 1987. One political lesson of the 1981 episode was that it was better to devise mechanisms which forced universities themselves to take unpopular decisions than to make them centrally: where odium was concerned, university autonomy was welcome.

The 1981 crisis also underlined the absence of a body to represent the full spectrum of university opinion. The CVCP was a club of university leaders, well suited to negotiating behind the scenes in a consensual atmosphere, less so when a strong collective voice or a bold initiative was needed. In 1943, the wartime minister of education R. A. Butler had observed that academics generally tried 'to avoid trouble with the government. This is carried to an extreme by the Vice-Chancellors' Committee, who ... are so keen to avoid trouble with the government that they either go and bury their heads in the sand of the UGC ... or they let matters affecting the universities slide away on every occasion when a stand might be made.'[20] In 1981, though individual vice-chancellors did take a stand, as a body they acted more as managers adjusting to the inevitable than as defenders of the endangered values of institutional and scientific autonomy. In this managerial role, the vice-chancellors scored something of an own goal in 1984 by agreeing to set up the Jarratt committee to report on 'efficiency' in university adminis-tration and on how long-term planning could be improved. Alex Jarratt was a leading industrialist; his committee's recommendations for a business style of top-down management in place of decision-making through academic committees and collegiate consensus were widely adopted, and endorsed by the government in a 1985 Green Paper which was notable for its crude espousal of economic instrumentalism, its business-oriented rhetoric, and its refusal to acknowledge the wider cul-tural role of universities and the special character of academic inquiry.[21] Jarratt led, if not to leaner and fitter universities, at least to a burgeon-ing of managerial posts and jargon, and added to the demoralization of academic staff following the 1981 cuts.[22] More significantly, the shift of power to 'managers' who thought primarily in financial rather than aca-demic terms (unlike the civil-service style 'administrators' whom they replaced) made the universities far more responsive, whether in com-pliance or in ingenious evasion, to the financial incentives and performance indicators which were now the state's preferred means for cajoling them into line.

One of the UGC's innovations after 1981 had a long-term future. The block grant had always been meant to cover both teaching and research, supporting the research done by individuals as part of their scholarly obligation. In addition, under the so-called 'dual support' sys-tem, much research in medicine, the natural sciences and social science was financed by grants from the research councils and other bodies. The UGC now split the block grant between core funding and a separate research-related element which could be distributed in a more discrim-inating way, to reward and support research-intensive universities.

The first 'research selectivity exercise' was introduced in 1985; renamed Research Assessment Exercise (RAE), and supported by an elaborate mechanism of peer-review panels, it has since taken place about every five years and become a central feature of university life. It encouraged the separate conceptualization of teaching and research, and ideas began to circulate – even before the end of the binary system – about classifying universities as teaching or research institutions. In 1987 the Advisory Board of the research councils proposed a classification of universities into 'R' (research, limited to about fifteen), 'T' (teaching) and 'X' (those with research strength in selective fields).[23] The idea provoked a hostile reaction, but did not go away. It appealed naturally to scientists, for whom externally funded research was already partly uncoupled from teaching, but seemed a threat to the humanities, and many branches of social science, where the traditional combination of teaching and research was still the norm.

Teaching was subject to another type of audit, Teaching Quality Assessment, run by the Quality Assurance Agency. This was another own goal by the CVCP, acting under government pressure, and was much less sympathetic than the RAE to the universities' own values. By contrast with RAE, a good performance in TQA was not rewarded with significant financial benefits. The exercise was intended to show that 'quality' was being maintained despite progressive underfunding. The QAA's bureaucratic methods and time-consuming inspections and gradings caused so much criticism that it was eventually curbed, though not abolished. Its definitions of quality bore little relation either to the experience of professional teachers, or to the findings of pedagogic research. They were based rather on a crude and amateurish adaptation of managerial theory, in which every teaching operation was broken down into a series of defined and testable 'outcomes'. This was accompanied by an entire new jargon in which, for example, the word 'student', having done service since the middle ages, had to be replaced by 'learner'. There was little room in this mechanical reduction of education to a set of skills and competences for the spirit of original inquiry, the subtleties of the personal relationship between scholar and pupil, or the notion of partnership in the pursuit of truth.[24] Like all 'league table' exercises, it encouraged a compliance culture, and tended to squeeze out experiment and innovation. It was also difficult to reconcile with the status of academics as professionals owing allegiance to ethical and intellectual standards independent of their status as employees. But the approach proved infectious, and spilled over into other aspects of university regulation.

The 1985 Green Paper was followed up by a White Paper in 1987 and legislation in 1988, by which time Kenneth Baker had replaced Keith Joseph. After the ad hoc policy-making of the early Thatcher years, clear policies now emerged in which the stress on business values reached its peak. The centrepiece of the Education Reform Act was the abolition of the UGC, replaced by a Universities Funding Council. The change of terminology indicated that the UFC would distribute funds, but control of policy would remain firmly in government hands. The act also created a Polytechnics and Colleges Funding Council (PCFC) to oversee the 'public sector'. The polytechnics had long chafed under local authority control, and this was now abolished and replaced by independent governing bodies. Elected local authorities were one of the Thatcher government's bugbears, and another prejudice was satisfied by weighting the membership of the polytechnic 'corporations', like that of the two funding councils, in favour of business interests. Nevertheless, the polytechnics were gaining autonomy while the universities were losing it, and this reduced the distinction, already very blurred in functional terms, between the two sides of the binary system.

The 1988 act included the abolition of 'tenure' for university staff, which was seen to stand in the way of restructuring and redundancies. This aroused alarm about academic freedom, since tenure protected staff from dismissal for unpopular or inconvenient views, and it was Max Beloff in the House of Lords who succeeded in introducing a clause giving constitutional protection to academic freedom, an innovation in Britain, though it was common in European countries. Academics should be free 'to question and test received wisdom, and to put forward new ideas and controversial or unpopular opinions' without fear of repercussions.[25] Significantly, this was designed to protect individuals not against the state, but against the university which employed them. In the new age of managerialism critical independence was less welcome, especially where it might offend private funders and potential donors.

The 1988 settlement, with its parallel funding councils, was inherently unstable, and also nationally asymmetrical, since the UFC covered Scotland and the PCFC did not. A Scottish inquiry in 1985 had already recommended a single 'planning and funding council' for the whole of higher education, and this now seemed the logical outcome for the whole country.[26] The Further and Higher Education Act of 1992 abolished the binary system. All polytechnics, and a few other colleges which met criteria of size and quality, were now able to take the title of university and to award their own degrees, including postgraduate degrees; the CNAA was abolished, and colleges still without degree powers had to seek validation from a university. The act raised the number of universities in the United Kingdom from forty-seven to eighty-eight.[27] They were to be financed through separate Funding Councils for England, Wales and Scotland, with the Northern Ireland Department of Education retaining direct responsibility in that province. This decision by a government which opposed political devolution in Wales and Scotland was one of several puzzling features of the act which await the attention of historians. The binary line had been supported by university conservatives who saw it as a defence against egalitarianism and a shield for academic excellence, but the government now seemed to defy its natural supporters. And while Crosland had been criticized in 1965 for the contradiction between comprehensive secondary education and binarism in higher education, now a party which was still suspicious of comprehensive education and nostalgic for the grammar schools introduced comprehensive higher education, ignoring any special claims from elite universities.

In the eyes of critics, the abolition of the binary system was intended to save money by driving all universities down to the level of polytechnics, with disastrous results for the quality of education and research, and for the international reputation of the British system.[28] Now all universities, new and old, had the same formal status and were funded on the same basis, related essentially to student numbers. In practice, behind the common label, a hierarchy of functions and prestige survived, as did great differences in the weight and quality of research and in the standard of degrees. The old binary system had outlived its usefulness, but had become accepted simply because it was the product of history. Any attempt to reinstate it by formally recognizing different types of university, particularly at the topmost level, would provoke a storm of controversy and open governments to the accusation of 'elitism'. The answer to this problem was to allow an informal hierarchy to re-emerge through discretionary payments allocated according to formally objective criteria, of which the RAE was the most significant. Beyond this, universities could be encouraged to seek extra revenue independent of the state. A mixture of pseudo-market incentives within what remained a state-funded system and entrepreneurial activities outside it might allow universities to sort themselves into a new differentiated system, with winners and losers. But would this be enough to preserve the quality of Britain's best universities, at a time when both research and teaching were becoming globally competitive?

A further paradox of 1992 was that the binary system, which had always been defended for its cheapness, was now abolished by a government hostile to public expenditure. Colleges which became universities naturally had expensive ambitions, and this added to the financial strain caused by rising numbers. The policies developed between 1985 and 1988 still assumed demographic stagnation, and much of the debate of that time was about numbers. In fact between 1984 and 1993, the last year when statistics were published separately for the 'old' universities, enrolments rose by 54 per cent (from 305,000 to 470,500). The polytechnics were also growing rapidly, and in the newly unified system there were over a million students.[29] The resulting financial strains led the government once more to clamp down on growth, and brought student fees and grants back onto the agenda. Maintenance grants had been preserved since the 1960s, though their real value had fallen steadily. Fees were still nominal, being paid by the state, and in 1984 an attempt to make better-off parents contribute to them had been hastily abandoned after protests by Conservative back-benchers. But in 1990 the maintenance grant was frozen at its existing level, and a system of national 'top-up' loans introduced on which students would have to depend for future increases. This was strongly opposed by Labour. Student finance was a political minefield, where action risked offending both middle-class parents and those on the left who saw free higher education as a vital achievement of the welfare state, and feared that its abolition would reverse the opportunities opened up since Robbins (more correctly, since Anderson). These problems were remitted in 1996

to a committee of inquiry under the businessman Ron Dearing, charged
with recommending how higher education should develop over the next
twenty years. It reported in 1997, just after the election which brought
Labour to power.

The Dearing Committee, composed of a mixture of business and university leaders (but not active scholars or teachers), was the first
wide-ranging inquiry since Robbins, and collected a mass of evidence.
There was a subcommittee for Scotland, and Northern Ireland was also
covered. But the committee had to work within tightly drawn terms of
reference, for such bodies were not now expected to have an independent influence on public opinion as Robbins had. Structural issues had
been decided in 1992, and Dearing was told that there would be no extra
funding from the government. Nevertheless, the report put forward a
coherent vision. Its clumsy title, 'Higher Education in the Learning
Society' reflected the new idea of a 'knowledge-based society' in which
individuals needed to be fitted for 'lifetime learning'. Both research and
teaching were now conceived within a global framework, in which it
was vital for Britain to retain its competitive edge as part of a Europe
in contention with the United States on one hand, China and India on
the other. The Robbins Report had used arguments about Britain
falling behind other advanced countries, but now the threat seemed
more comprehensive.

The inquiry's terms of reference included a Robbins-like statement
that 'higher education continues to have a role in the nation's social,
moral and spiritual life; in transmitting citizenship and culture in all
its variety; and in enabling personal development for the benefit of
individuals and society as a whole'. Tribute was paid to developing
the powers of the mind, disinterested inquiry, and scholarship and
research. The committee itself defined four purposes of higher education: to allow individuals to develop their capabilities to their highest
potential; to increase knowledge and understanding both for their
own sake and for their practical applications; to serve the needs of a
knowledge-based economy; and 'to play a major role in shaping a democratic, civilized, inclusive society'. The values of higher education
included 'respect for evidence; respect for individuals and their views;
and the search for truth'.[30] These pieties made a change from the

abrasive business-mindedness of the 1980s. The bulk of the report comprised a long list of recommendations directed at the government, the funding bodies and the universities themselves. The assumption was that these could be achieved directly through legislation, regulation or financial incentives: very much by contrast with Robbins, there was little deference to university autonomy.

Many of Dearing's recommendations were concerned with broadening access and breaking down the barriers to opportunity. Lifelong and part-time learning was emphasized, as were shorter degrees. It was noted that the current participation rate was 32 per cent, and 45 per cent was suggested as a reasonable target for twenty years ahead. Other sections dealt with the need to reassert the importance of teaching and improve its quality, and followed the QAA in seeing elaborate mechanisms of audit, benchmarking and target-setting as the way to achieve this. The report's belief that these bureaucratic mechanisms could preserve common degree standards within a mass system seemed at odds with reality, and indeed with Dearing's own advocacy of diversity of missions, where some universities would specialize in research and others in teaching, some would have 'world class', others regional or local status. Funding, the report recommended, should reflect these varying missions.

'Only market romantics seriously believed that, by a combination of belt-tightening, better management, better teaching with modern methods, and attracting private money and foreign students, the value of a University degree in a hugely expanded system could continue unimpaired', wrote a former Conservative minister for higher education in 1996.[31] The hard-headed businessmen and administrators of the Dearing committee indulged this romanticism. But their report departed from its cautious remit in warning that the long-term underfunding of universities was causing serious damage to their quality, and that this must be reversed. In the past twenty years, student numbers had more than doubled, but public funding had increased by only 45 per cent, and expenditure per student had fallen by 40 per cent. If this situation was to change, new sources of income had to be found. This led Dearing to the argument that since graduates were the main beneficiaries of their own education, they should make a contribution through 'top-up' fees, additional to the fee element already paid directly by the state. Various contribution scenarios were considered in detail, and their impact on families at different income levels assessed. The final recommendation was a fee contribution of 25 per cent of real cost, which meant about £3000. It should be a flat fee, not varying according to institution or subject, to avoid the danger of distorting the choices made by the less well-off. The fee contribution would be made available as a loan, to be repaid on an 'income-contingent' basis; the alternative of a graduate tax was considered and rejected. Maintenance should continue to be supported by both loans and grants, each counting for half; since the grant element was to be means-tested, this would help poorer families.

To justify these proposals, much emphasis was put on the differential earning power of graduates. Dearing seemed to see higher education as mainly a benefit for the individual, which conformed with the emphasis on students as consumers and customers which was already a part of managerial rhetoric, but played down the many other interests (or 'stakeholders') and public purposes which universities served, and was at odds with other aspects of the report: if higher education is so vital to the economy, for example, why should business not make a contribution too? And as participation in higher education increases, the graduate premium in lifetime earnings seems likely to diminish.

The political response to the Dearing Report focused almost exclusively on student loans and fees. When the Blair government came to power in 1997, it had to make a quick decision on these matters, and for no clear reason it rejected the Dearing recommendations in favour of a combination which seemed less favourable to poorer families: an 'upfront' flat fee of £1000, which was hardly enough to solve the universities' financial crisis, and a complete replacement of the remaining maintenance grant by loans. When the new Scottish Parliament acquired power over universities, it reversed this and introduced a scheme closer to Dearing, with wide public support: the upfront fee was abolished, but graduates paid a fixed sum into a 'graduate endowment' fund, and limited grants were reintroduced for poorer students. The other decision of the Blair government, again without much stated rationale, was to raise the target participation rate to 50 per cent of eighteen- to thirty-year-olds by 2010. Further thoughts by the

Westminster government had to await a White Paper in 2003, leading to legislation in 2004.

On most detailed policy matters, the White Paper followed Dearing quite closely, including its highly prescriptive line on teaching and the organization of research. It incorporated the new participation target, but most of the increase was to be through two-year 'foundation degrees', an idea which went back via Dearing to Shirley Williams's thirteen points in 1969, but which stretched the traditional definition of a degree to the limit; as these degrees were to be 'work focused' (or 'employer focused'), how they differed from existing vocational diplomas was not clear. The central point in the White Paper was the government's revised policy on fees. The upfront uniform fee was now jettisoned, to be replaced by fees repayable on an income-contingent basis as recommended by Dearing, but charged at variable rather than flat rates, up to a maximum of £3000. The original intention seems to have been to allow only selected universities to charge these, as a way of indirectly favouring an elite group, but this element did not survive, nor was it logical, for the costs of teaching vary according to discipline rather than the type of university. In the event nearly all universities announced that they would charge the maximum fee for all subjects. This recalled a manoeuvre in 1990, when the universities foiled an attempt by the short-lived and business-minded Universities Funding Council to make universities bid downwards for student numbers in order to drive down costs – the universities colluded to name identical 'guide prices'.[32] It looked, therefore, as if the fees due to be introduced in 2006 would effectively be at a flat rate, yet the government had expended much political capital to drive variable fees through.

Top-up fees were welcomed by many within the universities, as a source of extra income, but proved highly controversial politically. They were introduced by Labour (which had promised not to do so in its 2001 manifesto), and opposed by the Liberal Democrats (who had supported graduate repayment as part of the Scottish coalition government) and by the Conservatives (the party of market solutions and individual responsibility). More damagingly for the government, they were opposed by the Labour left, and only passed into law in 2004 after a large backbench rebellion. Fees of any kind were felt to be a reversal of the principle of free higher education and a symbolic blow to the postwar settlement; there was also a well-justified feeling that aversion to debt would deter working-class students. Against this it could be argued that a limited fee contribution was a redistributive measure, given that higher education still mainly benefited the middle classes, but a New Labour government was reluctant to make this case. In order to get its legislation through, however, the government made a variety of concessions and exemptions designed to help the less well-off, including an obligation on universities to offer bursaries, and the restoration of a small maintenance grant for poorer students. The outcome would depend on how these measures worked in detail, which was difficult to predict, and they threatened to reintroduce the jungle of awards and admissions criteria which had been abolished in the 1960s. But Labour victory in the 2005 election (in which the Conservatives promised the abolition of all fees) meant that the principle of a graduate contribution was unlikely to be reversed; attention switched to whether future governments would raise or remove the £3000 'cap', in the face of pressure from elite universities to be allowed to charge full market rates.

The political furore over the fees paid by full-time students sidelined the interests of postgraduates and part-timers and Dearing's emphasis on lifelong learning. Two other significant issues in the White Paper were also lost to sight. One was its discussion of the 'social class gap', the underuse of higher education by 'lower income families'. Even if the document could not bring itself to use the term 'working class', this was a significant return to traditional Labour concerns.[33] Secondly, there was a proclaimed intention to concentrate research, particularly at the internationally competitive or 'world class' level. There should be 'an honest recognition of universities' different roles', and movement to 'a funding regime which enables each institution to choose its mission and the funding streams necessary to support it'. The Research Assessment Exercise had distorted priorities, it was admitted, and the government should 'steer' universities which are not research-intensive to other parts of their mission. 'Scholarship' is necessary for good teaching, but research may not be. The White Paper pointed out that in the United States only 200 out of 1600 four-year universities have the power to award research degrees.[34] Although the government did not proceed to remove this power from existing universities, in 2005 it allowed six English colleges to achieve university status without it, and three other candidates were waiting in the wings. The White Paper thus went further than Dearing in questioning the uniformity of 1992 and allowing universities to find their own level in a semi-market system. If the government sticks to this intention, it is likely to find stiff resistance from universities which see their status threatened, with research as the battleground once the RAE cycle which lasts until 2008 is completed. The White Paper also accepted more clearly than Dearing that the state 'is overwhelmingly the biggest funder of higher education', and that other sources can only be supplementary. It claimed that the Labour government had begun to reverse long-term underfunding (though only after six years in power), and would continue to 'stand by students and universities in future spending reviews'.[35] Here, too, only time will tell. If top-up fees lead governments to make a corresponding reduction in other grants, universities will gain little from the new diversity of income streams.

In 1964, 32 per cent of university academics voted Conservative, and in 1976 the figure was still 29 per cent, but it fell to 18 per cent in 1989 and 10 per cent in 2005. Labour support remained fairly stable (43, 40, 37 and 41 per cent respectively), but the Liberal Democrats moved into the vacant space, and attracted 44 per cent in 2005.[36] Thatcher's policies had a permanently alienating effect for her party, but Labour's record after 1997 failed to enthuse the academic world. Despite the presence in its ranks of former student activists like Gordon Brown and Jack Straw, the Blair government did not break with the broad lines of existing university policy. This was not, or not only, because Thatcher had changed the rules of the game, but because university development had moved into a new phase. The golden age was not to return: it was already further off than many acknowledged, for university folk-memory easily forgets that financial crises and cuts have been a feature of life since 1973.

Specific policies apart, the Labour government made no break with the changes in political culture and style characteristic of the 1980s and 1990s, notably the intense politicization of decision-making and the propensity to intervene in detail in all areas of life subject to central authority. The Thatcher governments, while squeezing public expenditure, hardly 'rolled back' the state. Ministers are now less likely to be railroaded by mandarins of the Toby Weaver type, but the influence of civil servants has been replaced by that of ideologically motivated political advisers. Royal commissions designed to balance a wide variety of views, which collect factual evidence and listen to the opinions of experts and of those with practical experience of the subject being investigated, went out of fashion. Dearing was, to some extent, a revival of this type of inquiry, but the 2003 White Paper was a striking example of the new politics. It was notably badly written, adding New Labour jargon to the established managerial neologisms – the Treasury mandarins could at least write. Where traditionally one would speak of the 'state', the White Paper speaks of the 'government', as in 'Government also has to retain a role because it is the only body that can balance competing interests between the different stakeholders.'[37] This is more than a linguistic point: the 'state' is an impartial entity representing the permanent and collective interests of the community, the 'government' is not.

Many critics have identified as the most negative legacy of the Thatcher years the hollowing out of the public realm, the depreciation of the professional and public-service ethos, the exaltation of individual over collective interests, and the extension of market values to every sphere of life. Universities were a classic expression of the values of the 'public domain', created and consolidated, like the impartial civil service, by the great reforms of the Victorian era.[38] In that era, universities took their place among other institutions, notably local government, which worked in partnership with the central state, but were responsive to local demands and interests. The lay councils of the civic universities embodied this kind of accountability, to local elites if not to the mass electorate. Pluralist self-government was a key tradition of British liberalism, but the current political culture, intent on enforcing uniform national standards, seems unable to accommodate the idea of shared or devolved authority. Every aspect of public life is now potentially subject to central direction, and this is to be accomplished by financial incentives and proxy markets; the impression is sometimes given that without constant prodding and monitoring universities would not function at all. But social institutions can and do work independently of the state, following their own traditions and priorities, expressed in their collective life and passed from one generation to another through their professional ethos. The creation of the new universities in the 1960s and of the Open University showed how a living university ideal could be reproduced. In the days of the UGC, moreover, autonomy was collective and belonged to the sector as a whole. This has been dismantled, and universities are expected to respond individually to student demand and the challenges of the market, which leaves them much more vulnerable to outside pressures.

This matters because of the commitment of universities to the pursuit of truth and critical and independent thinking, which differentiates them from other social institutions, and provides a counterweight to other centres of power – politics, the media, or big business. The value of higher education to the economy has dominated political discourse on universities since the 1960s, sometimes as part of a world view in which no activities without a money-making purpose seem truly legitimate.[39] But the incessant use of such language is ultimately corrupting and demoralizing, and other legitimate purposes of the university, social, cultural and intellectual, need to be re-emphasized. Documents like the Dearing Report use some of the old language, but without the same conviction as in the days of Robbins.

Style and vocabulary matter, and not only because the fastidious use of language is, or should be, one of the academic values which universities exist to defend. Change in British universities was as profound in the 1980s and 1990s as in the Robbins era, but it was handled by governments very differently. Necessary but painful adjustments might have been accomplished no less effectively through a political culture which harnessed the universities' own ideals and purposes instead of challenging and devaluing them. The universities, in a more benign atmosphere, might have responded more positively and flexibly to changing conditions. There are signs in the 2003 White Paper of recognition that British universities are among the world's best, a national asset to be 'celebrated' and nourished; not just another public service to be pummelled into shape, but part of a European tradition with eight hundred years of history behind them. However, a real revolution in values is unlikely to happen without the return of political life itself to the pursuit of collective ends and ideals.

12

Past and Present

'The universities of all countries and all ages are in reality adaptations under various conditions of one and the same institution', wrote Hastings Rashdall, who saw a direct line running from medieval Bologna and Paris to the new English universities of the 1890s. 'The university ... represents an attempt to realize in concrete form an ideal of life in one of its aspects. Ideals pass into great historical forces by embodying themselves in institutions.'[1] Since the university is indeed 'the only European institution which has preserved its fundamental patterns and its basic social role and functions over the course of history',[2] there is a temptation (largely resisted by Rashdall) to see university ideals as timeless, or to interpret all past developments as leading up to the modern university and its values and priorities. In fact, of course, universities reflect the political, social and intellectual conditions of their time, and so does writing their history. When Lawrence Stone and others established scholarly university history on social and cultural lines in the 1960s and 1970s, this was related to the contemporary democratization of what had been privileged, elite bodies. Today that meritocratic revolution is in the past, and seems more limited than it did at the time; other issues such as the contribution of higher education to the economy, the rival claims of state and market and of collective and individual benefit, or the ways in which education relates to tensions between national cultural identity and globalization seem more pertinent.

When Eric Ashby published a study of Haldane in 1974, the debate in Haldane's time over 'whether education should be a responsibility of the state or should be left as far as possible to private agencies encouraged by the state' could be seen as 'quite unreal' to the modern reader. Dependence on the state was taken for granted, as were a number of axioms including the Humboldtian view that 'the teacher is not there for the sake of the student – both are there for the sake of knowledge'.[3]

Robbins seemed to have extended those values successfully to a new clientele, and the future promised gentle and manageable expansion on the same lines. The Robbins Report itself foresaw that by 2025, 15 per cent of the working population would have received higher education; even in 1988, the age-cohort projection for 2000 was 20 per cent.[4] But Dearing in 1997 found that it was already 33 per cent, and predicted a rise to 45 per cent over the next twenty years. In fact it was 48 per cent in 2002, though this was still lower than the OECD average of 53 per cent, and was exceeded in several European countries as well as the USA (63 per cent) and Australia (68 per cent).[5] The rise in participation is no doubt due partly to the reclassification of what counts as a university and as university work, but that is itself a significant change. If university and student finance and the traditions, autonomy and professional values of the older universities have come under unprecedented strain since the 1980s, this reflects the painful move towards a mass, if not a universal, system of higher education rather than any malign political agenda. Whether the best framework has been chosen for managing that transition is another matter.

Rashdall also said that 'in education as in other matters some knowledge of the past is a condition of practical wisdom in the present'.[6] It might be argued that in the age of the mass university there are few such lessons to be learnt from the past, that the elite university which could trace its origins to the middle ages has now run its course. Is there anything relevant today in the ideas of Newman, Arnold or Huxley? Can the rhetoric of the community of scholars, of teachers and students as partners in a common search for truth, of university education as a conversation about liberal culture, rhetoric which still had some force even in the 1960s, today evoke more than nostalgia or embarrassment? Current political debate discourages such questions, and interprets higher education as a handmaid to the economy, or as a consumer good through which individuals improve their earning power rather than their minds. But this closing down of debate can be challenged, and some at least of the questions to be asked about the scope and nature of university education are perennial. Moreover, it is difficult to understand the specific problems of British higher education without reference to its historic development since at least the mid-nineteenth century. Three episodes were particularly significant: the successful reform of Oxford and Cambridge in the mid-Victorian period, assuring their superiority within a hierarchy of prestige; the development of state action between around 1900 and 1919, creating a relatively homogeneous national system of universities, fenced off from their rivals by an elitist conception of what university education was; and the move to meritocracy in the 1940s and 1950s, creating a right to university education which required centralized and impartial methods of selection, further enforced by the universal funding brought in by the Anderson Report. The Robbins Report built on these foundations, but created a model of expansion which was out of line with practice in comparable countries and which ultimately proved financially unsustainable.

Can the past provide more specific guidance on current problems? The context of these is the 1992 Act, the Dearing Report, the 2003 White Paper and the endorsement of Labour plans in the 2005 election. These plans acknowledge that the state (or the 'government') must retain a directing role in the system, but do not envisage a return to open-ended state funding. Part of the burden of financing the years of study must pass to students themselves, and universities must seek alternative resources in the market-place. That market is partly a real one, in which change will be driven by student demand, and partly a proxy market in which the state pushes the universities in the directions thought desirable by a variety of financial sticks and carrots, backed up by audits, targets and performance indicators.

Many of these incentives and interventionist forms of funding are only necessary because formally, since the end of the binary system in 1992, all universities are equal. But can the hierarchy of prestige created by history be abolished by legislative fiat, and can the traditional definitions of the nature and purpose of the university, notably the commitment to the unity of research and teaching, survive within a system expanded in this way? De facto divisions have already appeared, though they do not necessarily coincide with the old binary line. A new form of academic drift is eroding the distinctive ideals for which the polytechnics once stood. Some post-1992 universities have remained faithful to the old polytechnic ethos (though jettisoning the title, once a badge of honour), others have developed more grandiose ambitions, sometimes abandoning campuses in the very communities which they were created to serve. The CVCP, fashionably renamed 'Universities UK', has embraced the new universities, but rival groups have appeared within it. In the self-selected Russell Group of nineteen 'research-intensive' universities, antiquity still counts: only one of the new universities of the 1960s, Warwick, is a member, and none founded later.

The White Paper is surely right to claim that Britain needs such a group where large-scale, internationally competitive research can be concentrated. Germany and Italy, countries where universities were traditionally of equal status, are moving painfully to the same conclusion. British university policy reflects the obsession of the British political class with American models, yet some of the lessons of America are ignored. There is no attempt there to claim that all universities are equal or that all degrees meet the same 'gold standard'. The state systems in California and Wisconsin are structured on a three-tier basis – research universities, universities mainly devoted to teaching, and community colleges – which allows for diversity of needs and the movement of individual students from one tier to another. Haldane might have approved, but nothing so rational now seems politically possible in Britain. Micro-intervention is accompanied by a lack of strategic planning, in the hope that decisions taken by universities themselves in response to market pressures will relieve the government from taking unpopular decisions, and produce 'diversity', seen as a virtue in itself, but all too easily turning into incoherence.

The politically fraught question of student loans and fees is likely to fade into the background, if only because student generations are short, and the days of free higher education are already a distant memory. Historically, it cannot be claimed that there is a long tradition of free higher education. Students (or rather their parents) always paid fees until the 1960s. On the other hand, they hardly ever paid the full market rate, and there were always scholarships and bursaries of various kinds. To establish a genuine market in higher education would be a real revolution, but to expect students to pay part of the cost of their education, on a deferred basis, and to back this up with means-tested financial aid, is in line with developments in the earlier twentieth century: this is, of course, exactly what worries critics of the policy, who see a historic reversal of what had seemed permanent acquisitions of the welfare state.

In fact, as we have seen, the Robbins Committee considered student loans, and the decision against them was a narrow one. Whether critics of loans and top-up fees are justified depends partly on survival of the equality of access also guaranteed by the welfare state, and this is a matter of university structures.

Here it may be helpful to think again in terms of polarized American and European models, representing market and state respectively. British universities fall between them. They are not run centrally as part of the state machine, as they have been in France and other countries marked by the Napoleonic stamp, yet they are public rather than private bodies. Britain shares in the European state tradition, but because history has created a hierarchy of prestige the continental norm of open entry to any university which the student chooses could not work. It is in the American direction that current tendencies seem to be driving, yet there are dangers in attempting simply to transfer any model which has grown organically in very different political, social and cultural conditions.

Historically, it is towards the European 'social model' that Britain has been moving since at least the late nineteenth century.[7] The state has indeed been interested in British universities ever since their foundation. In the sixteenth and seventeenth centuries, rulers expected them to instil political and religious orthodoxy, and intervened with a heavy hand when they did not. In the eighteenth century, the English universities were left alone, but only because they could be trusted to uphold the existing order. If the Scottish ones were more vigorous, this was due in part to prodding by local elites. In England, stagnation and religious monopoly aroused the state to action again by 1850. Oxford and Cambridge were restored to their position as national institutions, and Gladstone claimed with justification that parliament was giving them a new freedom from obsolete religious and constitutional restrictions. As elsewhere in Europe, the nineteenth-century liberal state sought to emancipate thought from the oppression of religious dogma, to expose every area of national life to the invigorating power of enlightened public opinion, and to introduce principles of merit that would check the old power of birth and the new power of money. Oxford and Cambridge had ever since their origins been embedded in national networks of political and social power through their graduates; now this relationship was extended as they produced an administrative class for the modern national and imperial state, and an 'intellectual aristocracy' to temper democracy. The European idea of the state as a creative cultural force, instilled into the British elite by Arnold and by Oxford idealism, and strengthened by the experience of two world wars, retains its relevance. It includes a specifically British emphasis on fairness and social solidarity, for once higher education was conceived as a right rather than a privilege the state assumed a new role as guarantor of equity and impartial selection.

The introduction of Treasury grants in England in 1889 and the creation of the UGC in 1919 were thus only stages in a long story. They reflected concern for international competition, national efficiency, and the importance of science. The creation of the UGC implied a compact: the universities recognized their obligation to serve national needs, and in return were allowed a very large measure of autonomy in the way they conducted their teaching and research. National funding helped to free the newer universities from local pressures. After the Second World War, when the UGC's remit was reworded and strengthened, the balance in this alliance shifted towards seeing universities as public institutions enjoying unusual autonomy rather than independent bodies to which the state extended aid. Expansion after Robbins did not at first seem to threaten the compact, but in due course, whether rightly or wrongly, the universities were held not to have risen to the challenge of meeting national needs, and the UGC was abolished. But neoliberalism did not seem to result in more liberty for the universities. The reduction or even elimination of state funding is no guarantee that state intervention will itself be abandoned. Independent endowment did not save nineteenth-century Oxford and Cambridge from being reformed, legitimately, as national institutions. Nor does the state refrain from regulating many 'private' bodies today, from trade unions to banks, insurance companies and privatized utilities. Whatever the attractions of returning higher education to the market-place, it is unlikely that any government in an advanced, democratic state will surrender the power to regulate a social institution which is so central not only to economic performance and scientific research, but to the quality of the nation's leadership, the standards and effectiveness of its professions, and its citizens' perceptions of social justice. Such public concern is more rather than less likely as higher education becomes a matter affecting the majority of families.

The 2003 White Paper acknowledges that there is no real alternative to the state as the main source of university finance. In the post-Robbins period, Britain spent more per student than comparable countries, but this anomaly has now been corrected; by international standards, over-all expenditure on higher education is not high, and a disproportionate amount still goes in aid to individual students. In the United States, whose appeal to many politicians is the supposed prevalence of private financing, the percentage of GDP spent in *public* funding of higher edu-cation is higher than in Britain, and when private resources are added American expenditure is more than double the British percentage.[8] Diversity of funding may be the best way of guaranteeing universities' freedom, but brings its own forms of dependence – American univer-sity commentators worry as much about corporate pressures as British ones do about bureaucratization. If the economic and social benefits which universities are expected to deliver are to be realized, the com-munity has in the end to pay for them, and the traditions which stimulate private giving in the United States cannot easily be reproduced in Britain. At the same time, the populist hostility to taxation for col-lective purposes stoked up in the Thatcher years remains strong. Public services dependent on taxation are liable to chronic underfunding even when, like the National Health Service, they enjoy popular support. Thus if the better-off are not prepared to pay more taxes to maintain higher education as a universal benefit, it seems only just that their pockets should be hit instead through top-up fees, and to introduce these was an act of political courage. In the 1960s, subsidies to the mid-dle class seemed justified when there was an urgent national need to expand higher education, but in a more consumerist society, where the benefits of university education for the individual are clear, they are more contentious. In continental countries where free or near-free higher education has been the norm, the raising of fees has proved an equally controversial challenge to middle-class expectations from the welfare state.

The equivalent of the former UGC block grant, which provided three-quarters or more of the universities' income in the 1960s, is now down to 30–40 per cent, comparable to what it was in the 1930s, or indeed the 1900s – but there has been no corresponding return to the universities' prewar autonomy. It is certainly desirable that universities should find alternative sources of income such as endowments and alumni appeals, overseas students and fee-paying postgraduates, but reliance on these types of income favours universities with wealthy alumni and international cachet, and so widens the gap between the elite and the rest. It would become still wider if top-up fees were 'uncapped'. Oxford and Cambridge now share their dominance of the academic world with other elite universities, but their names remain potent brands, and they could charge fees at a market level which went far beyond the real cost of teaching, paying for extra staffing and resources which would make their position even more impregnable.

Wealthy benefactors helped to found and maintain the Victorian civic universities, but their record was a patchy one, and these universities soon needed far more resources than endowments supplied. Few wealthy businessmen today have the local roots and loyalties of their Victorian predecessors, as independent firms collapse or become merged into national or multinational companies. Most of the companies which supported the foundation of East Anglia in the 1960s have since vanished or lost their local identity,[9] and if Buckingham failed to become a British Stanford, this is because there was no Leland Stanford waiting in the wings. The wealthy are as likely to endorse existing models of success as to sponsor innovation, and here again Oxford and Cambridge can outdo any rivals, offering the ultimate prize of a college to immortalize the donor's name.

Two remedies have been popular on the political right in an attempt to reduce state responsibility for financing universities. One is the idea that universities should be given a once-for-all endowment to provide an independent income. Apart from its political improbability – if the huge sums needed somehow became available, what chancellor would not prefer to use them for cutting taxes, or for more popular causes than universities? – this has been floated before, in Scotland in the 1880s. The sum proposed then was intended to yield about £40,000 a year, and it is unlikely that even the legendary wizardry of the Edinburgh financial community could have turned this into the £842 million which the Scottish Higher Education Funding Council spent in 2005. Endowments, by their nature, cannot anticipate new developments, and in the end, as Oxford and Cambridge found in the nineteenth century, call forth state intervention to ensure they are not misspent.

A second imaginary device is the educational voucher. The state would abandon direct financing and give each student a fixed sum which could then be spent, topped up by private resources, to make free choices in the university market. Institutions would compete healthily for student custom. A favourite of the Institute of Economic Affairs, vouchers have often been proposed for secondary schools, but always come up against the problem: what if 10,000 parents want to send their children to Eton? What if everyone wants to go to Oxford or Cambridge, which like Eton are not expandable without losing their character? The answer, of course, is that popular universities would have to select their students, and since the voucher money would come from the state, this could hardly be on anything but a meritocratic basis. So vouchers would only be a roundabout way of recreating the system which we already have; it would increase the proportion of university income coming from fees, and destabilize the system as unpopular universities faced financial crisis, but would not necessarily save the state any money. Nor is it likely that the state would renounce its right to regulate what it is ultimately paying for – one reason why independent schools have never shown enthusiasm for the idea. If greater responsiveness to student demand is needed, this is already envisaged in the pseudo-market thinking of Dearing and the 2003 White Paper. Besides, the fees for which vouchers would be a substitute are only one part of university funding, and students paying for their education can hardly be expected also to support scientific research, for which the state has been acknowledged as the prime funder since the First World War.

Students are not the only 'customers' of universities, and there are limits to which even they can be regarded in this light. The analogy has been fashionable since the mid-1980s, but it breaks down at several points. Even if the idea of a community of scholars no longer seems convincing, education is a process requiring active participation on both sides. Its effectiveness depends as much on what students put in as on what teachers hand out. Universities are agents of the community in maintaining intellectual standards and in awarding classed degrees which have value in the competitive labour market, and this must give

them an authority as public and professional organizations independent
of their 'customers'. Higher education cannot be multiplied (like cars or
tins of salmon?) as a uniform object of consumption, but is a positional
good which buys status and a right to income, with differential outcomes: half of all jobs may now be 'graduate' jobs, but they are as
diverse as they were before 1992, and the university attended and the
degree obtained still matter. Within the spectrum of occupations, there
will always be elite positions, and it is in the interests of national efficiency as well as social justice that these should be filled by the ablest
people, not just those from the best-endowed families.

The 2003 White Paper rightly draws attention to the 'social class gap'.
Students from the top three social strata are almost three times as likely
to enter universities as those from the bottom three, and between professionals and the unskilled working class the gap is more than fivefold.[10]
Such figures are all too familiar to the historian, because they are similar to those for the 1950s and 1960s which Robbins used against the 'pool
of ability' theory, or even those before 1914.[11] Since the 1960s, all social
classes have made more use of university education, to the point where
among the top group it is all but universal, but the gap itself has
remained the same, or even widened. This can be used as an argument
against free higher education, as introduced in 1962, which does not
seem to have had the egalitarian effects claimed by its defenders. It also
suggests that inequalities are deeply rooted in the British social structure
and school system, and it seems doubtful that this can be changed by
improvements to 'access' or by the battery of recruitment-related incentives, targets, benchmarks and penalties proposed by the White Paper.
However sincere the desire to widen participation, these are no substitute for a politics which engages directly with the distribution of
privilege, wealth and power.

The nature of choice in the context of universities is another doubtful question. Much of the detailed regulation of teaching is designed to
allow students an 'informed choice' – they 'should be able to draw on
up to date and robust assessments of the quality of learning and teaching'.[12] But neither Dearing nor the White Paper confront the issue of
selection: when universities vary in quality and prestige, it is the university which chooses the student, and the quality of secondary

education becomes a vital issue. Selection depends on specific examination grades, and private education and coaching will always give those who can afford them an edge; however much state schools are improved, independent schools will strive to keep ahead because their market depends on it. Here debate is distorted because the position of these schools is completely off the political agenda, though they create a fundamental difference between Britain and elsewhere.

Left to themselves, free markets in education will reproduce the structures of social inequality from one generation to another, since wealth can buy education of better quality if not counteracted by a controlling mechanism of some kind. Where state secondary schooling is universal or nearly so, equality of treatment can be guaranteed until the level of entry to higher education, so that free choice can operate thereafter. In Britain, on the other hand, secondary schooling has both a privileged sector and great variations of quality within the state sector; but impartial selection at eighteen-plus is perceived as fair, even if the results are in fact socially conditioned. The distribution of students within the school system is not based on merit, but within the university system it is, and on the university benches class and background are ignored. (In the same way, one might add, the secularism of universities, a nineteenth-century conquest, is an essential corrective to the divisiveness of religious denominationalism in schools.) Divided secondary education followed by unitary higher education works in Britain, while unitary secondary education followed by diversified and open higher education works in the United States, and in countries like France with its division of students after the baccalaureate between ordinary universities and elite engineering and business schools chosen by rigorous intellectual competition. Family ambition, cultural capital and knowledge of how the system works will always give the middle classes advantages which cannot be entirely removed. But those advantages would be maximized rather than controlled if socially divided secondary education was followed by socially divided higher education; a completely free market would surely produce this in Britain, with elite universities drawing their students from the independent schools, and with the rich able to bypass selection. There would no doubt be scholarships for the talented poor, but this would be a return to the situation before the 1960s, when higher education was much less vital than today for careers.

Within the current university hierarchy, there are already signs of a two-tier system, with older universities offering professional and liberal studies for affluent families, and newer ones providing vocationally oriented education for the rest. Down to the 1960s, when participation was still hardly more than 4 per cent, university education was an option for the middle classes, relevant only to certain careers, while working-class students were a privileged minority depending on scholarships. Today, it might be suggested, the university clientele falls into three segments. The upper middle classes, with inherited cultural capital and traditions of university attendance, are acutely aware of the benefits which higher education brings, and if state schools cannot promise access to it they will spend whatever is needed to give their children advantages. The importance of getting into a 'good' university, and acquiring a 'good' degree, have already made university entry and graduation into sites of acute social strain. In the broad middle strata of society, which have absorbed the prosperous working class, university education remains an option rather than an obsession, a desirable and achievable goal for which state schools and new universities provide an acceptable path. Below that level, higher education remains more or less closed to families mired in multiple social disadvantage.

A market vision of higher education posits a nation of self-sufficient individualists, creating their own destinies, striving to improve themselves and competing on merit for the rewards of ambition. This has its own attractions, and is compatible with traditional ideas of academic standards and achievement. But it is unlikely to work well in a country which lacks the American optimistic myth of an open society, and where economic efficiency is already hampered by social inequality and class privilege. The importance of schooling has already been stressed. It is surely also important that the best university education should be open to the best students from whatever class, and that the state should intervene positively to equalize access across the university hierarchy and to prevent it becoming a mirror-image of social inequalities. This means maintaining the integrity of the national university system, as it was established in the postwar settlement, though not necessarily the over-elaborate mechanisms of centralized admission. These were devised for school leavers in the age of the elite university, and are less attuned to lifelong learning. Today more students are content to study near their homes (or forced to do so when loans have replaced grants), and for many universities and disciplines the problem is to recruit students rather than to select them. The state might best serve equity and choice by ensuring the rational geographical provision of subjects and types of university; and if more flexible systems of selection could be devised, school-leaving examinations could be freed for their real purpose of ensuring a balanced school curriculum. The survival of equitable selection would be threatened, however, if the globalization of services forced governments to give private enterprise a free hand. It would also be incompatible with the privatization of Oxbridge, for which some siren voices call. The Victorian reformers rightly insisted that the ancient universities were public and national institutions; so did the 'Oxford and the Working Class' movement in the 1900s, and the historian of Oxford in the 1920s who said that Oxford and Cambridge are 'national possessions', which must share with all their 'kingdom of opportunity and power'.[13] These universities have done much to increase their recruitment from state schools, but this would surely not survive their conversion into enclaves for the international rich.

Another sensitive issue raised by the White Paper is the relationship between teaching and research. Since 1992 the need for the two activities to be combined in all university contexts has become an article of faith for the new universities, which do not want to see their new status clawed back as soon as it has been achieved. Yet the end of the binary system brought into the university sphere a mass of vocational teaching, where the relevance of research to practice is much less direct than in older university disciplines, and the requirement for every teacher to be an original researcher seems less obvious. The Research Assessment Exercise, because it is almost the only way for universities to gain substantial extra funding, has created an obsession with research output.[14] The essence of universities has always been learning, scholarship, the life of the mind and the transmission of culture, but the specific ideal of the fusion of teaching and research came from Germany in the nineteenth century, and specialized scientific and scholarly research in its modern form was adopted late and with some suspicion in Britain. In the 1940s Truscot was still complaining about its absence in the redbricks. But this soon changed, and by the 1950s and 1960s there were new complaints that only research counted when staff were appointed or promoted, that the research fetish was responsible for the exaggerated cult of the specialized honours degree, that too many academics 'regard research as their primary function, and teaching as an annoying interruption of it', and that scholarship ('keeping up with the subject') should be considered just as valuable a function.[15] The Robbins Report discussed and partly endorsed these complaints.[16] The new universities of the 1960s focused on innovation in teaching, and the champions of a 'polytechnic philosophy' saw teaching and the practical application of knowledge, not research, as the polytechnics' special mission. Thus there is nothing new in the White Paper's attempt to steer some universities away from research and to re-emphasize the value of teaching. As for Humboldtian principles, the unity of teaching and research was practicable when research was a personal choice, but in science today research is generally a collaborative enterprise, and the demand for research outweighs the demand for teaching. Nearly a third of all academic staff are now engaged purely in research. If it is wrong for teachers not to be active researchers, it is an equal departure from the Humboldtian ideal for these researchers not to teach.

The Research Assessment Exercises have imposed distortions of their own. They have been based on a very narrow definition of research, the sort which results in specialized publication; they have failed to give credit for other ways in which universities contribute to the intellectual life of the community (creative work in the arts, consultancy and public expertise, adult education in the WEA tradition, the diffusion of research through textbooks and communication to non-academic audiences, and so on); and they have adopted research models better suited to science than to the humanities.[17] As a proxy market device, the RAE exerts financial pressures which may well conflict with student demand, or with the national and regional spread of subject provision. What was originally intended to identify and encourage research throughout the system has become a tool of ruthless discrimination between and within universities, reducing rather than expanding choice. Departments have been closed down simply because they do not reach the highest RAE grade; the closure of chemistry and physics departments even in some major universities (due also, it is true, to falling student demand) would have astonished the policy-makers of the Robbins era. If financial benefits flowed to good teaching as they do to good research, the pattern of status and prosperity among British universities might be very different – for the universities which benefit least from RAE tend to be those which teach 'non-traditional' students, who need more skilled and intensive teaching, while those which benefit most usually have students who are already highly motivated and well prepared. There is little logical coupling between 'research intensiveness' and the costs of teaching.

Despite the interest in regulating and assessing teaching, the critique of over-specialization, still strong at the time of Robbins, has dropped out of public debate. Experiments with new curricula, of the type popular in the new universities of the 1960s, now seem to be absent, and discussions of liberal education are quite out of fashion. Governments, too, are less interested than in the 1970s or 1980s in steering subject choices in utilitarian directions, being content to leave this to the market; bolstered by the British tradition of the arts degree as an all-round preparation, the humanities and social sciences have profited from this freedom, as they have in research, where the RAE process has never discriminated between subjects.

Yet the problem of specialization in schools has worsened since Lionel Robbins described it as 'almost without parallel in the rest of the civilized world'. It has been encouraged by the spread of 'choice' within secondary education and by school league tables which depend almost entirely on examination grades. Difficult subjects are discouraged, and the consequences for mathematics, physics or modern languages are felt in the universities; premature choice is in reality a restriction of choice, closing off the range of subjects which students are in a position to choose. Yet when governments have been offered proposals for baccalaureate systems which would remedy the over-specialization of A Levels, rebalance the intellectual content of secondary schooling, and give vocational and academic subjects equal status – by the Howie Report in Scotland in 1992 and the Tomlinson Report in England in 2004 – the opportunity for creative reform has been rejected.

The question of specialization is in turn connected with the length of undergraduate degrees. The English three-year degree, a product of nineteenth-century Oxbridge, turned out graduates efficiently when elite students were initiated into academic values by their schools, when staff–student ratios were low, and when students were not distracted by having to take paid work, in vacations or during term. These conditions are now far from universal. Teaching Quality Assessment was an attempt to convince the world that traditional 'standards' were intact despite the rapid expansion of enrolments and the fall in per capita expenditure. Few within universities were convinced. Yet top-up fees and loans, by leaving students with a heavier debt at the time of graduation, further discourage a longer period of study, and post-graduate work is an expensive venture unless it has direct vocational value. Britain is a signatory to the 'Bologna process' which seeks to harmonize European degree structures on the basis of a three-year bachelor's degree followed by a two-year master's. The Scottish degree conforms to the overall five-year structure, the English one does not. Moreover, while for most English students the bachelor's degree is the exit point, in other European countries it is seen as the first cycle in a system where the master's degree is the norm. In the United States, the four-year degree followed by graduate school gives much the same outcome. There must be serious doubt whether the three-year degree is now equipping British students to compete effectively on the international stage. The combination of financial incentives, reformed degree structures and changed outlooks which would somehow encourage more open-ended and less narrowly specialized study remains to be found.

The constraints of the short degree are characteristic of a supposedly market-based system in which the state is not willing either to trust universities to respond to national needs as public bodies working within a pluralist society, or to let market forces work with genuine freedom, but succumbs to the itch to find an interventionist micro-solution to every newly discovered problem. It is true, nonetheless, that universities retain much real autonomy. Their legal independence from the state survives, and has protected them from enforced privatization or from endless bureaucratic reorganization: the National Health Service, similar in being an employer of professionals, but where existing institutions were fully nationalized in 1948, again provides an instructive contrast. In universities the appointment of staff, the admission of students and the organization of teaching remain free of direct government control, as they are not in many countries. There are multiple sources of funding, and the public money which comes from both research councils and the

RAE is dispensed by panels of academics on peer-review principles, leaving universities to determine their research priorities. Even the funding councils have returned in many respects to the 'arm's length' style of the UGC, although their own independence from political control is less. There are rewarding opportunities, as well as difficulties, in negotiating the new world of markets and consumerist demand. If universities and academics do not appreciate this freedom, it is partly due to a strong and continuing sense that competition is alien to the ethos of universities, and that they should stand or fall together – as shown by the 'guide prices' episode of 1990 and the reaction to variable fees; partly to continued underfunding, and salaries which have fallen behind those in the private sector; partly to management styles which are inappropriate for creative organizations with strong traditions of collegiality and collective decision-making; and partly to the reluctance of both government and university leaders to abandon narrowly economic justifications of the university's mission, with the accompanying dispiriting vocabulary.

Both Robbins and Dearing defined four purposes of the university. They were not quite the same, but they stressed the university's multiple role as a cultural, social and intellectual powerhouse. These were responses to the perceived needs of their age, but the historian can see some of these themes running through the centuries, both before and after the shaping of the modern British system began in the mid-nineteenth century. They include the role of universities in forming a leadership elite and moulding and transmitting the national culture (once religious, later secular); their service to the state and the collective interests of the community; their importance as sources of independent expertise and critical thought; and more recently, their function as channels of opportunity and social equity, crowning the educational edifice and countering the power of birth and money. The openness and responsiveness of the alternative tradition developed in the nineteenth century and later taken up by the polytechnics and the Open University contributed yet another strand. But if there is one theme which is common to conservative, liberal and socialist university traditions in Britain, it is that universities exist for the self-development of the individual, through training of the mind within a community of learning and

culture, and not for instrumental ends. This forms a distinctive contribution, shaped by prophets like Newman and Arnold, to the idealist
history of the western university. No one today talks of universities giving spiritual leadership to a society in crisis, nor would it be convincing
if they did. The age when universities shaped only a narrow elite and
represented their class-bound culture is over. Yet there must be more to
university education than the pursuit of individual ambition or economic utility. To make the old ideal live in an expanded and necessarily
differentiated university system, where it has to coexist with vocational
training and with research driven by outside needs rather than the self-
sufficient pursuit of truth, is a challenge. If it is to succeed, it can only
be by going with the grain of the universities' own traditions and values, and there is surely still inspiration, in a society of unprecedented
complexity and cultural pluralism, to be drawn from the usable past.

Notes

Notes to Chapter 1: Serving Church and State

1. A. B. Cobban, *The Medieval English Universities: Oxford and Cambridge to c. 1500* (Aldershot, 1988), p. 409.
2. Ibid., pp. 118–19.
3. T. Evans, 'The Number, Origins and Careers of Scholars', in J. I. Catto and R. Evans (eds), *The History of the University of Oxford*, ii, *Late Medieval Oxford* (Oxford, 1992), pp. 485–538; T. H. Aston et al., 'The Medieval Alumni of the University of Cambridge', *Past and Present*, 86 (1980), pp. 40–51.
4. H. Rashdall, *The Universities of Europe in the Middle Ages*, ed. F. M. Powicke and A. B. Emden (London 1936; original edn, 1895), iii, p. 456.
5. Cobban, *Medieval English Universities*, pp. 14–15, 161.
6. F. D. Logan, 'The First Royal Visitation of the English Universities, 1535', *English Historical Review*, 106 (1991), pp. 861–88.
7. See chapters by J. McConica and J. M. Fletcher in J. McConica (ed.), *The History of the University of Oxford*, iii, *The Collegiate University* (Oxford, 1986).
8. Ibid., p. 52.
9. L. Stone, 'The Educational Revolution in England, 1560–1640', *Past and Present*, 28 (1964), pp. 41–80.
10. K. Charlton, *Education in Renaissance England* (London, 1965), pp. 149–50; J. H. Hexter, 'The Education of the Aristocracy in the Renaissance', in *Reappraisals in History: New Views on History and Society in Early Modern Europe* (New York, 1961), pp. 45–70.
11. J. Simon, 'The Social Origins of Cambridge Students, 1603–1640', *Past and Present*, 26 (1963), pp. 58–67; R. O'Day, *Education and Society, 1500–1800: The Social Foundations of Education in Early Modern Britain* (London, 1982), pp. 81–88.
12. J. McConica in L. Stone (ed.), *The University in Society*, i, *Oxford and*

Cambridge from the Fourteenth to the Early Nineteenth Century (Princeton, 1975), p. 175.

13. D. R. Leader, *A History of the University of Cambridge*, i, *The University to 1546* (Cambridge, 1988), p. 35; Cobban, *Medieval English Universities*, p. 122; Aston et al., 'Medieval Alumni', pp. 85–86; T. H. Aston, 'Oxford's Medieval Alumni', *Past and Present*, 74 (1977), p. 7.

14. Charlton, *Education in Renaissance England*, pp. 135–36; N. Tyacke (ed.), *The History of the University of Oxford*, iv, *Seventeenth-Century Oxford* (Oxford, 1997), pp. 40, 45; V. Morgan, 'Cambridge University and "The Country", 1560–1640', in Stone, *University in Society*, i, p. 226.

15. Stone, 'Educational Revolution', p. 57.

16. L. Stone, 'The Size and Composition of the Oxford Student Body, 1580–1910', in Stone, *University in Society*, i, pp. 6, 89, 91–92, 110; Tyacke, *Seventeenth-Century Oxford*, pp. 31–34.

17. Stone, 'Educational Revolution', p. 69.

18. Ibid., p. 175; Tyacke, *Seventeenth-Century Oxford*, pp. 182–83.

19. Message to Oxford University, 1636: K. Sharpe, 'Archbishop Laud and the University of Oxford', in H. Lloyd-Jones et al. (eds), *History and Imagination: Essays in Honour of H. R. Trevor-Roper* (London, 1981), p. 152.

20. C. Cross in McConica, *Collegiate University*, p. 117.

21. Ibid., p. 330.

22. J. Twigg, *The University of Cambridge and the English Revolution, 1625–1688* (Woodbridge, 1990), p. 60.

23. Ibid., pp. 212–33.

24. Cited in J. Gascoigne, *Cambridge in the Age of the Enlightenment: Science, Religion and Politics from the Restoration to the French Revolution* (Cambridge, 1989), p. 18.

25. M. H. Curtis, 'The Alienated Intellectuals of Early Stuart England', *Past and Present*, 23 (1962), pp. 25–49.

26. Humphrey Prideaux, dean of Norwich, cited in J. Gascoigne, 'Church and State Allied: The Failure of Parliamentary Reform of the Universities, 1688–1800', in L. Beier et al. (eds), *The First Modern Society: Essays in English History in Honour of Lawrence Stone* (Cambridge, 1989), p. 411.

27. Ibid., p. 417 (1733).

28. S. Vance, 'Poverty and the Pursuit of Learning: Poor Scholars in Seventeenth-Century Aberdeen', *History of Universities*, 18, no. 2 (2003), pp. 90–146.

29. M. Lynch et al., *The University of Edinburgh: An Illustrated History* (Edinburgh, 2003), pp. 35–36.

30. C. A. McLaren, *Aberdeen Students, 1600–1860* (Aberdeen, 2005), p. 52.

31. J. Carter, 'British Universities and Revolution, 1688–1718', in P. Dukes and J. Dunkley (eds), *Culture and Revolution* (London, 1990), pp. 15–18; D. B. Horn, *A Short History of the University of Edinburgh, 1556–1889* (Edinburgh, 1967), pp. 36–40.

32. Stone, 'Educational Revolution', pp. 79–80; Tyacke, *Seventeenth-Century Oxford*, p. 2. This volume includes pioneering chapters by M. Feingold on the curriculum.

33. Curtis, *Oxford and Cambridge*, p. 228; R. Porter, 'The Scientific Revolution and Universities', in H. de Ridder-Symoens (ed.), *A History of the University in Europe*, ii, *Universities in Early Modern Europe, 1500–1800* (Cambridge, 1996), p. 548.

Notes to Chapter 2: Currents of Change

1. *Supplement to the Fourth, Fifth and Sixth Editions of the Encyclopaedia Britannica* (Edinburgh, 1824), i, p. 16.

2. M. Sanderson, *The Universities in the Nineteenth Century* (London, 1975), p. 67.

3. R. L. Emerson, 'Scottish Universities in the Eighteenth Century, 1690–1800', *Studies on Voltaire and the Eighteenth Century*, 167 (1977), pp. 456, 473; P. Searby, *A History of the University of Cambridge*, iii, *1750–1870* (Cambridge, 1997), p. 11.

4. Cited in M. Lynch et al., *The University of Edinburgh: An Illustrated History* (Edinburgh, 2003), p. 71.

5. P. Wood, *The Aberdeen Enlightenment: The Arts Curriculum in the Eighteenth Century* (Aberdeen, 1993), p. 71.

6. W. M. Mathew, 'The Origins and Occupations of Glasgow Students, 1740–1839', *Past and Present*, 33 (1966), pp. 74–94.

7. *The Autobiography and Correspondence of Edward Gibbon, the Historian* (London, 1869; original edn 1796), pp. 25, 27, 49.

8. H. Kearney, *Scholars and Gentlemen: Universities and Society in Pre-Industrial Britain, 1500–1700* (London, 1970), pp. 158–59, 171.

9. Cited in L. S. Sutherland and L. G. Mitchell (eds), *The History of the University of Oxford*, v, *The Eighteenth Century* (Oxford, 1986), p. 467.

10. J. Gascoigne, *Cambridge in the Age of the Enlightenment: Science, Religion and Politics from the Restoration to the French Revolution* (Cambridge, 1989), p. 21.

11. Ibid., p. 19; J. Cannon, *Aristocratic Century: The Peerage of Eighteenth-Century England* (Cambridge, 1984), p. 47; M. G. Brock and

M. C. Curthoys (eds), *The History of the University of Oxford*, v, *Nineteenth-Century Oxford*, part 1 (Oxford, 1997), pp. 478–79.

12. Gascoigne, *Cambridge*, p. 22; L. Colley, *Britons: Forging the Nation, 1707–1837* (London, 1994), p. 167.

13. P. Searby, *A history of the University of Cambridge*, iii, *1750–1870* (Cambridge, 1997), pp. 562–65.

14. C. Stray, 'From Oral to Written Examinations: Cambridge, Oxford and Dublin, 1700–1914', *History of Universities*, 20, no. 2 (2005), pp. 76–130.

15. H. W. Becher, 'The Social Origins and Post-Graduate Careers of a Cambridge Intellectual Elite, 1830–1860', *Victorian Studies*, 28 (1984–85), pp. 97–127; S. Rothblatt, 'The Student Sub-Culture and the Examination System in Early 19th Century Oxbridge', in L. Stone (ed.), *The University in Society*, i, *Oxford and Cambridge from the Fourteenth to the Early Nineteenth Century* (Princeton, 1975), pp. 280–96.

16. D. A. Winstanley, *Later Victorian Cambridge* (Cambridge, 1947), p. 147.

17. Gascoigne, *Cambridge*, p. 2.

18. Searby, *University of Cambridge*, pp. 298–303; M. M. Garland, *Cambridge before Darwin: The Ideal of a Liberal Education, 1800–1860* (Cambridge, 1980), p. 57.

19. H. H. Bellot, *University College London, 1826–1926* (London, 1929), p. 48.

20. S. Rothblatt, 'London: a Metropolitan University?', in T. Bender (ed.), *The University and the City: From Medieval Origins to the Present* (New York, 1988), pp. 119–49.

21. Humboldt, cited in R. D. Anderson, *European Universities from the Enlightenment to 1914* (Oxford, 2004), p. 56. For this background, see also L. Brockliss, 'The European University in the Age of Revolution, 1789–1850', in Brock and Curthoys, *University of Oxford*, vi, pp. 77–133.

22. K. Jaspers, *The Idea of the University* (London, 1960), pp. 52, 65, 67, 129.

23. A. J. Engel, *From Clergyman to Don: The Rise of the Academic Profession in Nineteenth-Century Oxford* (Oxford, 1983), pp. 21–22.

24. Cited in Anderson, *European Universities*, p. 58.

25. W. Hamilton, *Discussions on Philosophy and Literature, Education and University Reform* (London, 1852), p. 343.

26. *The Scotsman*, 6 January 1858; J. S. Blackie, *Education in Scotland: An Appeal to the Scottish People on the Improvement of their Scholastic and Academical Institutions* (Edinburgh, 1846), p. 5.

Notes to Chapter 3: Oxbridge Reformed

1. M. G. Brock and M. C. Curthoys (eds), *The History of the University of Oxford*, vi, *Nineteenth-Century Oxford*, part 1 (Oxford, 1997), p. 145.

2. L. Goldman, *Dons and Workers: Oxford and Adult Education since 1850* (Oxford, 1995), p. 17; J. Sparrow, *Mark Pattison and the Idea of a University* (Cambridge, 1967), p. 94.

3. W. R. Ward, *Victorian Oxford* (London, 1965), p. 123.

4. V. H. H. Green, *Oxford Common Room: A Study of Lincoln College and Mark Pattison* (London, 1957), pp. 239–43.

5. Quoted (1835) in Brock and Curthoys, *University of Oxford*, vi, p. 219.

6. W. M. Thackeray, *The History of Pendennis*, Nelson edn (London, 1899), pp. 34, 213.

7. N. Annan, *Leslie Stephen: The Godless Victorian* (New York, 1984), p. 25.

8. J. Gascoigne, *Cambridge in the Age of the Enlightenment: Science, Religion and Politics from the Restoration to the French Revolution* (Cambridge, 1989), pp. 272–74; P. Searby, *A History of the University of Cambridge*, iii, *1750–1870* (Cambridge, 1997), p. 185.

9. H. Lloyd-Jones, *Blood for the Ghosts: Classical Influences in the Nineteenth and Twentieth Centuries* (London, 1982), p. 82. Cf. C. Stray, *Classics Transformed: Schools, Universities and Society in England, 1830–1960* (Oxford, 1998), p. 60.

10. Whewell quoted (1849) in Searby, *University of Cambridge*, p. 517; M. G. Brock and M. C. Curthoys (eds), *The History of the University of Oxford*, vii, *Nineteenth-Century Oxford*, part 2 (Oxford, 2000), p. 68.

11. A. D. Culler, *The Imperial Intellect: A Study of Newman's Educational Ideal* (New Haven, 1955), p. 38. Cf. S. Rothblatt, *Tradition and Change in English Liberal Education: An Essay in History and Culture* (London, 1976), p. 130.

12. M. Sanderson, *The Universities in the Nineteenth Century* (London, 1975), p. 68.

13. M. M. Garland, *Cambridge before Darwin: The Ideal of a Liberal Education, 1800–1860* (Cambridge, 1980), p. 45.

14. Cited (1854) in M. Richter, *The Politics of Conscience: T. H. Green and his Age* (London, 1964), p. 61.

15. T. Hughes, *Tom Brown's School Days*, new edn (London, 1890), p. 100.

16. H. S. Jones in Brock and Curthoys, *University of Oxford*, vii, p. 532.

17. J. Roach, 'Victorian Universities and the National Intelligentsia', *Victorian Studies*, 3 (1959–60), p. 145.

18. Cited in E. G. W. Bill, *University Reform in Nineteenth-Century Oxford: A Study of Henry Halford Vaughan, 1811–1885* (Oxford, 1973), p. 86.

19. L. Brockliss, in Brock and Curthoys, *University of Oxford*, vi, pp. 132–33. Cf. F. Ringer in W. Rüegg (ed.), *A History of the University in Europe*, iii, *Universities in the Nineteenth and Early Twentieth Centuries, 1800–1945* (Cambridge, 2004), pp. 249–50.

20. J. Prest (ed.), *The Illustrated History of Oxford University* (Oxford, 1993), p. 196; D. A. Winstanley, *Later Victorian Cambridge* (Cambridge, 1947), p. 340.

21. C. N. L. Brooke, *A History of the University of Cambridge*, iv, *1870–1990* (Cambridge, 1993), p. 103.

22. A. J. Engel, *From Clergyman to Don: The Rise of the Academic Profession in Nineteenth-Century Oxford* (Oxford, 1983), pp. 113–14.

23. H. McLeod, *Secularisation in Western Europe, 1848–1914* (Basingstoke, 2000), pp. 75–76.

24. Brock and Curthoys, *University of Oxford*, vii, p. 56.

25. J. S. Mill, *On Liberty and Other Essays*, ed. J. Gray (Oxford, 1991), p. 39.

26. R. Soffer, *Discipline and Power: The University, History, and the Making of an English Elite, 1870–1930* (Stanford, 1994), p. 91.

27. S. Rothblatt, *The Revolution of the Dons: Cambridge and Society in Victorian England* (London, 1968), p. 231; J. Smith and C. Stray (eds), *Teaching and Learning in Nineteenth-Century Cambridge* (Woodbridge, 2001), pp. 114–15; cf. Brock and Curthoys, *University of Oxford*, vii, pp. 133–35, B. Harrison (ed.), *The History of the University of Oxford*, viii, *The Twentieth Century* (Oxford, 1994), pp. 127–33.

28. Brooke, *University of Cambridge*, p. 290.

29. M. C. Curthoys and H. S. Jones, 'Oxford Athleticism, 1850–1914: A Reappraisal', *History of Education*, 24 (1995), pp. 305–17; Rothblatt, *Tradition and Change*, p. 136.

30. Brock and Curthoys, *University of Oxford*, vi, p. 370; G. W. Roderick and M. D. Stephens (eds), *Where Did We Go Wrong? Industrial Performance, Education and the Economy in Victorian Britain* (Lewes, 1981), pp. 192–93; cf. Brooke, *University of Cambridge*, pp. 295–96.

31. Prest, *Illustrated History*, p. 319.

Notes to Chapter 4: Effortless Superiority

1. J. Jones, *Balliol College: A History, 1263–1939* (Oxford, 1988), p. 226.

2. M. Richter, *The Politics of Conscience: T. H. Green and his Age* (London, 1964), p. 12.

3. M. G. Brock and M. C. Curthoys (eds), *The History of the University of Oxford*, vii, *Nineteenth-Century Oxford*, part 2 (Oxford, 2000), p. 329.

4. G. M. Young, *Victorian England: Portrait of an Age* (Oxford, 1960), p. 96.

5. E. Abbott and L. Campbell, *The Life and Letters of Benjamin Jowett* (London, 1897), i, p. 151.

6. Trevelyan cited in W. D. Rubinstein, 'The End of "Old Corruption" in Britain, 1780–1860', *Past and Present*, 101 (1983), p. 78; Gladstone to Lord John Russell, 1854, cited in J. Roach, *Public Examinations in England, 1850–1900* (Cambridge, 1971), p. 193.

7. See R. D. Anderson, *Universities and Elites in Britain since 1800* (2nd edn, Cambridge, 1995), pp. 31–41. Recent statements of the second tendency include E. J. Hobsbawm, 'The Example of the English Middle Class', in J. Kocka and A. Mitchell (eds), *Bourgeois Society in Nineteenth-Century Europe* (Oxford, 1993), pp. 127–50; F. M. L. Thompson, *Gentrification and the Enterprise Culture: Britain, 1780–1980* (Oxford, 2001), pp. 122–42.

8. H. W. Becher, 'The Social Origins and Post-Graduate Careers of a Cambridge Intellectual Elite, 1830–1860', *Victorian Studies*, 28 (1984–85), p. 125.

9. R. N. Soffer, 'The Modern University and National Values, 1850–1930', *Historical Research*, 60 (1987), p. 166.

10. D. Cannadine, *G. M. Trevelyan: A Life in History* (London, 1993), p. 236.

11. 'The Intellectual Aristocracy', reprinted in N. Annan, *The Dons: Mentors, Eccentrics and Geniuses* (London, 1999), pp. 304–41.

12. S. Rothblatt, *The Revolution of the Dons: Cambridge and Society in Victorian England* (London, 1968), pp. 86–93.

13. V. A. McClelland, *English Roman Catholics and Higher Education, 1830–1903* (Oxford, 1973), p. 207.

14. C. Harvie, *The Lights of Liberalism: University Liberals and the Challenge of Democracy, 1860–86* (London, 1976), p. 14.

15. L. Dowling, *Hellenism and Homosexuality in Victorian Oxford* (Ithaca, 1994), p. 123.

16. Hobsbawm, 'Example of the English Middle Class', p. 138; R. D. Anderson, *European Universities from the Enlightenment to 1914* (Oxford, 2004), p. 149.

17. Jones, *Balliol College*, p. 227.

18. R. Jenkins, *Asquith* (London, 1964), p. 519.

19. Brock and Curthoys, *University of Oxford*, vii, p. 572.

20. R. Symonds in ibid., p. 706.

21. L. Stone, 'The Size and Composition of the Oxford Student Body, 1580–1910', in L. Stone (ed.), *The University in Society*, i, *Oxford and Cambridge from the Fourteenth to the Early Nineteenth Century* (Princeton, 1975), p. 68.

22. Brock and Curthoys, *University of Oxford*, vii, pp. 554, 566–68.

23. C. Brooke, *A History of Gonville and Caius College* (Woodbridge, 1996), p. 207.

24. Stone, 'Size and Composition', pp. 66–67, 103; Brock and Curthoys, *University of Oxford*, vii, p. 578; B. Harrison (ed.), *The History of the University of Oxford*, viii, *The Twentieth Century* (Oxford, 1994), p. 56; H. Jenkins and D. C. Jones, 'Social Class of Cambridge University Alumni of the Eighteenth and Nineteenth Centuries', *British Journal of Sociology*, 1 (1950), p. 99.

25. E. Waugh, *Decline and Fall* (1928), 'Prelude'.

26. Brock and Curthoys, *University of Oxford*, vii, p. 633.

27. J. Howarth, ' "In Oxford but … not of Oxford": the Women's Colleges', in ibid., pp. 237–307. Cf. F. Perrone, 'Women Academics in England, 1870–1930', *History of Universities*, 12 (1993), pp. 339–67.

28. Ibid., p. 126.

29. Ibid., pp. 14, 163.

30. Cited (1867) in ibid., p. 204.

31. Cited in Brock and Curthoys, *University of Oxford*, vi, p. 726.

32. Anderson, *European Universities*, pp. 199, 207.

33. V. Brittain, *Testament of Youth*, Fontana edn (Glasgow, 1979), pp. 59–63.

34. L. Goldman, *Dons and Workers: Oxford and Adult Education since 1850* (Oxford, 1995), pp. 127–28.

35. S. Harrop (ed.), *Oxford and Working-Class Education* (reprint, Nottingham, 1987), pp. 142, 146.

36. Hansard, 4th series, 178, cols 1527–29 (24 July 1907).

37. Cited (1914) in R. D. Anderson, *Education and Opportunity in Victorian Scotland: Schools and Universities* (Oxford, 1983), pp. 250–51.

38. Goldman, *Dons and Workers*, pp. 87, 105; L. Goldman, 'Intellectuals and the English Working Class, 1870–1945: The Case of Adult Education', *History of Education*, 29 (2000), pp. 281–300.

39. H. Rashdall, *The Universities of Europe in the Middle Ages*, ed. F. M. Powicke and A. B. Emden (London 1936; orig. 1895), i, p. 533.

40. *Hansard*, 3rd series, 132, cols 767 (7 April 1854), 954, 959, 975 (27 April 1854).

Notes to Chapter 5: Province and Metropolis

1. E. Shils, *The Intellectuals and the Powers, and Other Essays* (Chicago, 1972), p. 145 (originally in *Encounter*, 1955).

2. R. Lowe, 'The Expansion of Higher Education in England', in K. H. Jarausch (ed.), *The Transformation of Higher Learning, 1860–1930: Expansion, Diversification, Social Opening, and Professionalization in*

England, Germany, Russia, and the United States (Chicago, 1983), p. 45; R. D. Anderson, *Education and Opportunity in Victorian Scotland: Schools and Universities* (Oxford, 1983), p. 351.

3. University Grants Committee, *Report for the Period 1929–30 to 1934–35* (London, 1936), pp. 52–53.

4. F. M. Turner, *Contesting Cultural Authority: Essays in Victorian Intellectual Life* (Cambridge, 1993), p. 175.

5. J. S. Maclure, *Educational Documents, England and Wales, 1816–1963* (London, 1965), p. 110.

6. Anderson, *Education and Opportunity*, pp. 98–102.

7. J. Roach, *Public Examinations in England, 1850–1900* (Cambridge, 1971), p. 4.

8. B. Simon, 'Systematisation and Segmentation in Education: The Case of England', in D. Müller et al. (eds), *The Rise of the Modern Educational System: Structural Change and Social Reproduction, 1870–1920* (Cambridge, 1987), pp. 88–108.

9. G. Sutherland, 'The Movement for the Higher Education of Women: Its Social and Intellectual Context in England, c. 1840–80', in P. J. Waller (ed.), *Politics and Social Change in Modern Britain: Essays Presented to A. F. Thompson* (Brighton, 1987), pp. 97–98.

10. T. Kelly, *For Advancement of Learning: The University of Liverpool, 1881–1981* (Liverpool, 1981), pp. 35–37.

11. F. M. L. Thompson (ed.), *The University of London and the World of Learning, 1836–1986* (London, 1990), pp. xvii–xix.

12. T. N. Bonner, *To the Ends of the Earth: Women's Search for Education in Medicine* (Cambridge, Massachusetts, 1992), pp. 133–37.

13. F. M. G. Willson, *The University of London, 1858–1900: The Politics of Senate and Convocation* (Woodbridge, 2004), p. 1; F. M. G. Willson, *Our Minerva: The Men and Politics of the University of London, 1836–1858* (London, 1995), pp. 178–79.

14. C. E. Whiting, *The University of Durham, 1832–1932* (London, 1932), p. 97.

15. E. Fiddes, *Chapters in the History of Owens College and of Manchester University, 1851–1914* (Manchester, 1937), p. 51.

16. E. Ives, D. Drummond and L. Schwarz, *The First Civic University: Birmingham, 1880–1980: An Introductory History* (Birmingham, 2000), p. 58; Fiddes, *Chapters*, p. 85.

17. A. W. Chapman, *The Story of a Modern University: A History of the University of Sheffield* (London, 1955), pp. 202–4.

18. K. Vernon, *Universities and the State in England, 1850–1939* (London, 2004), pp. 115–23.

19. H. G. Wells, *Experiment in Autobiography*, i (London, 1934), p. 201.

20. W. H. G. Armytage, *Civic Universities: Aspects of a British Tradition* (London, 1955), pp. 229–30.

21. M. Argles, *South Kensington to Robbins: An Account of English Technical and Scientific Education since 1851* (London, 1964), p. 40.

22. R. D. Anderson, 'Universities and Elites in Modern Britain', *History of Universities*, 10 (1991), p. 238.

23. D. H. Lawrence, *The Rainbow*, ch. 15.

24. Anderson, 'Universities and Elites', pp. 238–39.

25. A. C. Wood, *A History of the University College, Nottingham, 1881–1948* (Oxford, 1953), pp. 38–40, 46–54.

26. D. H. Lawrence, 'Nottingham's New University'.

27. Ives, Drummond and Schwarz, *First Civic University*, pp. 12–13.

28. T. H. Huxley, *Science and Education: Essays* (London, 1910), p. 157.

29. Ives, Drummond and Schwarz, *First Civic University*, pp. xv, 66, 98, 245–46.

30. D. R. Jones, *The Origins of Civic Universities: Manchester, Leeds and Liverpool* (London, 1988), p. 3; Armytage, *Civic Universities*, p. 243.

31. Kelly, *Advancement of Learning*, pp. 52, 60, 83; Jones, *Origins*, pp. 66–72.

32. A. H. Halsey and M. Trow, *The British Academics* (London, 1971), pp. 39–41; R. Lowe, 'The Expansion of Higher Education in England', in Jarausch, *Transformation of Higher Learning*; R. Lowe, 'Structural Change in English Higher Education, 1870–1920', in Müller, *Rise of the Modern Educational System.*

33. J. Garnett in C. Matthew (ed.), *The Nineteenth Century: The British Isles, 1815–1901* (Oxford, 2000), p. 213; M. Sanderson, 'The English Civic Universities and the "Industrial Spirit", 1870–1914', *Historical Research*, 61 (1988), pp. 90–104.

34. Kelly, *Advancement of Learning*, pp. 149–51.

35. M. Sanderson, *The Universities and British Industry, 1850–1970* (London, 1972), pp. 184–213; E. W. Vincent and P. Hinton, *The University of Birmingham: Its History and Significance* (Birmingham, 1947), pp. 136–37.

36. F. Bédarida, *A Social History of England, 1851–1990* (2nd edn, London, 1991), pp. 48, 151–52.

37. Anderson, 'Universities and Elites', p. 233.

38. A. H. Halsey, J. Floud and C. A. Anderson (eds), *Education, Economy and Society: A Reader in the Sociology of Education* (New York, 1961), p. 462.

39. Vernon, *Universities and the State*, p. 134. Cf. K. Vernon, 'Calling the Tune: British Universities and the State, 1880–1914', *History of Education*, 30 (2001), pp. 251–71.

40. UGC, *Report for the Period 1929–30 to 1934–35*, pp. 52–53.

41. R. D. Anderson, *European Universities from the Enlightenment to 1914* (Oxford, 2004), p. 126.

42. Maclure, *Educational Documents*, pp. 150, 153.

43. P. Gosden, *Education in the Second World War: A Study in Policy and Administration* (London, 1976), p. 389.

44. H. C. Dent, *Universities in Transition* (London, 1961), p. 107.

45. M. G. Brock and M. C. Curthoys (eds), *The History of the University of Oxford*, vii, *Nineteenth-century Oxford*, part 2 (Oxford, 2000), p. 555.

46. W. B. Childs, *Making a University: An Account of the University Movement at Reading* (London, 1933), pp. 167–84.

47. E. Ashby and M. Anderson, *Portrait of Haldane at Work on Education* (London, 1974), pp. 45–46, 63, 113. (The term 'tertiary' never really caught on.)

48. R. B. Haldane, *Education and Empire: Addresses on Certain Topics of the Day* (London, 1902), pp. ix–x, 44–45, 75.

49. R. B. Haldane, *Universities and National Life: Three Addresses to Students* (London, 1910), pp. 95, 109.

50. Thompson, *University of London*, p. 68.

51. F. J. C. Hearnshaw, *The Centenary History of King's College, London, 1828–1928* (London, 1929), pp. 341–42, 354, 408.

52. Haldane cited in Ashby and Anderson, *Portrait of Haldane*, p. 126.

53. P. Alter, *The Reluctant Patron: Science and the State in Britain, 1850–1920* (Oxford, 1987), pp. 138–90. Cf. G. R. Searle, *A New England? Peace and War, 1886–1918* (Oxford, 2004), pp. 626–35.

54. Vernon, *Universities and the State*, p. 148.

55. Chapman, *Story of a Modern University*, p. 255.

56. Ibid., pp. 201, 249.

57. Anderson, *Education and Opportunity*, p. 289.

58. Searle, *A New England?*, p. 630.

59. Ashby and Anderson, *Portrait of Haldane*, pp. 92–93, 114–19.

60. G. Sherington, *English Education, Social Change and War, 1911–20* (Manchester, 1981), passim.

Notes to Chapter 6: National Identities

1. Notably E. J. Hobsbawm and Ernest Gellner: see R. D. Anderson, *European Universities from the Enlightenment to 1914* (Oxford, 2004), pp. 138–39.

2. R. D. Anderson, *Education and Opportunity in Victorian Scotland: Schools and Universities* (Oxford, 1983), pp. 260, 289.

3. D. Withrington, 'The Idea of a National University in Scotland,

c. 1820–*c.* 1870', in J. Carter and D. Withrington (eds), *Scottish Universities: Distinctiveness and Diversity* (Edinburgh, 1992), pp. 40–55.

4. *Report ... by a Royal Commission of Inquiry into the State of the Universities of Scotland* (London, 1831), pp. 9, 11.

5. *General Report of the Commissioners under the Universities (Scotland) Act, 1858* (Edinburgh, 1863), p. xxix.

6. Anderson, *Education and Opportunity*, pp. 74–77, 283–84.

7. Ibid., p. 301.

8. Notably in the very influential but controversial G. Davie, *The Democratic Intellect: Scotland and her Universities in the Nineteenth Century* (2nd edn, Edinburgh, 1964; orig. edn 1961). Cf. R. D. Anderson, *Scottish Education since the Reformation* (Dundee, 1997), pp. 30–35.

9. R. D. Anderson, *The Student Community at Aberdeen, 1860–1939* (Aberdeen, 1988), p. 11.

10. Anderson, *Education and Opportunity*, pp. 348–56.

11. R. D. Anderson, *Education and the Scottish People, 1750–1918* (Oxford, 1995), pp. 274–78.

12. R. D. Anderson, 'In Search of the "Lad of Parts": The Mythical History of Scottish Education', *History Workshop*, 19 (1985), pp. 82–104.

13. Anderson, *Education and Opportunity*, pp. 148–61, 294–335.

14. W. C. Davies and W. L. Jones, *The University of Wales and its Constituent Colleges* (London, 1905), p. 91.

15. J. S. Maclure, *Educational Documents, England and Wales, 1816–1963* (London, 1965), pp. 113, 119.

16. Ibid., p. 120.

17. R. D. Anderson, *Universities and Elites in Britain since 1800* (2nd edn, Cambridge, 1995), pp. 234–35.

18. J. G. Williams, *A History of the University of Wales*, ii, *The University of Wales, 1893–1939* (Cardiff, 1997), pp. 295, 361–64.

19. K. O. Morgan, *Rebirth of a Nation: Wales, 1880–1980* (Oxford, 1981), p. 111.

20. M. Sanderson, *The Universities and British Industry, 1850–1970* (London, 1972), pp. 121–45; G. W. Roderick, 'Education, Culture and Industry in Wales in the Nineteenth Century', *Welsh History Review*, 13 (1986–87), pp. 438–52; G. W. Roderick and D. A. Allsobrook, 'Welsh Society and University Funding, 1867–1914', *Welsh History Review*, 20 (2000), pp. 34–61.

21. C. Harvie, 'The Folk and the *Gwerin*: The Myth and the Reality of Popular Culture in Nineteenth-Century Scotland and Wales', *Proceedings of the British Academy*, 80 (1991), pp. 19–48.

22. Davies and Jones, *University of Wales*, p. xi; A. C. Fryer, *Llantwit Major: A Fifth-Century University* (London, 1893), p. 26.

23. J. G. Williams, *A History of the University of Wales*, i, *The University Movement in Wales* (Cardiff, 1993), pp. 57, 93–94, 99–100, 182, 189–90.

24. R. B. Haldane, *Universities and National Life: Three Addresses to Students* (London, 1910), p. 31.

25. Peel (1844), cited in T. W. Moody and J. C. Beckett, *Queen's Belfast, 1845–1949: The History of a University* (London, 1959), p. 1.

26. Ibid., p. 140.

27. Cited in F. McGrath, *Newman's University: Idea and Reality* (London, 1951), p. 456.

28. R. F. Foster, *W. B. Yeats: A Life*, i, *The Apprentice Mage 1865–1914* (Oxford, 1998), p. 35; cf. R. B. McDowell and D. A. Webb, *Trinity College Dublin, 1592–1952: An Academic History* (Cambridge, 1982), pp. 324–25, 507.

29. McDowell and Webb, *Trinity College Dublin*, p. 364.

30. Anderson, 'Universities and Elites', p. 233.

31. T. W. Moody, 'The Irish University Question of the Nineteenth Century', *History*, 43 (1958), p. 109.

Notes to Chapter 7: Ideas of the University

1. J. H. Newman, *The Idea of a University Defined and Illustrated*, ed. M. J. Svaglic (New York, 1960), pp. 76, 135.

2. Ibid., p. 92.

3. Ibid., pp. xxxvii, xl.

4. M. Arnold, *Essays in Criticism: First Series* (London, Macmillan, 1928; orig. 1865), p. xi; 'dreaming spires' in his poem 'Thyrsis'.

5. S. T. Coleridge, *On the Constitution of the Church and State According to the Idea of Each*, Everyman edn (London, 1972), p. 34.

6. R. D. Anderson, 'Education and the State in Nineteenth-Century Scotland', *Economic History Review*, 2nd series, 36 (1983), pp. 532–33; R. D. Anderson, *Education and Opportunity in Victorian Scotland: Schools and Universities* (Oxford, 1983), pp. 57–58.

7. M. Arnold, *Schools and Universities on the Continent*, Complete Prose Works, ed. R. H. Super (Ann Arbor, 1964), iv, p. 288.

8. M. Arnold, *Democratic Education*, Complete Prose Works, ed. R. H. Super (Ann Arbor, 1962), ii, p. 157 (orig. 1861).

9. Ibid., p. 315 (orig. 1864).

10. Arnold, *Schools and Universities*, pp. 322–23.

11. M. Arnold, *Culture and Anarchy*, ed. J. D. Wilson (Cambridge, 1932), p. 6; Sophocles, in Arnold's sonnet 'To a Friend', 'saw life steadily ...'

12. F. M. Turner, *Contesting Cultural Authority: Essays in Victorian Intellectual Life* (Cambridge, 1993), p. 44.

13. John Morley, quoted in C. Harvie, *The Lights of Liberalism: University Liberals and the Challenge of Democracy, 1860–86* (London, 1976), p. 11.

14. Arnold, *Democratic Education*, p. 324.

15. C. Harvie, in M. G. Brock and M. C. Curthoys (eds), *The History of the University of Oxford*, vi, *Nineteenth-Century Oxford*, part 1 (Oxford, 1997), pp. 718–21.

16. Cited (1868) in V. H. H. Green, *Oxford Common Room: A Study of Lincoln College and Mark Pattison* (London, 1957), p. 242.

17. J. Sparrow, *Mark Pattison and the Idea of a University* (Cambridge, 1967), p. 118; Arnold, *Schools and Universities*, p. 68.

18. Arnold, *Schools and Universities*, p. 318.

19. Ibid., pp. 299–300.

20. Useful extracts are in M. Sanderson, *The Universities in the Nineteenth Century* (London, 1975), pp. 115–41.

21. Arnold, *Schools and Universities*, p. 292.

22. Sanderson, *Universities*, pp. 127–29.

23. Anderson, *Education and Opportunity*, p. 86.

24. R. D. Anderson, 'Scottish University Professors, 1800–1939: Profile of an Elite', *Scottish Economic and Social History*, 7 (1987), pp. 42–46.

25. R. Simpson, *How the PhD Came to Britain: A Century of Struggle for Postgraduate Education* (Guildford, 1983).

26. J. Demogeot and H. Montucci, *De l'enseignement supérieur en Angleterre et en Écosse* (Paris, 1870), p. 348. Cf. S. Rothblatt, 'Historical and Comparative Remarks on the Federal Principle in Higher Education', *History of Education*, 16 (1987), pp. 151–80.

27. F. M. G. Willson, *The University of London, 1858–1900: The Politics of Senate and Convocation* (Woodbridge, 2004), pp. 222, 269–70.

28. C. E. Mallet, *A History of the University of Oxford*, iii, *Modern Oxford* (London, 1927), p. 450; cf. W. R. Ward, *Victorian Oxford* (London, 1965), p. 294.

29. Cf. S. Rothblatt, 'State and Market in British University History', in S. Collini et al. (eds), *Economy, Polity and Society: British Intellectual History, 1750–1950* (Cambridge, 2000), pp. 224–42.

Notes to Chapter 8: Interwar Conservatism

1. J. Carswell, *Government and the Universities in Britain: Programme and Performance, 1960–1980* (Cambridge, 1985), p. 12.

2. C. H. Shinn, *Paying the Piper: The Development of the University Grants Committee, 1919–46* (Lewes, 1986), p. 128.

3. E. Ashby, *Technology and the Academics: An Essay on Universities and the Scientific Revolution* (London, 1958), p. 91.

4. P. Gosden, *Education in the Second World War: A Study in Policy and Administration* (London, 1976), p. 151.

5. A. Flexner, *Universities American, English, German* (New York, 1930), p. 251.

6. C. G. Robertson, *The British Universities* (2nd edn, London, 1944), p. 53 (orig. 1930).

7. A. W. Chapman, *The Story of a Modern University: A History of the University of Sheffield* (London, 1955), p. 67.

8. L. Robbins, *The University in the Modern World and Other Papers on Higher Education* (London, 1966), p. 48.

9. R. O. Berdahl, *British Universities and the State* (London, 1959), p. 77; Carswell, *Government and the Universities*, p. 13.

10. K. Vernon, *Universities and the State in England, 1850–1939* (London, 2004), p. 190.

11. A. C. Wood, *A History of the University College, Nottingham, 1881–1948* (Oxford, 1953), p. 119.

12. R. D. Anderson, *Universities and Elites in Britain since 1800* (2nd edn, Cambridge, 1995), pp. 15–16.

13. Chapman, *Story of a Modern University*, pp. 369–70.

14. Carswell, *Government and the Universities*, p. 3.

15. W. A. C. Stewart, *Higher Education in Postwar Britain* (Basingstoke, 1989), p. 271.

16. B. Simon, *The Politics of Educational Reform, 1920–1940* (London, 1974), pp. 363–64; R. D. Anderson, 'Education and Society in Modern Scotland: A Comparative Perspective', *History of Education Quarterly*, 25 (1985), p. 475.

17. T. Kelly, *For Advancement of Learning: The University of Liverpool, 1881–1981* (Liverpool, 1981), p. 182.

18. R. Ollard, *A Man of Contradictions: A Life of A. L. Rowse* (London, 1999), pp. 26–27.

19. See M. Sanderson, *Educational Opportunity and Social Change in England* (London, 1987), pp. 18–44; C. Dyhouse, 'Family Patterns of Social Mobility through Higher Education in England in the 1930s', *Journal of Social History*, 34 (2001), pp. 817–42; C. Dyhouse, 'Going to University in England between the Wars: Access and Funding', *History of Education*, 31 (2002), pp. 1–14.

20. A. H. Halsey, *No Discouragement: An Autobiography* (Basingstoke, 1996), pp. 26–27, 47.

21. See W. D. Rubinstein, 'Education and the Social Origins of British Elites, 1880–1970', *Past and Present*, 112 (1986), pp. 163–207; R. D. Anderson, 'Universities and Elites in Modern Britain', *History of Universities*, 10 (1991), pp. 225–50.

22. Rubinstein, 'Education and the Social Origins', pp. 183–95. Cf. H. Perkin, *The Rise of Professional Society: England since 1880* (London, 1989), pp. 258–66.

23. B. Harrison (ed.), *The History of the University of Oxford*, viii, *The Twentieth Century* (Oxford, 1994), p. 56.

24. H. Lange, *Higher Education of Women in Europe* (New York, 1901), pp. 28–29, 31.

25. V. Woolf, *A Room of One's Own. Three Guineas*, World's Classics edn (Oxford, 1992), p. 22. Cf. H. Lee, *Virginia Woolf* (London, 1997), pp. 564–65.

26. C. Dyhouse, *No Distinction of Sex? Women in British Universities, 1870–1939* (London, 1995).

27. T. Begg, *The Excellent Women: The Origins and History of Queen Margaret College* (Edinburgh, 1994); W. Thompson and C. McCallum, *Glasgow Caledonian University: Its Origins and Evolution* (East Linton, 1998).

28. 1936 report, cited in Shinn, *Paying the Piper*, p. 254.

29. K. Vernon, 'A Healthy Society for Future Intellectuals: Developing Student Life at Civic Universities', in C. Lawrence and A. Mayer (eds), *Regenerating England: Science, Medicine and Culture in Inter-War Britain* (Amsterdam, 2000), pp. 179–202.

30. W. H. G. Armytage, *Civic Universities: Aspects of a British Tradition* (London, 1955), p. 268; H. Perkin, *Key Profession: The History of the Association of University Teachers* (London, 1969), pp. 60–64.

31. B. Simon, *A Student's View of the Universities* (London, 1943).

32. W. Rüegg (ed.), *A History of the University in Europe*, iii, *Universities in the Nineteenth and Early Twentieth Centuries, 1800–1945* (Cambridge, 2004), pp. 339–40.

33. Robertson, *British Universities*, pp. iv, 14, 40–41, 44, 51.

34. H. Martin (ed.), *The Life of a Modern University* (London, 1930), p. 20.

35. Flexner, *Universities*, pp. 5, 29, 263.

36. B. Truscot, *Red Brick University* (Harmondsworth, 1951), pp. 65, 70. Cf. H. Silver, 'The Universities' Speaking Conscience: "Bruce Truscot" and *Redbrick University*', *History of Education*, 28 (1999), pp. 173–89.

37. Truscot, *Red Brick University*, pp. 267–68, 273.

38. J. Baillie, *The Mind of the Modern University* (London, 1946), pp. 10, 19–20.

39. R. Livingstone, *Some Thoughts on University Education* (London, 1948).

40. W. Moberly, *The Crisis in the University* (London, 1949), esp. pp. 106–47.

41. J. Ortega y Gasset, *Mission of the University* (London, 1946), pp. 48, 62. Another volume in the Routledge series was W. F. Connell, *The Educational Thought and Influence of Matthew Arnold* (1950).

42. Robertson, *British Universities*, pp. 56–57, 85.

43. Ashby, *Technology and the Academics*, pp. 40–41, 77.

44. Reprinted in C. P. Snow, *The Two Cultures*, ed. S. Collini (Cambridge, 1993).

45. Reprinted in F. R. Leavis, *Nor Shall My Sword: Discourses on Pluralism, Compassion and Social Hope* (London, 1972).

46. F. R. Leavis, *Education and the University: A Sketch for an 'English School'* (London, 1943), pp. 24, 28.

47. Leavis, *Nor Shall My Sword*, p. 104.

48. G. Ortolano, 'Two Cultures, One University: The Institutional Origins of the "Two Cultures" Controversy', *Albion*, 34 (2002), pp. 606–24.

Notes to Chapter 9: Postwar Revolution

1. *Higher Education: Report of the Committee Appointed by the Prime Minister* (London, 1963), p. 8.

2. E. Shils, *The Intellectuals and the Powers, and Other Essays* (Chicago, 1972), p. 145 (orig. in *Encounter* 1955).

3. *Minerva*, 8 (1970), pp. 242–50.

4. R. D. Anderson, *Universities and Elites in Britain since 1800* (2nd edn, Cambridge, 1995), p. 15; W. A. C. Stewart, *Higher Education in Postwar Britain* (Basingstoke, 1989), p. 279.

5. H. C. Dent, *Universities in Transition* (London, 1961), p. 76.

6. R. O. Berdahl, *British Universities and the State* (London, 1959), p. 201; P. Gosden, *Education in the Second World War: A Study in Policy and Administration* (London, 1976), pp. 422–30.

7. Stewart, *Higher Education*, pp. 268, 271.

8. C. H. Shinn, *Paying the Piper: The Development of the University Grants Committee, 1919–46* (Lewes, 1986), p. 221.

9. E.g. W. H. G. Armytage, *Civic Universities: Aspects of a British Tradition* (London, 1955); Berdahl, *British Universities*; Dent, *Universities in Transition*. Cf. R. Lowe, *Education in the Post-War Years: A Social History* (London, 1988), pp. 159–60.

10. Dent, *Universities in Transition*, pp. 128–29.

11. Leicester was the paradigmatic provincial town, being the setting also for

William Cooper's *Scenes from Provincial Life* (1950) and the early novels in C. P. Snow's cycle.

12. Using their present university names, they were Aston, Bath, Bradford, Brunel, City (former Northampton Polytechnic), Loughborough, Salford, Surrey (former Battersea Polytechnic). Chelsea (former Polytechnic) has since been merged with King's College London, and Cardiff with the university.

13. Lowe, *Education in the Post-War Years*, pp. 57–59; Dent, *Universities in Transition*, p. 77.

14. A. H. Halsey (ed.), *British Social Trends since 1900: A Guide to the Changing Social Structure of Britain* (Basingstoke, 1988), p. 281.

15. J. Carswell, *Government and the Universities in Britain: Programme and Performance, 1960–1980* (Cambridge, 1985), p. 34.

16. For a good case study, see I. G. C. Hutchison, *The University and the State: The Case of Aberdeen, 1860–1963* (Aberdeen, 1993), pp. 85–137; J. D. Hargreaves and A. Forbes (eds), *Aberdeen University, 1945–1981: Regional Roles and National Needs* (Aberdeen, 1989), pp. 4–14.

17. W. B. Gallie, *A New University: A. D. Lindsay and the Keele Experiment* (London, 1960), pp. 73–77.

18. A. Sampson, *Anatomy of Britain* (London, 1962), pp. 210, 217; *Anatomy of Britain Today* (London, 1965), pp. 234–38; *The New Anatomy of Britain* (London, 1971), pp. 165–67; *The Changing Anatomy of Britain* (London, 1982), pp. 130, 142.

19. Dent, *Universities in Transition*, pp. 139–40, 172.

20. M. Shattock, *The UGC and the Management of British Universities* (Buckingham, 1994), pp. 81–97.

21. E. P. Thompson (ed.), *Warwick University Ltd: Industry, Management and the Universities* (Harmondsworth, 1970).

22. M. Sanderson, *The History of the University of East Anglia, Norwich* (London, 2002), p. 120.

23. B. Pullan and M. Abendstern, *A History of the University of Manchester, 1951–73* (Manchester, 2000), p. 99.

24. A. Briggs, 'A Founding Father Reflects', *Higher Education Quarterly*, 45 (1991), pp. 311–32; *The Collected Essays of Asa Briggs*, iii, *Serious Pursuits: Communications and Education* (Hemel Hempstead, 1991), pp. 327–85.

25. Stewart, *Higher Education*, p. 285.

26. For a more critical judgement, H. Perkin, 'Dream, Myth and Reality: New Universities in England, 1960–1990', *Higher Education Quarterly*, 45 (1991), pp. 294–310.

27. L. Robbins, *The University in the Modern World and Other Papers on*

Higher Education (London, 1966), pp. 29–30. Cf. *Higher Education*, pp. 210–12.

28. *Grants to Students: Report of the Committee Appointed by the Minister of Education* (London, 1960), pp. 92–94. Cf. Carswell, *Government and the Universities*, pp. 23–25.

29. E. W. Vincent and P. Hinton, *The University of Birmingham: Its History and Significance* (Birmingham, 1947), pp. 2, 205–6.

30. P. Morgan, *The University of Wales, 1939–1993* (Cardiff, 1997), pp. 3, 45, 86.

31. T. H. Marshall, *Citizenship and Social Class, and Other Essays* (Cambridge, 1950), pp. 63, 65–66. Cf. A. H. Halsey, *Change in British Society* (new edn, Oxford, 1986), p. 62.

32. G. Walden, *We Should Know Better: Solving the Education Crisis* (London, 1996), p. 169.

33. S. Caine, *British Universities: Purpose and Prospects* (London, 1969), p. 177.

34. M. Young, *The Rise of the Meritocracy, 1870–2033* (Harmondsworth, 1961).

Notes to Chapter 10: The Robbins Era

1. 'Lone Voices. Views of the Fifties', *Encounter*, 15/1 (July 1960), pp. 8–9.

2. *The Future of Higher Education* (London, 2003), p. 12.

3. Texts of 1949–50 in T. Fuller (ed.), *The Voice of Liberal Learning: Michael Oakeshott on Education* (New Haven, 1987), pp. 100, 129.

4. C. G. Robertson, *The British Universities* (2nd edn, London, 1944), pp. 74–76.

5. Cited (1971) in P. Scott, *The Crisis of the University* (London, 1984), p. 60.

6. K. Jaspers, *The Idea of the University* (London, 1960), p. 120.

7. *Higher Education: Report of the Committee Appointed by the Prime Minister* (London, 1963), pp. 49–54.

8. 'Modes of Social Ascent through Education: Sponsored and Contest Mobility' (1960), reprinted in A. H. Halsey, J. Floud and C. A. Anderson (eds), *Education, Economy and Society: A Reader in the Sociology of Education* (New York, 1961), pp. 121–39.

9. *Higher Education*, pp. 11–12, 16, 42, 45–47, 69.

10. Ibid., pp. 8, 48, 65–66, 70, 87, 166.

11. Ibid., pp. 6–7.

12. Ibid., p. 224.

13. Article reprinted in M. Shattock (ed.), *The Creation of a University System* (Oxford, 1996), p. 126.

14. Ibid., pp. 75–78, 83–84.

15. L. Robbins, *The University in the Modern World and Other Papers on Higher Education* (London, 1966), pp. 95, 97.

16. *Higher Education*, pp. 89–97, 104.

17. Ibid., p. 1.

18. Ibid., pp. 15–16.

19. Ibid., pp. 8–9.

20. Ibid., p. 160.

21. Ibid., pp. 154–55.

22. List in W. A. C. Stewart, *Higher Education in Postwar Britain* (Basingstoke, 1989), p. 140. There were various reshufflings and renamings in later years. The current universities which derive from the initial batch are: Brighton, Central England, Central Lancashire, Coventry, De Montfort, East London, Glamorgan, Greenwich, Hertfordshire, Huddersfield, Kingston, Leeds Metropolitan, Liverpool John Moores, London Metropolitan (merging North London and London Guildhall), Manchester Metropolitan, Middlesex, Northumbria, Nottingham Trent, Oxford Brookes, Plymouth, Portsmouth, Sheffield Hallam, South Bank, Staffordshire, Sunderland, Teesside, Westminster, West of England and Wolverhampton. Anglia Ruskin (formerly Anglia Polytechnic), Bournemouth, Lincoln and Thames Valley derive from polytechnics created later.

23. C. D. Godwin, 'Origin of the Binary System', *History of Education*, 27 (1998), pp. 182, 184, 190–91.

24. Robbins, *University in the Modern World*, p. 151, and cf. 147–48.

25. T. Burgess et al., *Degrees East: The Making of the University of East London* (London, 1995), p. 161.

26. Brosan in G. Brosan et al., *Patterns and Policies in Higher Education* (Harmondsworth, 1971), pp. 61–75. North-East London Polytechnic became a constituent of East London University.

27. Burgess et al., *Degrees East*, pp. 107–10, 154.

28. J. Carswell, *Government and the Universities in Britain: Programme and Performance, 1960–1980* (Cambridge, 1985), pp. 171–72; Stewart, *Higher Education*, p. 278. Stewart has useful statistics for both universities and public sector.

29. Stewart, *Higher Education*, p. 279.

30. Carswell, *Government and the Universities*, pp. 43–44, 163. As a former secretary of the UGC, Carswell was a well-informed critic.

31. Stewart, *Higher Education*, pp. 160–61; the thirteen points are listed in Shattock, *Creation of a University System*, pp. 174–75.

32. *Education: A Framework for Expansion* (London, 1972), p. 35.

33. Stewart, *Higher Education*, p. 285.
34. M. Shattock, *The UGC and the Management of British Universities* (Buckingham, 1994), pp. 10–11.
35. A. Sampson, *The Changing Anatomy of Britain* (London, 1982), p. 132.
36. D. King and V. Nash, 'Continuity of Ideas and the Politics of Higher Education: Expansion in Britain from Robbins to Dearing', *Twentieth Century British History*, 12 (2001), p. 188.
37. A. H. Halsey and M. Trow, *The British Academics* (London, 1971), p. 83; A. H. Halsey, *Decline of Donnish Dominion: The British Academic Professions in the Twentieth Century* (Oxford, 1992), pp. 1–19; Trow in 1987, reprinted in Shattock, *Creation of a University System*, pp. 202–24. Cf. R. Lowe, *Education in the Post-War Years: A Social History* (London, 1988), pp. 200–2.
38. N. Annan, 'The Reform of Higher Education in 1986', *History of Education*, 16 (1987), pp. 218, 220. Cf. N. Annan, *Our Age: The Generation that Made Post-War Britain*, Fontana edn (London, 1991), pp. 502–8.

Notes to Chapter 11: State or Market?

1. R. O. Berdahl, *British Universities and the State* (London, 1959), p. 171.
2. W. A. C. Stewart, *Higher Education in Postwar Britain* (Basingstoke, 1989), p. 219.
3. B. Pullan and M. Abendstern, *A History of the University of Manchester, 1973–90* (Manchester, 2004), pp. 197–206.
4. R. Dahrendorf, *LSE: A History of the London School of Economics and Political Science, 1895–1995* (Oxford, 1995), p. 501, and cf. 497; A. H. Halsey, *Decline of Donnish Dominion: The British Academic Professions in the Twentieth Century* (Oxford, 1992), pp. 178–84.
5. J. A. Soares, *The Decline of Privilege: The Modernization of Oxford University* (Stanford, 1999), passim.
6. H. Perkin, *The Rise of Professional Society: England since 1880* (London, 1989), pp. 436–54; H. Perkin, 'Dream, Myth and Reality: New Universities in England 1960–1990', *Higher Education Quarterly*, 45 (1991), p. 303.
7. Memorandum by Hugh Gaitskell and Ernest Bevin, 1950, cited in C. Barnett, *The Verdict of Peace: Britain Between her Yesterday and the Future* (London, 2001), p. 34.
8. M. Sanderson, *The History of the University of East Anglia, Norwich* (London, 2002), pp. 304–5; M. Sanderson, *Educational Opportunity and Social Change in England* (London, 1987), p. 134.
9. C. B. Cox and A. E. Dyson (eds), *Fight for Education: A Black Paper*

(London, n.d. [1968]); *Black Paper Two: The Crisis in Education* (London, n.d. [1969]); *Black Paper Three: Goodbye Mr Short* (London, n.d. [1970]). Further *Black Papers* appeared in 1975 and 1977.

10. A. H. Halsey, *No Discouragement: An Autobiography* (Basingstoke, 1996), p. 124 (attributed to E. Midwinter).

11. Perkin, 'Dream, Myth and Reality', p. 295.

12. Raphael Samuel in T. C. Smout (ed.), *Victorian Values* (Oxford, 1992), p. 21.

13. R. E. Bell, in R. E. Bell and A. J. Youngson (eds), *Present and Future in Higher Education* (London, 1973), pp. 24–25.

14. M. Beloff, 'British Universities and the Public Purse', *Minerva*, 5 (1966–67), pp. 520–32.

15. J. and J. Pemberton, *The University College at Buckingham: A First Account of its Conception, Foundation and Early Years* (Buckingham, 1979).

16. *Higher Education into the 1990s: A Discussion Document* (London, 1978), appendix 2.

17. Sanderson, *University of East Anglia*, pp. 271, 392.

18. M. Shattock, *The UGC and the Management of British Universities* (Buckingham, 1994), pp. 20–25.

19. Ibid., p. 28. Cf. P. Moore, 'University Financing, 1979–86', in M. Shattock (ed.), *The Creation of a University System* (Oxford, 1996), pp. 187–201.

20. P. Gosden, *Education in the Second World War: A Study in Policy and Administration* (London, 1976), p. 423.

21. D. King and V. Nash, 'Continuity of Ideas and the Politics of Higher Education: Expansion in Britain from Robbins to Dearing', *Twentieth Century British History*, 12 (2001), pp. 200–1. Cf. D. Ryan, 'The Thatcher Government's Attack on Higher Education in Historical Perspective', *New Left Review*, 227 (1998), pp. 23–25; P. Scott, *Knowledge and Nation* (Edinburgh, 1990), p. 115.

22. Pullan and Abendstern, *University of Manchester, 1973–90*, pp. 216–19.

23. Shattock, *The UGC*, p. 43.

24. N. Johnson, 'Dons in Decline: Who Will Look After the Cultural Capital?', *Twentieth Century British History*, 5 (1994), pp. 377–78.

25. B. Salter and T. Tapper, *The State and Higher Education* (Ilford, 1994), p. 69.

26. *Future Strategy for Higher Education in Scotland* (Edinburgh, 1985).

27. Including the Scottish equivalents of the polytechnics: Abertay (Dundee), Glasgow Caledonian, Napier (Edinburgh), Paisley and Robert Gordon (Aberdeen).

28. Halsey, *No Discouragement*, p. 129.

29. UK, full-time, undergraduate and postgraduate: from figures published by Higher Education Statistics Agency.

30. Report cited from the summary in *Times Higher Education Supplement*, 25 July 1997.

31. G. Walden, *We Should Know Better: Solving the Education Crisis* (London, 1996), p. 172.

32. Sanderson, *University of East Anglia*, pp. 354–55.

33. *The Future of Higher Education* (London, 2003), p. 8.

34. Ibid., pp. 13, 20, 26, 54.

35. Ibid., p. 77.

36. Halsey, *Decline of Donnish Dominion*, pp. 235–38, 306–7; survey in *THES*, 29 April 2005.

37. *Future of Higher Education*, p. 21.

38. E.g. D. Marquand, *Decline of the Public: The Hollowing-Out of Citizenship* (London, 2004), pp. 76–77.

39. King and Nash, 'Continuity of Ideas', pp. 185–207.

Notes to Chapter 12: Past and Present

1. H. Rashdall, *The Universities of Europe in the Middle Ages*, ed. F. M. Powicke and A. B. Emden (London 1936; orig. 1895), i, pp. 3–4.

2. W. Rüegg, in H. de Ridder-Symoens (ed.), *A History of the University in Europe*, i, *Universities in the Middle Ages* (Cambridge, 1992), p. xix.

3. E. Ashby and M. Anderson, *Portrait of Haldane at Work on Education* (London, 1974), pp. 15, 173.

4. *Higher Education: Report of the Committee Appointed by the Prime Minister* (London, 1963), pp. 70–71; D. King and V. Nash, 'Continuity of Ideas and the Politics of Higher Education: Expansion in Britain from Robbins to Dearing', *Twentieth Century British History*, 12 (2001), p. 198.

5. Most recent OECD figures, for participation at entry as distinct from graduation, in *Times Higher Education Supplement*, 16 September 2005.

6. Rashdall, *Universities of Europe*, iii, p. 464.

7. S. Rothblatt and M. Trow, 'Government Policies and Higher Education: A Comparison of Britain and the United States, 1630–1860', in C. Crouch and A. Heath (eds), *Social Research and Social Reform: Essays in Honour of A. H. Halsey* (Oxford, 1992), pp. 173–215.

8. *The Future of Higher Education* (London, 2003), pp. 13, 18; *THES*, 17 September 2004. Current OECD average 1.4 per cent, UK 1.1 per cent (of which 0.8 per cent public), USA 2.6 per cent (of which 1 per cent public).

9. M. Sanderson, *The History of the University of East Anglia, Norwich* (London, 2002), pp. 55–56.

10. *Future of Higher Education*, pp. 17–18.

11. R. D. Anderson, *Universities and Elites in Britain since 1800* (2nd edn, Cambridge, 1995), p. 58; A. H. Halsey (ed.), *British Social Trends since 1900: a Guide to the Changing Social Structure of Britain* (Basingstoke, 1988), pp. 264, 291; J. H. Farrant, 'Trends in Admissions', in O. Fulton (ed.), *Access to Higher Education* (Guildford, 1981), pp. 42–88.

12. *Future of Higher Education*, pp. 47–48.

13. C. E. Mallet, *A History of the University of Oxford*, iii, *Modern Oxford* (London, 1927), p. 495.

14. N. Johnson, 'Dons in Decline: Who Will Look After the Cultural Capital?', *Twentieth Century British History*, 5 (1994), p. 380.

15. H. C. Dent, *Universities in Transition* (London, 1961), p. 163; S. Caine, *British Universities: Purpose and Prospects* (London, 1969), p. 36; cf. D. Logan, *Universities: The Years of Challenge* (Cambridge, 1963), p. 27.

16. *Higher Education*, pp. 181–85.

17. See for example G. Bernard, 'History and Research Assessment Exercises', *Oxford Review of Education*, 26 (2000), pp. 95–106.

Guide to Further Reading

INTRODUCTION

This guide is meant for the general reader. Articles in scholarly journals are not included, but many of them are cited in the footnotes. For those who want more advanced guidance, books with useful bibliographies are indicated here, and regular lists of new publications may be found in the journal *History of Universities*. There are many celebratory or inward-looking histories of individual universities and colleges, and only a selection of recent works is given below.

GENERAL HISTORY

There is no single-volume history of British, or even English, higher education. Since for centuries Oxford and Cambridge were the only English universities, see the section below which covers them.

V. H. H. Green, *British Institutions: The Universities* (Harmondsworth, 1969: bibliography) combined a useful history with discussion of contemporary problems, but was never updated. W. H. G. Armytage, *Civic Universities: Aspects of a British Tradition* (London, 1955), was much wider than its title indicated, constituting a rather unsystematic general history. For a selection of more modern scholarship, see T. Bender (ed.), *The University and the City: From Medieval Origins to the Present* (New York, 1988), and N. Phillipson (ed.), *Universities, Society and the Future* (Edinburgh, 1983).

R. E. Bell took a refreshing view of some myths of British university history in R. E. Bell and A. J. Youngson (eds), *Present and Future in Higher Education* (London, 1973) and in R. E. Bell and N. Grant, *A Mythology of British Education* (St Albans, 1974).

For the European context, three out of four volumes have now appeared of a large collective *History of the University in Europe* (Cambridge). These are i, *Universities in the Middle Ages*, ed. H. de Ridder-Symoens (1992); ii,

Universities in Early Modern Europe, 1500–1800, ed. H. de Ridder-Symoens (1996); iii, *Universities in the Nineteenth and Early Twentieth Centuries, 1800–1945*, ed. W. Rüegg (2004). The treatment is thematic, and material on Britain has to be searched out. Britain has a separate chapter in R. D. Anderson, *European Universities from the Enlightenment to 1914* (Oxford, 2004: bibliography).

MIDDLE AGES TO EARLY NINETEENTH CENTURY

This book gives only the briefest sketch of the medieval universities, but a good introduction is now A. B. Cobban, *English University Life in the Middle Ages* (London, 1999: bibliography), a popular version of his *The Medieval English Universities: Oxford and Cambridge to c. 1500* (Aldershot, 1988).

The early modern period was the focus of efforts in the 1970s to treat university history with contemporary scholarly techniques. The journal *Past and Present* was especially important, as was Lawrence Stone. The fruits of a project directed by him are in L. Stone (ed.), *The University in Society*, i, *Oxford and Cambridge from the Fourteenth to the Early Nineteenth Century* (Princeton, 1975), and ii, *Europe, Scotland, and the United States from the Sixteenth to the Twentieth Century* (Princeton, 1974).

For this period, a good introduction is R. O'Day, *Education and Society, 1500–1800: The Social Foundations of Education in Early Modern Britain* (London, 1982: bibliography). Older works include K. Charlton, *Education in Renaissance England* (London, 1965); M. H. Curtis, *Oxford and Cambridge in Transition, 1558–1642* (Oxford, 1959); and H. Kearney, *Scholars and Gentlemen: Universities and Society in Pre-Industrial Britain, 1500–1700* (London, 1970), which includes coverage of Scotland and Ireland.

NINETEENTH AND EARLY TWENTIETH CENTURIES

The best introduction is now K. Vernon, *Universities and the State in England, 1850–1939* (London, 2004: bibliography). M. Sanderson, *The Universities in the Nineteenth Century* (London, 1975: bibliography) is a valuable combination of first-hand sources and commentary.

Sanderson discussed a major issue in M. Sanderson, *The Universities and British Industry, 1850–1970* (London, 1972). Other books on science, technology, and the alternative tradition of higher education include M. Argles, *South Kensington to Robbins: An Account of English Technical and Scientific Education since 1851* (London, 1964); D. S. L. Cardwell, *The Organisation of Science in England* (new edn, London, 1972); E. Ashby, *Technology and the Academics: An*

Essay on Universities and the Scientific Revolution (London, 1958); and R. Bell and M. Tight, *Open Universities: A British Tradition?* (Buckingham, 1993).

On the cultural background to university history, see B. Knights, *The Idea of the Clerisy in the Nineteenth Century* (Cambridge, 1978); R. Williams, *Culture and Society, 1780–1950* (Harmondsworth, 1961); C. Harvie, *The Lights of Liberalism: University Liberals and the Challenge of Democracy, 1860–86* (London, 1976); and F. M. Turner, *Contesting Cultural Authority: Essays in Victorian Intellectual Life* (Cambridge, 1993). T. Heyck, *The Transformation of Intellectual Life in Victorian England* (London, 1982: bibliography) is standard for the professionalization of academic subjects. A. D. Culler, *The Imperial Intellect: A Study of Newman's Educational Ideal* (New Haven, 1955) is the best study of this subject. S. Rothblatt, *The Modern University and its Discontents: The Fate of Newman's Legacies in Britain and America* (Cambridge, 1997) deals with much besides Newman, and reprints some key articles by this leading scholar. See also his *Tradition and Change in English Liberal Education: An Essay in History and Culture* (London, 1976).

For the modern social history of higher education, see R. D. Anderson, *Universities and Elites in Britain since 1800* (2nd edn, Cambridge, 1995: bibliography) and M. Sanderson, *Educational Opportunity and Social Change in England* (London, 1987: bibliography). Detailed scholarly work has especially focused on the impact of industrialization, often within a comparative context. See F. Ringer, *Education and Society in Modern Europe* (Bloomington, 1979), and two books with titles calculated to deter any but the most determined reader: K. H. Jarausch (ed.), *The Transformation of Higher Learning, 1860–1930: Expansion, Diversification, Social Opening, and Professionalization in England, Germany, Russia, and the United States* (Chicago, 1983), and D. Müller et al. (eds), *The Rise of the Modern Educational System: Structural Change and Social Reproduction, 1870–1920* (Cambridge, 1987).

A general study of women and universities is badly needed. M. Vicinus, *Independent Women: Work and Community for Single Women, 1850–1920* (London, 1985) has material on Oxbridge, while C. Dyhouse, *No Distinction of Sex? Women in British Universities, 1870–1939* (London, 1995: bibliography) looks at other universities. Dyhouse's work has pioneer value for the interwar years. Good biographies of scholars are M. Berg, *A Woman in History: Eileen Power, 1889–1940* (Cambridge, 1996) and M. Beard, *The Invention of Jane Harrison* (Cambridge, Massachusetts, 2000).

Student life is another neglected subject: E. Ashby and M. Anderson, *The Rise of the Student Estate in Britain* (London, 1970) does not go very far.

The period around the First World War has been covered by P. Alter, *The Reluctant Patron: Science and the State in Britain, 1850–1920* (Oxford, 1987) and

G. Sherington, *English Education, Social Change and War, 1911–20* (Manchester, 1981). Haldane's central role makes E. Ashby and M. Anderson, *Portrait of Haldane at Work on Education* (London, 1974) an important study. S. Wallace, *War and the Image of Germany: British Academics, 1914–1918* (Edinburgh, 1988) discusses the intellectual impact of the war.

C. H. Shinn, *Paying the Piper: The Development of the University Grants Committee, 1919–46* (Lewes, 1986) is a thorough treatment of policy between the wars. P. Gosden, *Education in the Second World War: A Study in Policy and Administration* (London, 1976) is a standard work, but has comparatively little on universities. The title of R. Simpson, *How the PhD Came to Britain: A Century of Struggle for Postgraduate Education* (Guildford, 1983) is self-explanatory, as is that of H. Perkin, *Key Profession: The History of the Association of University Teachers* (London, 1969).

<h2 style="text-align:center">SINCE 1945</h2>

Two standard histories are R. Lowe, *Education in the Post-War Years: A Social History* (London, 1988) and W. A. C. Stewart, *Higher Education in Postwar Britain* (Basingstoke, 1989), but Lowe does not go beyond 1964. Otherwise the main books have been written by participants: J. Carswell, *Government and the Universities in Britain: Programme and Performance, 1960–1980* (Cambridge, 1985) and M. Shattock, *The UGC and the Management of British Universities* (Buckingham, 1994). There are also studies of policy-making by political scientists, notably B. Salter and T. Tapper, *The State and Higher Education* (Ilford, 1994: bibliography).

The first fifty years of the periodical *Universities Quarterly*, founded in 1946, are anthologized in M. Shattock (ed.), *The Creation of a University System* (Oxford, 1996). Peter Scott was editor of the *Times Higher Education Supplement* in the 1980s, and collected his thoughts in *The Crisis of the University* (London, 1984) and *Knowledge and Nation* (Edinburgh, 1990).

A. H. Halsey has been an important sociological observer, and surveys of academic opinion were the starting-point for A. H. Halsey and M. Trow, *The British Academics* (London, 1971) and A. H. Halsey, *Decline of Donnish Dominion: The British Academic Professions in the Twentieth Century* (Oxford, 1992). A very different and entertaining guide is N. Annan, *Our Age: The Generation that made Post-War Britain*, Fontana edn (London, 1991), while in *Ancient Cultures of Conceit: British University Fiction in the Post-War Years* (London, 1990) I. Carter uses campus novels to illuminate the wider scene.

OXFORD AND CAMBRIDGE

Oxford and Cambridge have both published multi–volume histories, but Oxford chose collective and Cambridge single authorship. The Oxford history in particular is a huge scholarly achievement. Details are: *The History of the University of Oxford*, i, *The Early Oxford Schools*, ed. J. I. Catto (1984); ii, *Late Medieval Oxford*, ed. J. I. Catto and R. Evans (1992); iii, *The Collegiate University*, ed. J. McConica (1986); iv, *Seventeenth-Century Oxford*, ed. N. Tyacke (1997); v, *The Eighteenth Century*, ed. L. S. Sutherland and L. G. Mitchell (1986); vi, *Nineteenth-Century Oxford*, part 1, ed. M. G. Brock and M. C. Curthoys (1997); vii, *Nineteenth-Century Oxford*, part 2, ed. M. G. Brock and M. C. Curthoys (2000); viii, *The Twentieth Century*, ed. B. Harrison (1994). *A History of the University of Cambridge*, i, *The University to 1546*, by D. R. Leader (1988); ii, *1546–1750*, by V. Morgan and C. Brooke (2004); iii, *1750–1870*, by P. Searby (1997); iv, *1870–1990*, by C. N. L. Brooke (1993).

Histories in one volume are J. Prest (ed.), *The Illustrated History of Oxford University* (Oxford, 1993) and E. Leedham-Green, *A Concise History of the University of Cambridge* (Cambridge, 1996).

Important works for Cambridge on the period before 1850 are J. Twigg, *The University of Cambridge and the English Revolution, 1625–1688* (Woodbridge, 1990); J. Gascoigne, *Cambridge in the Age of the Enlightenment: Science, Religion and Politics from the Restoration to the French Revolution* (Cambridge, 1989); and M. M. Garland, *Cambridge before Darwin: The Ideal of a Liberal Education, 1800–1860* (Cambridge, 1980).

The best studies of the nineteenth-century reforms are S. Rothblatt, *The Revolution of the Dons: Cambridge and Society in Victorian England* (London, 1968) and A. J. Engel, *From Clergyman to Don: The Rise of the Academic Profession in Nineteenth-Century Oxford* (Oxford, 1983). W. R. Ward, *Victorian Oxford* (London, 1965) is still useful, and particular aspects are dealt with in R. Symonds, *Oxford and Empire: The Last Lost Cause?* (Oxford, 1986); R. Soffer, *Discipline and Power: The University, History, and the Making of an English Elite, 1870–1930* (Stanford, 1994); and L. Goldman, *Dons and Workers: Oxford and Adult Education since 1850* (Oxford, 1995). L. Dowling, *Hellenism and Homosexuality in Victorian Oxford* (Ithaca, 1994) discusses two civilizing forces. On modern Cambridge, see J. Smith and C. Stray (eds), *Teaching and Learning in Nineteenth-Century Cambridge* (Woodbridge, 2001) and R. McWilliams-Tullberg, *Women at Cambridge* (Cambridge, 1998). The wider influence of Cambridge can be traced in W. C. Lubenow, *The Cambridge Apostles, 1820–1914: Liberalism, Imagination and Friendship in British Intellectual and Professional Life* (Cambridge, 1998), and G. Werskey, *The Visible College: A*

Collective Biography of British Scientists and Socialists of the 1930s (London, 1988).

N. Annan gives an account of modern Oxbridge personalities in *The Dons: Mentors, Eccentrics and Geniuses* (London, 1999). Useful studies of individuals are N. Annan, *Leslie Stephen: The Godless Victorian* (New York, 1984); B. Schultz, *Henry Sidgwick, Eye of the Universe: An Intellectual Biography* (Cambridge, 2005); G. Faber, *Jowett: A Portrait with Background* (London, 1957); M. Richter, *The Politics of Conscience: T. H. Green and his Age* (London, 1964); and V. H. H. Green, *Oxford Common Room: A Study of Lincoln College and Mark Pattison* (London, 1957), which is more solid than J. Sparrow, *Mark Pattison and the Idea of a University* (Cambridge, 1967).

For the adaptation of Oxbridge to postwar policies, see J. A. Soares, *The Decline of Privilege: The Modernization of Oxford University* (Stanford, 1999), which is valuable for recent history generally, and T. Tapper and B. Salter, *Oxford, Cambridge and the Changing Idea of the University: The Challenge to Donnish Domination* (Buckingham, 1992).

OTHER ENGLISH UNIVERSITIES

A painless introduction to London University is N. Harte, *The University of London, 1836–1986: An Illustrated History* (London, 1986). A similar illustrated history is N. Harte and J. North, *The World of UCL, 1828–1990* (London, 1991). Apart from R. Dahrendorf, *LSE: A History of the London School of Economics and Political Science, 1895–1995* (Oxford, 1995) the London colleges lack substantial modern histories. The administrative history of the University is covered exhaustively in F. M. G. Willson, *Our Minerva: The Men and Politics of the University of London, 1836–1858* (London, 1995) and *The University of London 1858–1900: The Politics of Senate and Convocation* (Woodbridge, 2004). F. M. L. Thompson (ed.), *The University of London and the World of Learning, 1836–1986* (London, 1990) discusses various aspects of teaching.

For the early history of the civic universities, see D. R. Jones, *The Origins of Civic Universities: Manchester, Leeds and Liverpool* (London, 1988). The best histories of individual universities are T. Kelly, *For Advancement of Learning: The University of Liverpool, 1881–1981* (Liverpool, 1981); E. Ives, D. Drummond and L. Schwarz, *The First Civic University: Birmingham, 1880–1980. An Introductory History* (Birmingham, 2000); and H. Mathers, *Steel City Scholars: The Centenary History of the University of Sheffield* (London, 2005). Among older ones A. W. Chapman, *The Story of a Modern University: A History of the University of Sheffield* (London, 1955) is still useful. For recent history, see S. Harrop, *Decade of Change: The University of Liverpool, 1981–1991* (Liverpool, 1994) and the two volumes by B. Pullan and M. Abendstern, *A History of the University of Manchester, 1951–73* (Manchester, 2000) and *A History of the University of Manchester, 1973–90* (Manchester, 2004). The absence of any modern history of Manchester before 1951 is a serious gap.

Among the new universities of the 1960s, only East Anglia has a substantial history: M. Sanderson, *The History of the University of East Anglia, Norwich* (London, 2002). T. Burgess and others, *Degrees East: The Making of the University of East London* (London, 1995) makes a start for the post-1992 universities.

SCOTLAND

There is no history of Scottish universities covering all periods, but a useful introductory collection of essays is J. Carter and D. Withrington (eds), *Scottish Universities: Distinctiveness and Diversity* (Edinburgh, 1992). For the nineteenth century there is R. D. Anderson, *Education and Opportunity in Victorian Scotland: Schools and Universities* (Oxford, 1983: bibliography), and the story is continued in L. Paterson, *Scottish Education in the Twentieth Century* (Edinburgh, 2003: bibliography). G. E. Davie, *The Democratic Intellect: Scotland and her Universities in the Nineteenth Century* (2nd edn, Edinburgh, 1964) expounds a thesis extended to the twentieth century in G. E. Davie, *The Crisis of the Democratic Intellect: The Problem of Generalism and Specialisation in Twentieth-Century Scotland* (Edinburgh, 1986).

For earlier centuries, the story can be traced through individual university histories: J. Durkan and J. Kirk, *The University of Glasgow, 1451–1577* (Glasgow, 1977); D. Stevenson, *King's College, Aberdeen, 1560–1641: From Protestant Reformation to Covenanting Revolution* (Aberdeen, 1990); P. Wood, *The Aberdeen Enlightenment: The Arts Curriculum in the Eighteenth Century* (Aberdeen, 1993); R. B. Sher, *Church and University in the Scottish Enlightenment: The Moderate Literati of Edinburgh* (Edinburgh, 1985); M. Lynch, N. Phillipson and R. Anderson, *The University of Edinburgh: An Illustrated History* (Edinburgh, 2003); and M. Moss, J. F. Munro and R. H. Trainor, *University, City and State: The University of Glasgow since 1870* (Edinburgh, 2000).

Other short histories are D. B. Horn, *A Short History of the University of Edinburgh, 1556–1889* (Edinburgh, 1967); A. L. Brown and M. Moss, *The University of Glasgow, 1451–1996* (Edinburgh, 1996); J. J. Carter and C. A. McLaren, *Crown and Gown, 1495–1995: An Illustrated History of the University of Aberdeen* (Aberdeen, 1994); R. G. Cant, *The University of St Andrews: A Short History* (3rd edn, St Andrews, 1992); and J. Butt, *John Anderson's Legacy: The University of Strathclyde and its Antecedents, 1796–1996* (East Linton, 1996).

Aberdeen celebrated its 500th anniversary in 1995 with a series of short studies, which include C. A. McLaren, *Aberdeen Students, 1600–1860* (Aberdeen, 2005); R. D. Anderson, *The Student Community at Aberdeen, 1860–1939* (Aberdeen, 1988); R. L. Emerson, *Professors, Patronage and Politics: The Aberdeen Universities in the Eighteenth Century* (Aberdeen, 1992); J. D. Hargreaves, *Academe and Empire: Some Overseas Connections of Aberdeen University, 1860–1970* (Aberdeen, 1994); I. G. C. Hutchison, *The University and the State: The Case of Aberdeen, 1860–1963* (Aberdeen, 1993); and L. Moore, *Bajanellas and Semilinas: Aberdeen University and the Education of Women, 1860–1920* (Aberdeen, 1991).

Scotland's oldest university, St Andrews, has been neglected, though for Dundee there is D. Southgate, *University Education in Dundee: A Centenary History* (Edinburgh, 1982).

WALES

The University of Wales is well served by an official history: J. G. Williams, *A History of the University of Wales*, i, *The University Movement in Wales* (Cardiff, 1993) and ii, *The University of Wales, 1893–1939* (Cardiff, 1997), completed by P. Morgan, *The University of Wales, 1939–1993* (Cardiff, 1997). See also G. H. Jenkins, *The University of Wales: An Illustrated History* (Cardiff, 1993). Good college histories are E. L. Ellis, *The University College of Wales Aberystwyth, 1872–1972* (Cardiff, 1972); J. G. Williams, *The University College of North Wales: Foundations, 1884–1927* (Cardiff, 1985); and D. T. W. Price, *A History of Saint David's University College Lampeter* (2 vols, Cardiff, 1977–90). But the urban colleges of Cardiff and Swansea have not found historians.

IRELAND

There is no single-volume history, but for the early centuries see R. B. McDowell and D. A. Webb, *Trinity College Dublin, 1592–1952: An Academic History* (Cambridge, 1982); the period 1793–1908 is covered by S. M. Parkes in W. E. Vaughan (ed.), *A New History of Ireland*, vi, *Ireland under the Union*, part 2, *1870–1921* (Oxford, 1996). T. W. Moody and J. C. Beckett, *Queen's Belfast, 1845–1949: The History of a University* (London, 1959) is an excellent source for the general university question as well as a college history. It is continued by L. A. Clarkson, *A University in Troubled Times: Queen's Belfast, 1945–2000* (Dublin, 2004).

F. McGrath, *Newman's University: Idea and Reality* (London, 1951) is good on the Catholic University, but there is less on its successor UCD. For Galway see T. Foley (ed.), *From Queen's College to National University: Essays on the Academic History of QUC/UCG/NUI Galway* (Dublin, 1999), and for Cork J. A. Murphy, *The College: A History of Queen's/University College Cork, 1845–1995* (Cork, 1995).

Index

London 14, 21, 71, 117
  Bedford College 72
  City and Guilds Institute 75
  Imperial College 84, 134, 153
  King's College 27–28, 72, 83–84,
    121–22
  London School of Economics 84,
    137, 164, 167
  medical schools 67–68, 72
  North-East London Polytechnic 157
  Queen Elizabeth College 122
  Royal College of Chemistry 33, 75
  Royal College of Science 75
  Royal Holloway College 72
  School of Mines 75
  technical education 75, 84
  University College 27–28, 72, 101
  University of 27–28, 60, 65–66,
    67–68, 72, 79, 83–84, 91, 103,
    110–11
  Westfield College 72
Longton 60, 136
Lorimer, James 102
Loss and Gain (1848) 42
Lowe, Robert 110–11, 164
Lucky Jim (1954) 133

Macaulay, Thomas 11, 40, 44
MacDonald, Ramsay 61
Macmillan, Harold 131
Manchester 10, 28, 65, 72, 73–74, 76,
  78, 125, 138, 153
Mansbridge, Albert 59
Marsden, Dennis 149
Marshall, Thomas H. 143
Mary I, queen 5, 10, 14
Mason, Josiah 66–67
Mason College, see Birmingham
Maxwell, James Clerk 66
Maynooth 95
Medical Research Committee 84
Melbourne, 2nd viscount 35
Mill, James 20

Mill, John Stuart 46, 71, 106, 109
Minerva 132, 167
Moberly, Walter 125–26, 128, 136, 148
Moore, G. E. 55
Morant, Robert 81, 84
Morris, William 60
Murray, Keith 136

national efficiency movement 80, 83,
  121
National Health Service 144, 189, 198
National Union of Students (NUS)
  123
Newcastle-upon-Tyne 73, 78
Newman, J. H. 38–39, 42, 96, 99–101,
  103, 106, 109, 111, 184, 200
Newton, Isaac 24, 68
Northcote–Trevelyan Report 36, 52
Northern Ireland see Ireland
North Staffordshire see Keele
Norwood Report 132
Nottingham 73–74, 76

Oakeshott, Michael 147–48, 163
Onslow, Arthur 12
Open University 141, 182, 199
Ortega y Gasset, José 127
Owens College, see Manchester
Oxbridge, origin of term 40
Oxford
  All Souls College 45, 114
  Arnold on 54, 101
  Balliol College 43, 51, 55, 58, 73
  Christ Church 4
  Jesus College 6
  Keble College 46
  Lady Margaret Hall 57
  Magdalen College 11
  New College 2
  Oriel College 42–43, 101
  origins 2
  'Oxford and the Working Class'
    59–61, 81, 195